"The complete how-to book of the decade…"

New! Even-More-Improved-Than-Ever 21st-Century Edition. Here are some comments from ad professionals, ad educators, and publications about Maxine Paetro's *How to Put Your Book Together and Get a Job in Advertising.*

"Great. Maxine answers every conceivable question and then some… I strongly recommend this book to all my students."

Richard Wilde, Co-Chairman
Media Arts, School of Visual Arts

"Read this book before you go to ad school. Max Paetro's advice is timeless."

Betsy Yamazaki, EVP, Creative Manager
Lowe, New York

"When I started out wanting to be a copywriter, How To Put Your Book Together *was my 'Bible.' I remember lying on my parents' couch reading this book, wondering how I was going to get the attention of that elusive creative recruiter.*

Now that I am one myself, I know what all my candidates are going through. So it's great to know that the 'How-to Bible' is still here to guide them, just as it did me."

Michele Daly
Bozell, New York

"Maxine Paetro makes a long overdue contribution to the agency world… hers is no stuffy, professorial tome. Instead, it's a conversationally written, witty primer on the agency hiring ABCs."

The New York Daily News

"There are two ways to embark on a career in advertising. One, buy Maxine Paetro's book. Two, buy a helmet. Number one is cheaper, faster and smarter."

Ed McCabe
Hall of Fame Copywriter

D0144678

"Having run the ad industry's largest, longest-running creative training program, I maybe hold the world record for hiring entry-level writers and art directors. I surely hold the record for recommending this book! If you're lucky enough to have a ticket to one of the great portfolio schools, read this book; if not, read it over and over again."

Flinn Dallis
SVP, Director of Creative Operations
Leo Burnett Company, USA

"Paetro's book is timeless... one of the classics of advertising brain building that reminds us there are no real rules, a few valuable guidelines, and lots of great common sense to take to heart if you want to make it as a creative."

Professor Deborah Morrison
University of Texas

"The unfortunate pilgrim, drifting in the big city, can heed her guidelines in all aspects of job hunting... this book offers a positive and supportive attitude to those struggling with the bewildering prospect of the hunt."

Advertising Techniques

"This is a remarkable book. It speaks directly to the young person for whom the message is intended."

Ron Seichrist
Miami Ad School

"Max is terrific! The book is an invaluable tool for young people starting in the creative side of the business — full of important tips that could make the difference in their approach to job interviews."

Judy Wald
The Judy Wald Agency

"You know those rare books that you read that actually change you, and the way you think, and you're never the same because it helps you grow and improve and gives you insight to a whole new way of 'being'... well, this is one of those books."

"A reader" on Amazon

HOW TO PUT YOUR BOOK TOGETHER AND GET A JOB IN ADVERTISING

MAXINE PAETRO

21st Century Edition
Published by The Copy Workshop

21st CENTURY EDITION

Copyright ©2002 Maxine Paetro
Published by The Copy Workshop
A division of Bruce Bendinger Creative Communications, Inc.
For further information contact: The Copy Workshop
2144 N. Hudson • Chicago, IL 60614 • 773-871-1179
FAX: 773-281-4643 • e-mail thecopyworkshop@aol.com
All rights reserved. Printed in the U.S.A.

Library of Congress Catalog Card Number: 91-137-839

ISBN: 1-887229-13-2
Illustrations: Giff Crosby
Cover Art and Design: Greg Paus
Author's Photo: Linda R. Chen

0 9 8 7 6 5 4 3 2

Publishing History:
First Printing © 1979 Maxine Paetro
Published by Executive Communications, New York
Second Printing 1980
Published by Hawthorne Books, a division of Elsevier-Dutton, New York
Third Printing 1984 Hawthorne Books, New York
Fourth Printing 1985 Hawthorne Books, New York
Fifth Printing 1987 Hawthorne Books, New York
New Improved Edition
First Printing 1990 The Copy Workshop, Chicago
Second Printing 1991 The Copy Workshop, Chicago
Third Printing 1993 The Copy Workshop, Chicago
Fourth Printing 1994 The Copy Workshop, Chicago
Fifth Printing 1995 The Copy Workshop, Chicago
Sixth Printing 1996 The Copy Workshop, Chicago
Even-More-Improved Edition
First Printing 1998 The Copy Workshop, Chicago
Second Printing 2000 The Copy Workshop, Chicago
21st Century Edition
First Printing 2002 The Copy Workshop, Chicago
Second Printing 2002 The Copy Workshop, Chicago

No part of this publication may be reproduced or transmitted in any form or by any means, electronic or mechanical, including photocopy, recording or any information storage and retrieval system now known or to be invented, without permission in writing from the publisher, except by a reviewer who wishes to quote brief passages in connection with a review written for inclusion in a magazine, newspaper or broadcast.

AUTHOR'S NOTE:

In 1978, I was a recruiter at Foote Cone and Belding, New York, and part of my job was to hire junior creative people.

There were very few schools teaching portfolio classes back then, and most of the "kids" who were looking for creative jobs had little idea about what the contents of a "book" should be.

So, I wrote a book called *How to Put Your Book Together and Get a Job in Advertising*. My intentions were to set down the basics, describe the portfolio format, help the would-be writer or art director eliminate – or at least shave down – the obligatory six months to a year of information-gathering, and enable him or her to use the interview process more productively for portfolio improvement, rather than for the collection of nuts and bolts.

Today, there are schools that specialize in teaching advertising to creative people, and computers have replaced magic markers and other artifacts of the '70s and '80s.

Most everyone who dreams of getting a creative job in advertising knows that they must have a portfolio of speculative ads with headlines, visuals, and tag lines. The portfolios recruiters see now are filled with ads that look like finished ads. The visuals are often brilliant photograpic images, married to dazzling type, spat out of the printer in colorful, double-page spreads.

But here's the complaint voiced most by advertising professionals who are in a position to hire: they say today's books fall flat because they are full of "ad-like objects," "heartless" ads, and imitations of ads that have won awards, instead of original ideas that spring from solid preparatory work and the creator's unique perspective.

To address this problem in particular, as well as to update old data and address the concerns of a more sophisticated advertising student, I've revised the original *How to…*

I still want to talk to those of you who've never thought about doing a book before, so I have left in all the basics of creating an ad, of product selection, and of portfolio format and execution. But I also want to talk with those of you who are deeply into the process of creating your portfolio.

The advertising media has changed dramatically since I started in the business. Ads look different; the use of type, the non-linear, more cinematic way many television commercial stories are told, reflect the visual orientation of a younger consumer.

The advent of the Internet, interactive television, and other venues yet to be invented are part of your now and your future.

It is your job to be aware of advancements in technology and new sensibilities. It's mine to tell you that at heart, the point of advertising remains the same.

Advertising is the message from the manufacturer of goods or services to the consumer. The point of advertising is to sell.

The consumer is not a faceless mass of people. He or she is a person who may buy a product or service if the message is convincing, both emotionally and logically.

Your portfolio must persuade a different consumer, in this case a person who can employ you, that you can do this job of convincing in an effective and original way.

As I originally intended, I want to save you time as you put your book together. There's more "stuff" in this revised edition, more questions and answers, more examples of good ads and bad.

I've also invited colleagues and friends, creative heads of some of the top agencies around, headhunters, creative managers, and junior creative people to write essays and supplement the text of this book with their comments, their stories, and examples from their portfolios. The contributions of these generous people are of enormous value, and I'm delighted to pass their advice on to you.

I hope this book encourages you. I hope it becomes a kind of map.

The first assault on the ad business is not for the chicken-hearted.

You can expect obstacles, disappointment, and infuriating inconsistency on the part of your evaluators.

It's very hard to get a creative job in an advertising agency, even if you are talented and have a good book.

I'm telling you this, not only because it's true, but because creative job seekers and agency "gatekeepers" have urged me to divulge this fact right up front.

An unofficial estimate is that five hundred beginning creatives get first jobs as junior copywriters and art directors in the United States every year. Most of that number get their jobs in the "major markets" – New York, Chicago, and Los Angeles.

The rest get jobs in agencies throughout the country. If you want to be one of those people badly enough, you will be. If not in your first year out, then in your second.

And many of you will find entry level jobs as studio assistants or creative assistants and get promoted into copy and art later on. Or you will get into a different aspect of advertising and communications, like promotion, design, direct response, or in-house advertising for a corporation. Or you will decide to go into a different business altogether.

If what you read in this book discourages you from pursuing a career in advertising, I'm glad I've saved you from what might have been years of frustration.

Don't feel badly about this, should it happen.

As we sometimes say, *"Hey. It's only advertising."* And we mean it.

The advertising business is just a business; a very small business, although a very visible one. That's why so many people want to be in it and why so few people get in. But for those who are suited to it, it's the very best business in the world.

That's why, with the help of many interested parties, I've written this book. If you want to join us, we want to help you.

I hope you get what you want.

Maxine Paetro

ACKNOWLEDGMENTS:

My enduring thanks to these wonderful people who helped me put the original version of this book together and whose contributions are very much evident in the revised edition:

Billy Foster, Giff Crosby, Ted Littleford, Mike Becker, David Liemer, Mary Ellen Cohen, Marshall Karp, Ken Charof, Mark Ross, John LaRock, Kerry O'Conner, Colleen Meehan, John Sarley, Susan Friedman, Gary Kott, Ed Vick, Charles McAleer, Peter Bregman, Judy Fitzgerald, Bruce Minniear, Jim Bozman, Linda Almgren, Susan DiLallo, Lisa Maxwell, Ted Luciani, Bobbi Goldin, Arthur Bijur, Owen Ryan, Joyce Harrington, Sylvia Laniado, Bill Chororos, the late Dale Fels, Ed Rogers, the late Ron Hoff, and especially the late Ed Buxton who blessed, edited, published, and sold the original edition.

And I wish to thank the following people without whose help the first revision would have been only a reprinting:

Marie Arteca, Erin Milhaven, the team; Giff Crosby who came through again with his humorous, apt, and accessible illustrations; and Flinn Dallis, Nancy Temkin, Ginny Howsam, Dany Lennon, Ed McCabe, Joe Conwell, Arthur Bijur, Judy Demillo, Dan Mountain, Neal Hughlett, Steve Penchina, Dennis Harkey, Mark Katz, Steven Hersh, Russ Cohen, Shelly Gewirtz, Charles Hall, Vivian Alford, Steven Miller, Dalton Padgett, Gary Goldsmith, Steven Herman, Pat Peduto, Leora Brayer, Kelly Trewartha, David Parson, Paul Brandenburger, Bill Karow, Loren Phillips, Howard Karp, Anders Rich, Tony Lauricella, Scott Smith, Mia Relyea, Ed Wax, Jean-Claude Kaufmann, Gregory Powell, Dianne Dean, Mary Dean, David Liemer, Carin Greenberg, John Colquhoun, Jean Govoni, Laura Shapiro, Ray Johnson, Cindy Chupack, Diana Kramer, Lee Kovel, Eric Mudich, and Renata Rizzo-Harvi, for allowing me to appropriate their stories, résumés, advice, and promotional ideas.

The revision you now hold in your hands has been advanced by the very valuable contributions of Betsy Yamazaki, Carol Vick, Pippa Seichrist, Lauren Slaff, Cathy St. Jean, Kathy Primozic, Michele Daly, Bertrand Garbassi, Tracy Sachs, Amy Krouse Rosenthal and David Jones, Chris Turner, Leslie Kay, Phil Theibert, Michael Cohen, and Curtis Smith.

And many thanks to Patrick Coyne of *Communication Arts* and Curtis Clarkson at *CMYK* who were kind enough to let us use essays that originally ran in their fine publications.

These marvelous people sat down in front of their blank screens and wrote dazzling, insightful, practical, and wise essays for this book. I'm very grateful to Luke Sullivan, Tom Cunniff, Rick Boyko, Greg DiNoto, Rod Goodman, Charles Hall, Ernie Schenck, Bruce Bendinger, Leora Brayer, Phil Dusenberry, Jim Durfee, Mark Fenske, Cliff Freeman, Gary Goldsmith, Jeff Goodby, Richard Kirshenbaum, Wayne Johnson, David Lubars, Deborah Morrison, Charlotte Moore, Lee Kovel, Alex Kroll, Bob Kuperman, Evelyn Monroe, Jim Patterson, Ross Sutherland, Robin Raj, Ron Seichrist, Susan Spiegel, Helayne Spivak, and Eric Weber for their wonderful essays and advice.

I wish to thank the department heads, instructors, and placement people at the Portfolio Center, the University of Texas, Syracuse University, the School of Visual Arts, Fashion Institute of Technology, L.A. Art Center, The Creative Circus, and the Miami Ad School for inviting me to speak on their campuses, and I also want to thank the students of these schools who have taught me, taken what I've dished out, and written in with their questions.

I'd like to thank my good friends Jim Patterson and Nancy Temkin, who gave me a room of my own at J. Walter Thompson, New York, so that I could complete this work.

Thanks to Geri Thoma, who has hung in through countless contracts and new editions.

And thanks, too, to Giff Crosby, creative director and cartoonist extraordinaire, for updating and creating new apt and funny illustrations for the millennium edition of this book.

Lastly and most sincerely, I'd like to thank the pros at the Copy Workshop: Bruce Bendinger, my tireless and good-humored editor, this edition's assistants, Arunas Statkus and Patrick Aylward, Lorelei Davis, one of the world's loveliest publishers, and the rest of the team for adopting this book, devoting themselves to it, and putting their time and money where their friendship was.

And thanks to all my friends and associates who taught me what I know about advertising.

TABLE OF CONTENTS:

PART III. A LITTLE HELP FROM SOME FRIENDS (CONT.)

INTRODUCTION:

This book was not written by a copywriter or an art director or a creative director. It was written by me, Maxine Paetro, a creative department manager, a recruiter, an administrator, whose job it was for many years to be concerned with the quality of life in an advertising agency creative department.

I have never written a word of advertising copy, nor have I designed an ad, or come up with an advertising idea.

What I have done in the course of my 20-plus years in advertising is to place or hire or recommend to be hired a whole lot of copywriters and art directors. And in the process of doing that I have seen many, many thousands of books.

I wish I could, but I can't actually teach you how to become a copywriter or an art director. (I assume you have decided on an advertising career and have taken courses in advertising.)

My purpose with this book is to help you become aware of what makes a great ad, help you think through the advertising process, give you some guidelines on how to present your work in the best possible light, assist you in getting to and impressing people who've seen as many portfolios as I've seen, and help you land a job.

The original *How to Put Your Book Together…* grew out of talks I'd given to students at art schools and universities.

This newest edition picks up from those talks and continues with questions asked by new generations of future advertising people.

As before, the questions are those of copy and art students. The answers are mine. I have kept the basic information in this revision; first-year issues concerning concepts and campaigns for those who have just begun to ask what this portfolio thing is all about.

I have added new questions and answers that I hope will help those about to graduate, those who are about to enter or have already entered the tougher-than-ever entry-level job competition.

Because I am but one voice in the wilderness, I've invited some of the best creative brains in advertising to express their point of view about the business, tell what they look for in a portfolio, and generally offer you a helping hand. You'll find these contributions in the third section of this book.

2

Finally, it is important to understand that in a business as subjective as advertising, there are often no wrong or right answers.

But I think you will agree, you have to know the rules in order to break them.

My hope is that you will incorporate the advice you get from this book with what you believe is right for you and, in the process, form your own good judgment.

If you can do that, you will have a better chance of getting your first job in advertising.

I have seen a lot of books.

PART I

HOW TO PUT
YOUR BOOK TOGETHER...

YOUR BOOK. THE BASICS.

Advertising agencies are looking for the very best portfolios they can find. What they want to see, primarily, are *ideas*.

They want to see that you can sell products, that you're an *advertising thinker*. When you hear a person described as being *"conceptual,"* this is what the speaker means.

There is an expectation that both copywriters and art directors should be conceptual.

At some point, agencies look for different skills in copy and art, but for the moment, let's talk about this thing called *concept*.

A concept, very simply, is an *idea*.

In terms of advertising, it's the central theme that underlies your advertising. It's the premise that is the foundation of your ad and your campaign.

The best way to express your concept is in a *campaign* format.

A campaign is a series of ads for a product (or service or company) that work individually and cumulatively to communicate the advertiser's message to the consumer.

A concept, very simply, is an idea.

First, a simple example. "Got Milk?" This campaign, created by Goodby Silverstein & Partners, reminds people in a variety of creative ways that there are some times when you really need to have milk.

The concept, the idea, remains the same in each ad. But the ads, part of the same set, change visuals each time. That's a decent working definition of a campaign.

Interestingly enough, there's a second campaign for milk created by Bozell – the "milk mustache." This campaign worked "to establish milk as a contemporary beverage alternative." Again, there is a unifying visual, celebrities wearing their "milk mustache." Along the way, the client decided to combine them.

Advertising can be like that. Create something one way – and it ends up another. Still, each campaign's creator also created a great professional reputation – and they were paid handsomely for it.

Two more clear examples of long-running campaigns are those for two credit card brands – VISA and MasterCard. Even though these two products are obviously very similar – identical, really – each developed a different and meaningful campaign approach.

VISA tells you they are "everywhere you want to be" in a variety of desirable ways. They connect with all the fun places you can spend money with a VISA card. Meanwhile, MasterCard talks about being part of your life with their "priceless" campaign – and the line, "There are some things money can't buy. For everything else, there's MasterCard."

Before we leave these campaigns, think about that set of words that comes at the end of the commercial or is at the bottom of the print ad. "Got Milk?" And "It's Everywhere You Want to Be."

What's hard at work here is a device called a *tag line,* sometimes called a base, theme, or logo line.

Used as a positioning statement, this line tells the consumer how the advertiser wants his product or company to be perceived, and this message is delivered in a neat package the consumer can take with him.

A tag line also serves as a signature for the advertiser, thereby helping you, the consumer, link up all the ads you've seen for this product or company so that the effect of each ad is enhanced by your memory of the whole campaign.

8

Not all campaigns use a tag line, but for your purposes, you may find it a useful technique for pulling your ads together into a campaign. Very often, if you have a good tag line, your ads may almost create themselves.

Can you think of some concepts that are so big, the agency could create (or "pool out") additional advertising around that concept for years? Does the advertiser use a tag line?

How about "Just Do It" for Nike. "Drivers Wanted" for Volkswagen. "Like a Rock" for Chevy. "Obey Your Thirst" for Sprite. "Do the Dew" for Mountain Dew.

Analyze your favorite campaigns.

Look at tag lines, and see which ones effectively sum up a campaign idea and give the consumer a phrase to remember.

Consider how tag lines can work for you.

And now, back to your book.

When we look at it, we want to see that you can come up with concepts and expand your ideas into campaigns.

Now, don't think that a technically complete campaign – three ads for the same product – is sufficient. You've all seen enough advertising to simply imitate a campaign by doing three similar ads in a series.

If you do that, the person who is reviewing your book is going to doze off. You need to come up with fresh ideas that jar that person awake. You want him to go tearing down the hall with your book under his arm shouting, "Let's give this kid a job!"

But putting together a book that gets people excited is hard to do.

How are you going to do it? Well, having talent is a must.

Being clever distinguishes you.

Being *thorough* is your starting point.

Your good friend, Drano.

To do good ads, you must be on very good terms with your products. You have to know what you're talking about and to whom you're directing your message.

That's why I suggest you *concentrate on products you know or products you want to know more about,* because the more you know about your product, the more you care about it, the more likely you are to have an inspired idea. And the truer your ads will ring.

To get started, pick a product you know.

Check out your medicine chest or the cabinet under your kitchen sink. Got any friends in there? Okay. Choose one. Say hello, and if you feel like it, give it a friendly pat.

Then think through what made you buy that product. When you know why you bought that product, you're on your way to coming up with an idea that will convince someone else to buy it.

Choose products you know.
Here's one source of inspiration.

Now ask yourself these questions:

- In what ways is your product similar to others in its category?
- In what ways is it different?
- What benefit does your product offer?
- What (truthful) promise can you make about your product that will differentiate it from others in its category?
- What is the "advertising problem" you're trying to solve?
- Who buys your product now? Should you be addressing the same consumer? Or should you focus on, expand, or change your target?

"Oh, no," you might be thinking. "I don't have to know that stuff. That's account exec territory."

Sorry, but knowing your product – what it has to offer, what competes with it, and who you can persuade to buy it – is absolutely fundamental to the process of doing advertising. You shouldn't even think of executing your ad until you've got some answers to these questions.

Here's another.

11

In an advertising agency, this foundation work is often called *"positioning"* the product and developing a *"strategy"* for the advertising.

In real life, the account executive on your account will be key to this part of the process and will work with you to help you arrive at these reference points.

No one expects you to have a degree in marketing, but since you must have some form of this basic information before you start to do your speculative ads, you'll have to pour the foundation yourself.

Now, how about doing some research on your product?

Advertising agencies talk to consumers. You can do the same.

The people who work in an agency's planning department probe the marketplace for insight into the consumer's tastes, values, loyalties, preferences. They design questions, analyze data, and interpret it for use by the creative department.

One frequently used research tool is the *"focus group."* In an informal setting, volunteer consumers answer questions about a specific product or product category. Sometimes they look at speculative advertising, answer questions about it, and as a result, the ads may be abandoned. Sometimes new ideas are born.

What am I suggesting now? That you become a planner? Don't worry. This is painless. Even fun.

Think about doing some research on your product.

12

Go to your neighborhood supermarket and ask the manager why one brand of dog food outsells the competing brands. Study the competition. Read the labels. Take notes.

Discuss your chosen products with family members, roommates, unsuspecting strangers in the pet food section.

Make new friends. Get some conversations going. Someone's offhand remark could spark that illuminating idea.

I know getting this involved with the product seems like a lot of work. It *is* a lot of work. And no one is expecting you to have all the answers. What we're hoping is that starting now you'll train yourselves to ask the questions.

Someday this process will be automatic. Upon meeting your new brand, your brain will strip-search it so fast, it won't even feel your fingerprints. Trust me on this. *All good creative people – whether they get their marketing information in a formal or informal way, through a hundred-page strategic brief or a hundred well-chosen words with the client – think "product" and "consumer" before they think "headline" and "visual."*

Get into a good habit now. Knowing the product and understanding your prospective consumer can help you come up with stronger ideas – ideas with impact. The better the ideas in your portfolio, the better the chance some creative director is going to come knocking at my door.

Your ideas must have impact.

Q. **What products should be represented in my portfolio? Should I work on a variety of accounts?**

A. It would certainly simplify things if there was an official list of product categories that you should cover. Then you could check off this list as you go, and when the list was done, you would be, too.

But there is no such list.

People judging your book care about the quality of your ideas, and they care about your craftsmanship. Showing that you can work on a variety of products suggests to the person reviewing your book how your talents might be applied to the agency's client list.

And now, here's something new to think about.

While most people who look at your book won't have a product checklist in mind, they may go back over the whole of your book – even if it's very, very good – and consider the degree of difficulty you set for yourself in problem-solving.

In a competitive situation, your book will be ranked accordingly.

It's kind of the way diving and skating competitions are judged in the Olympics. Straight tens go to the athletes who do the tough maneuvers perfectly. Easy maneuvers, even if perfectly done, only earn eights.

Q. **Having said that, what kind of products should I choose for my book? Should I work on a variety of accounts?**

A. As we've discussed previously, you're going to choose products you know or want to know.

But I wouldn't suggest filling up your book exclusively with ads for stereos, cameras, and motorcycles just because you love high-tech hard goods. A one-category book is drawing a pretty small box around yourself, don't you think? I'd suggest that you increase your range a bit. Is there a brand of detergent you can relate to? Are you dead loyal to Clean 'n' Shiny shampoo? Is there an antacid you always reach for when you've got a nasty stomach?

Maybe. But you don't want to do ads for an antacid, you say. All those shampoo ads look the same. You can't do good ads for detergents.

Tell that to Alka Seltzer. And tell it to Cheer. Bushels of awards have been won for the advertising for these two products, as well as for scouring pads, tomato sauce, and dog food.

But come to think of it, no award-winning shampoo advertising comes to my mind. So here, I think, is an opportunity for you to distinguish yourself.

The World's Toughest Product Category – Packaged Goods.

That shampoo I mentioned, along with the antacid and the detergent, etc., fall into a category of products called *"packaged goods."*

Packaged goods come in a box, tube, or a container of some sort – the package. You buy them in a grocery store or pharmacy.

Toothpaste, cleansers, baby peas – in fact all canned goods – are packaged goods.

You use the products up, and then you buy them again.

Advertising for packaged goods products represents many millions of dollars annually. Procter & Gamble alone spends something like *$2 billion* a year in ads and commercials.

About 75 percent of the ads you see are for packaged goods products, which means that doing advertising for clients that make packaged goods is big business for big agencies.

If I may take this thought a step further, the odds are pretty good that if you get into advertising, there's a packaged goods account somewhere in your future.

Now, to crank the difficulty factor up another notch, I'd like to introduce you to the word "parity." While it's tough to make startling ads for a straight-up packaged goods product, it's even tougher to take on a parity product.

A parity product is one that is just about the same as all other products in its category – a "me-too" product.

Let's compare the two types of products.

For instance, Crest is a toothpaste. It's a packaged goods product. Crest toothpaste is also more of a parity product. It has virtually the same properties and ingredients as the other major competitors.

Crest White Strips, on the other hand, are a much more distinctive product with an obvious and immediate benefit.

It is easier for you to do an ad for Crest White Strips than it is for you to do an ad for Crest. The strips have a few product differences you can get your brain around.

With Crest, on the other hand, you really have to push to differentiate it from Colgate, or others in its category.

Your mission, should you choose to accept it, is to look at that toothpaste from all angles, uncover a unique but truthful selling idea, and then execute that idea in a dazzling way.

And that's tough to do.

Come up with a great campaign for Crest White Strips, and we're happy. Come up with a new idea for Crest toothpaste, and we're more than happy, we're a little stunned.

Creating advertising for parity products is a major challenge for people in the advertising business. They deal with products that have tiny or nonexistent differences, and yet they are expected to create advertising that gives the product a unique quality.

Sometimes the biggest difference between two products is the advertising. This is the stuff of which the cola and burger wars are made, and carving out a position for a parity product is very difficult.

But, it can be done. I'm sure you've seen that classic commercial for Cheer detergent. A silent spokesman takes a lipstick-smeared hanky, puts it in a cocktail shaker of cold water and ice cubes, shakes it up for thirty seconds, and produces a clean hanky. "Nothing Washes Cleaner in Cold" is the line. This amusing and solid campaign successfully ran for many years.

Services also have parity – like insurance companies, banks, and airlines. For example, American Airlines, Delta Airlines, and United all have parity. Low fare airlines, like SouthWest and ATA have a different type of selling message – one that clearly differentiates them from "the big boys."

So, if we look at your book and we see ads that say SouthWest is cheaper, we hope your execution is great because the "product" difference makes coming up with a concept relatively easy.

Q. What if you're not ready to take on a parity product or service?

A. If you've tried, but the results are dull, back off for now.

Your objective is to set yourself as difficult a challenge in product selection as you can cope with. But most of us would rather see a book of ads for Crest White Strips and SouthWest Airlines executed brilliantly than an entire book of detergent ads done in a boring but competent way.

So what products should you choose?
Should you do work for a variety of accounts?

Here's what one advertising professional thinks on this subject. Dan Mountain, an award-winning copywriter/CD based in Los Angeles, offers the following tips on product category selection.

1. Pick a product you use every day, *a product you need but don't want.* Mouthwash, cereal, shoe polish. You choose.
2. Pick one product you buy quite often that you *want, don't need.* Candy bars, magazines, a CD, etc.
3. Pick a product that you don't buy more than once a year. *It's a considered purchase.* A car, a VCR, two weeks in the sun.

Ginny Howsam, a New York employment agent, suggests a fourth type of product.

4. Pick a product you *feel passionately about.* Anything, so long as your feelings about it are strong.

To sum up:

In real life, advertising agencies have many different accounts, and each of those accounts must be approached in a custom-tailored way.

So – do ads for a variety of accounts. Show some range.

Work on products you understand – big brands and small, hard goods and soft.

Try to do at least one campaign for a parity product or service. This is where you will find your toughest challenges.

Consider doing a campaign for a packaged goods product.

While you won't get points for doing a C+ bar soap ad, an A+ bar soap ad says you're special.

Finally, no agency will turn you away because you haven't done packaged goods, parity products, or because you haven't covered every product category. A book of splendid, original, captivating ads transcends any niggling concerns about product selection.

A QUIZ:

WHICH ONE ISN'T A PACKAGED GOOD?
(TAKE YOUR TIME)

WHICH ONE ISN'T A PARITY PRODUCT?

AND, FINALLY, WHICH ONE ISN'T A PARITY SERVICE?

A N S W E R S :

3. (upside-down biplane)   2. (upside-down Whitestrips)   1. (upside-down YetAnother Airline plane)

19

Q. What types of products or accounts should I avoid?

A. Again, there are no rules here, but here are some categories where "spec" ads may not be able to compete favorably with the real thing. My thoughts:

It's risky to do spec campaigns for products with advertising so outstanding, your chances of doing better work are quite slim.
In other words, your spec ads won't look so good by comparison.

One of those products is Absolut Vodka. The long-running Absolut campaign is a collection of elegant ads in which a swimming pool, a golf green, or some other witty visual effect is depicted in the shape of the Absolut bottle.

Each ad projects an iconic image of the product, involves the consumer in solving the visual puzzle, and summons up recollections of other ads in the campaign. This is about as good as a campaign can get.

I wouldn't go after Nike, either. Their image has been so impressed upon consumer America, we need only see their familiar "swoosh" logo and we call up rafts of Nike ads and television commercials from our memory banks.

Similarly, I wouldn't take on the Gap. If they've ever produced boring ads for their products, I can't remember any.

Good luck.

Perhaps you can think of campaigns for other products or services that have achieved first-class, indelible brand identities. If you are going to do a spec campaign for one of these classic accounts, make sure your campaign is a killer.

It's very difficult to create brilliant "image" campaigns without the use of great photography, music, production values.

A definition: "Image advertising" reflects the personality or look a client's target consumer relates to, or wants to emulate.

Rather than appealing to logic (as does the Cheer campaign), it persuades by inviting consumers to picture themselves in the ad

Beauty and fashion accounts frequently use image advertising to project their message, as do cigarette, liquor, and beer accounts.

When you think of Calvin Klein's advertising, or Ralph Lauren's or Lexus, I'll bet a picture and a mood comes to mind, but not a snappy line to take away.

The image ad usually depends on an intangible, emotional feeling expressed by an unusual graphic concept and rich production values. Most (although not all) great image campaigns are rooted in film, and this is why you, at home at your desk or keyboard, might be at a disadvantage.

Mercedes Benz gave us a herd of galloping rhinos. Pepsi, using the best television production money can buy, conveys their message with great music, Britney Spears, or fancy-trick camera work.

You've got less than a few million dollars to spend and are creating campaign awareness from scratch. Can you make a big production idea (as opposed to a big selling idea) come alive in your book? Can you do it without ripping off images that have already appeared in print for another product? It's a heck of a challenge.

Advertising portfolios coming out of schools that specialize in portfolio development have become very sophisticated.

These books can cost their creators a thousand bucks or more to produce. Scrap photos are imported into Macs, sized up and down, and altered. Exotic type fonts abound. Color copies are used extensively, and when there is an original concept behind these showy productions, images with impact can leap from that portfolio into a reviewer's mind.

So, I'm not saying don't try to create a compelling image campaign, because this could be an area where success is equal to a home run. But remember – conveying image in spec print is hard to do well, and if you only do a fair job, it may not be worth doing.

Don't do too many campaigns for local retailers.

If we don't understand the local lore and you assume we know it, we may miss the point of your campaign. If you must do ads for the campus pizza hangout down the road, keep in mind that Joe's Pizza doesn't run double page spreads in *Sports Illustrated* magazine. Do a small space ad campaign instead.

Don't do too much public service advertising.

A public service ad is one that pleads a cause, solicits money, recruits volunteers, or in other ways performs a not-for-profit information service. "Don't Wear Fur," "Don't Do Drugs," "Use Condoms," all fit into the public service category.

If parity products are on the high end of the difficult challenge scale, public service ads are on the low end. They are relatively easy to do because emotion is already built into the "product;" you don't have to create it. It's fine to do one public service ad or campaign for your book, but if your best headline is "Adopt These Puppies or We Will Kill Them," your book needs more solid work.

As with all rules, there are exceptions.

Charles Hall came up with this magnificent public service campaign. Picture a series of ads depicting steamy black and white close-ups; a women's bosom in a black lace bra, a stretch of creamy thigh gripped with a garter belt fastener, an exposed navel above lacy underwear. In tiny red letters that draw the reader in very close to the page is this caption "This is not an invitation to rape me."

This is a great, moving, simple campaign that might actually change human perceptions. Charles did a strong public service campaign for a cause he cares about, and his caring shows. (Read his essay in Part III of this book.)

If you decide to do a public service ad, do one for a cause that's important to you. Exploiting shock for shock's sake, and hitching a ride on the thing we fear most right now, is not reason enough to do a public service ad.

Q. What do you like to see most in a book?
What do you like to see least?

A. *I like to see ads that feel like they came from the heart of the creator;* ones that talk to a human being on a human level, ones that evoke an emotional response. I think of this kind of ad as having "heart."

An ad with heart will warm the reader, or scare him, or snap him to attention, or make his jaw drop, or make him laugh, or make him wonder.

And an ad with heart doesn't lie.

It supports its emotional message with facts, sometimes referred to as a "reason why." Sometimes as "permission to believe."

When a person reads an ad, he reads by himself. He (or she) should feel you are speaking just to him, not to a million other people at the same time. Your ads will have much more impact if you picture this individual reader in your mind.

Here's an example.

If you were writing a perfume ad, you could say, "This perfume is sexy." But Judy wrote, "Put It Where You Want to Be Kissed." See what I mean? That headline makes you feel something. Where do you want to be kissed?

Colleen, a beginning art director, did an ad for a new product she invented – a deep-cleansing soap. Her visual was two photos, one of a young woman and one of a newborn baby. Her headline was, "Your Skin Hasn't Been Clean Since the Day You Were Born."

Wow! Really? How come? She pulled me right into that ad by speaking to me. Her visual was compelling, and her few lines of copy described this new kind of soap. It made me focus on the condition of my skin.

I like humor that works.

Chris's campaign for an exotic pet shop shows a close-up of an alligator. The headline: "Sure, he'll catch a frisbee – if you tie a poodle to it."

Russ came up with this small-space coupon ad for Vick's Cough Drops. The ad is in cartoon-strip format. Imagine a couple in a darkened theater, in silhouette, their backs to us.

Coughs are emitted via voice balloon from the character on the right for a couple of frames, until the character on the left turns, and snaps, "Cut it out!"

A 25 cents-off coupon takes up the last frame.

I like smart, simple, grabby demos that make the product the star of the campaign.

Michael and Curtis did this clever ad for Turtle Wax.

Picture a beautiful landscape. Upon close inspection, you realize that the landscape is a reflection in the finish of the side of a car. The headline: "Scenery by Mother Nature. View by Turtle Wax." A perfect demonstration of the product.

I like ads that are founded on an original idea.

Andrea and Matt created a campaign for Rose's Lime Juice based on the personality of a sour character named Rose.

Rose is never pictured, but alongside a vivid, stylized visual of the bottle is snarky copy like this: "I hate beautiful weather. And beautiful thoughts. And beautiful teeth. I hate holding hands and all that crap. Happiness is coming back for a five-year reunion and finding all of you bald. I hope you are all miserable." – (Rose's graduation speech.)

The tag line is "Rose's Lime Juice. There Ain't Nothin' More Sour." I love this campaign because Andrea and Matt "get" the product and engage the consumer. They brought an ordinary product to life with intelligence and wit to create an original product personality.

I like ads that are well crafted.

I like visualizations and words that are honed, impactful, and reflect your individual point of view.

Kim and Bobby came up with this ad for Dial soap. Visual: an outstretched, naked male arm. Hovering around the armpit, is a small hummingbird. The Dial logo is in the bottom corner. This lovely, simple visual gets your attention, and sells the product.

24

Some general advice.

Art directors: Unless it really is the best way to go, you know to break away from the standard ad-like layout; headline on top, visual in the middle, body copy on the bottom. But beware of going too far off the wall in the other direction.

Layouts that have too many elements are hard to read.

Bizarre type in numerous fonts, colors, directions, and sizes confuses the message and therefore the reader.

You must communicate in order to sell, and no one likes to work hard to get your message. And, to state the obvious, for art directors, design counts as much as concept.

Copywriters: Really write! Create pictures in our minds.

Both of you: Come up with a headline that grabs, and a tag line that sums up your concept – one that gives your reader that little package to take home.

Now. What I like to see least.

I don't like to see a book filled with pun headlines.

A very good pun can work, but if creating them is your first instinct, your ads may be so slick they don't stick.

If they don't stick, they can't move the consumer, and they can't sell the product.

Here are some examples of pun headlines.

"Glove Me Tender." Insert name of glove line in ad. "Call in the Infant Tree." Insert plant nursery name in ad.

Do these headlines make you feel anything? Would they induce you to buy anything? Do you get the feeling some of these headlines were written even before the product was selected?

A rule. Never be clever at your product's expense.

Once in a while, we see a pun that showcases the product, that is, really makes the product the star of the ad. Here's what I mean.

Two juniors I know came up with this ad for Lifesavers. Visual: a clean, white page filled with colorful, bigger-than-life Life Saver candies. Headline: "Hole Sale."

To pay off the line, there's a coupon below that invites the consumer to buy two, get one free. This pun is about and for the product. So, a pun can be fun, but a whole book of puns signals heartless advertising.

I dislike the casual use of celebrity spokespersons.

If your chosen celebrity is very well matched to your product, okay, but just grafting a famous person onto your product doesn't impress anyone.

We want to see ideas.

Unless you're Gatorade, Michael Jordan isn't an idea. In real life, Shaq O'Neill might not be interested in selling your product, and even if he is, does he promote your message or make you think you don't need a message?

Celebrity artists, ditto. Be careful when your campaign depends on cartoons by Booth or Larsen or photos by Annie Liebowitz.

True, advertising people use celebrities and high-priced photographers all the time, but at this stage we're more interested in seeing your ideas – selling ideas, that is – and shortcuts can short-circuit the process.

The heartless ad: a friend to no one.

Heartless ads make me nuts.

This, the biggest problem we see in portfolios from New York to California and every state in between, is the result of picking up your markers or turning on your computer too soon.

The scenario can go like this. You had an idea for a visual and you've created a campaign around it.

Or you heard a headline in your head last night, and now you've picked a product to fit the headline and you're off and running.

Starting with an execution first is a sure way of creating heartless ads; sometimes called "ad-like objects." All the components of an ad are there: the headline, the visual, the body copy, and the tag line. Some of these elements can be kind of smashing.

But the piece still doesn't move anybody, and because nobody is moved, the ad doesn't sell.

Here's an example of a heartless ad for Gatorade. Visual: A jogger, jogging, and a product shot in the corner of the page. Headline: "More Miles per Gallon." The tag line: "Gatorade. The High-Octane Drink."

Well, what do you think?

Kind of clever, right? But do you feel anything? Do you get any sense that this writer understands you, the athlete, or that he is bringing anything new to your understanding of the product?

Compare this ad with one from the long-running and still effective campaign for Nike athletic shoes. Their message speaks to the part of each of us that hates to exercise. Then, Nike's theme line – "Just Do It." Feel that?

Again. The ad-making process always begins with the product and consumer. The execution follows. While you might be able to get away with a few clever-but-heartless ads, a whole book of them is going to work against you.

What else do I like least?

Walking Strategy Statements.

A "Walking Strategy Statement" – an "ad-like object" – is an ad with no craft. Like its cousin, the heartless ad, the walking strategy statement has a headline, a visual, and body copy, but it reads like a research report.

It has no zing. It strikes no chord.

I think this kind of work shows up when you've taken the opposite approach to doing your ads too fast.

In this case, you've paid so much homage to your strategy (the way the product should be marketed) that your "key fact" is right there in the headline – bald, naked, and wearing its hiking boots.

Here's an example. The ad is for Elan Frozen Yogurt. The visual is a product shot in the center of the page. The headline: "Tastes Great Like Haagen-Daz. Takes Out Fat and Calories That Haagen-Dazn't." The tag line seems to be yet another piece of the strategy: "Elan Frozen Yogurt. For Sundaes and Every Day."

Understand the strategy? Catch the pun? Feel anything?

If your book is filled with walking strategy statements, you've forgotten the consumer wants to be spoken to. Not lectured at.

Vulgar Advertising.

Keep it clean. Sexist, racist, and crude ads offend more people than they persuade. I can't think of any ads that offend people into buying the products, can you?

I interviewed a writer once who had created, perhaps innocently, this ad for Lender's Bagels. "So Nice and Jewy," said her headline. I think there was actually a visual of bagels, like quoits, on someone's nose. (I'm not sure, because I think I blacked out for a moment.) This is a true story.

In short, bad taste is bad news. What else?

Sloppy Ads.

You don't care about your book and it shows.

I'm not talking about last-minute ideas that you've roughed out. I'm talking about old ads with food stains.

If you don't care enough to give your very best, please don't waste my time. And what else?

Class Assignments.

If so, they'd better be terrific – not filler where you didn't even get top grades. Are you cocky? Lazy? Or what?

There's a competition going on here, remember?

And, frankly, we've seen an awful lot of ads for Post-it notes, dental floss, Fix-a-Flat, Lava Soap, Tabasco sauce, and your local zoo – to name some of the most common.

Naturally, you have a lot of class assignments in your book. If you were awarded gold stars and stickers, by all means keep those ads in. As for the rest, please take my advice.

Close your book on your class assignments and come up with a killer ad on your own. Then use it to replace your half-good, class-assigned campaign for a local beer joint that is adding nothing but weight to your portfolio.

Get sharp or get left behind.

Bottom line.

I do like ads that have an original idea, that are executed with thought and craft, that strike a chord with the reader.

I don't like ads that are offensive, slick, or sloppy, or where you've solved your advertising problem by taking the easiest path.

Q. What's a killer ad?

A. A killer ad is simple, dramatic, memorable.

It has heart, a brain, and sometimes a funnybone.

A killer ad is based on an original idea. It stands the test of time. When you see a killer ad, you wish you'd done it.

One killer ad that comes to my mind is the classic ad for Maxell recording tape. You know the one. A man is sitting in a chair in front of his tape deck. The sound, like wind, is blowing back his hair, his tie, the lampshade. Every time I see this ad, I get enthralled anew.

Have you seen the print ad of a partially eaten peanut butter and jelly sandwich bearing the headline "Got Milk?" for the Milk Advertising Board?

The concept of this campaign is to show intense milk deprivation situations. This one ad sums up the concept perfectly, stands alone, yet calls up the entire campaign to mind. Pretty darned great.

A killer TV spot for Jeep shows a car-sized object tunneling under the snow. It comes to a stop sign, signals for a turn, continues tunneling. We never see the Jeep, but we get the message. This vehicle is indomitable.

One student I know tapes this killer spec ad right by his computer and uses it as a touchstone. Visual: a broken crayon. Headline: "Toys Break. Crayons Multiply."

This ad was created by creative director, Gary Goldsmith (read his essay in Part III) when he, like you, was putting his book together.

Where to find more killer ads? Get your hands on some award annuals. The *One Show* book is one of the best. *Archive* takes you on an international advertising trip.

Or get the *Art Directors Annual*, the *Clio* book, the *Communication Arts Advertising Annual*. *Ad Age's Creativity Magazine* produces ten issues annually of current creative news and *AdWeek* showcases new work weekly. And now there's *CMYK* featuring the best student work.

Here's how to rate your ads for killerhood.

- Is your ad (or commercial or campaign) simple, dramatic, and memorable?
- Does it know to whom it is talking and what it wants to say?
- Does it stand on its own without depending upon fancy production or celebrity spokespersons?
- Does it arouse emotion?
- Does it satisfy logic?
- Does it have an original idea?

Well, okay! Come up with one more killer just to be sure.
Stick a couple more good campaigns between those two.

Now you've got a killer sandwich. If you constantly upgrade those merely good campaigns, soon you'll have a killer book.

When you go out looking for a job, you're going to be armed!

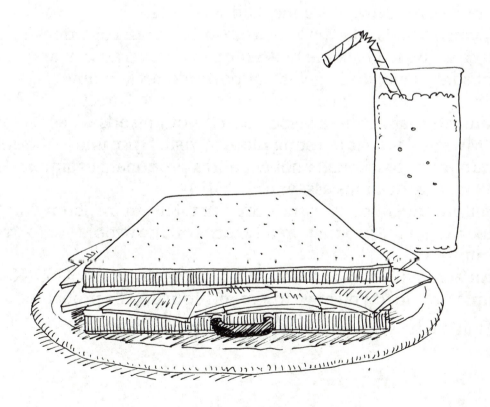

Now you've got a "Killer Sandwich!"

Q. **Why simple?**
Simple would put Steven Spielberg out of business.

A.   Steven Spielberg's concepts are simple. Stranded extra-terrestrial wants to go home. Man-created dinosaurs run amok.
And Spielberg has hours to tell his story.
You've got seconds.

Your *ideas* should be simple. You can execute your little heart out as long as you don't muddy your message. You're doing ads, you know. And the consumer doesn't want to have to work too hard to figure out what you're trying to sell. Or why he should buy it.
Simple doesn't mean *simple-minded.*

We're not looking for vapid, boring, condescending ads. We mean simple as in "pure." Better yet, pure gold.
Your goal is to crystalize a powerful thought in an instant.
I keep saying your ads must communicate quickly.
Think subway poster. You're standing on the platform when the subway comes in and stops before you. The door opens. Read the ad on the opposite side. The door closes. Did you get it?
Or think billboard. You're in your car driving on the freeway. See the billboard? Now, it's gone. Did you get it?
If your visuals take too long to absorb, if your copy doesn't grab, you're going to get some twisted up eyebrows and an apologetic, "I'm sorry. I just don't get it," at portfolio review time.
Jim Patterson, former Worldwide Creative Director of J. Walter Thompson, labels these personal, sell-nothing ads we see so much of "My mind is an interesting place to visit." (Jim is also the author of numerous blockbuster novels, and a proponent of simple, killer advertising. Read his essay in Part III.)
Self-indulgent body copy – copy that tells more about you than it does about the product – really turns off the people you're trying to impress.
An acronym from the world of communications: KISS. Keep it simple, stupid. If you have to explain your ad, it's probably a miss.

That's why your ads should be simple.

Q. **There isn't a packaged goods client within a thousand miles of the place I call home and where I want to work. Do I have to do ads for packaged goods?**

A. Heck no. Flinn Dallis, long-time Creative Manager of Leo Burnett, has this advice: *"Make your book match your market."*

By which she means: if there is very little packaged goods business in your city of choice, do ads for insurance companies, brokerage firms, real estate companies, retail businesses, restaurants, and automotive products, as well as the consumer goods you'd just plain like to take a crack at. When in Chicago, think food.

On the West Coast, there are more retailers and computer companies on agency client rosters than there are in New York. And you may want your campaigns to include outdoor advertising.

There isn't a packaged goods account within 1,000 miles.
Do you still need to do ads for them?

33

Actually, an outdoor ad is even welcome in Gotham, where we don't have too many billboards on display. A concept that has impact at fifty-five miles an hour is impressive anywhere.

Bruce Bendinger, Creative Guru, adds, *"Make your book match your skills."* By which he means: If your strength is posters for a rock concert or sales promotion pieces for your uncle's store, do those. Then you might want to pitch your book and yourself toward event marketers, hip design shops, sales promotion agencies, or even in-house advertising groups at places like The Gap or Starbucks. Go with what you know or want to know.

Ad great Steve Penchina suggests, *"Pick your camp."* By which he means: if you don't want to work at a pack-aged goods agency, don't do packaged goods ads. Concentrate your efforts and your energy in getting into one of those agencies that are constantly cited in the award annuals – be they in Portland, Minneapolis, Manhattan, or Tuscaloosa.

Marie Arteca, Creative Recruiter at J. Walter Thompson, N.Y., says, *"Don't do packaged goods for the sake of doing packaged goods no matter where you live."* She continues, "A great book is great for JWT and it's great for TBWA\Chiat\Day. We're all looking for original thinking, expressed brilliantly. But don't wimp out when you pick your products. Show us you've got some teeth."

I'd like to sum up here with another quote from Flinn Dallis of Leo Burnett. *"Make your book look like the job you want."*

I think that's excellent advice.

YOUR BOOK, FORMAT AND EXECUTION.

Scott was only months away from graduating from a good portfolio school when I met him. He was prolific and had created some dandy campaigns that were touching and funny. He'd picked products that varied in range from a cigarette campaign (!) to one for a local shop that sold only electric fans.

And Scott was a very devil with his fine-line Pentel. He could draw like crazy; his products and people were comic, detailed. In fact, I think Scott is a bit of a genius when it comes to drawing.

So, why is it that Scott has just been hired as a copywriter by one of the sharpest "hot" agencies in New York?

Because he's conceptual, verbal, and his *design skills*, despite the fact that he can draw well, are quite average.

The line between copywriters and art directors is very blurry. The computer has made it possible for writers to art direct and for art directors to leap tall buildings where once upon a time they had to carry their markers up the stairs. Because writers and art directors are both Mac fluent, they cross skills. Scott can become a writer, work with an art director, and never miss a beat in his career.

Still, there is a difference between the disciplines.

Art directors: You must have great visual/design sense. You should be able to write headlines. If you like to write copy, that's fine. Present yourself as an art director who can write. Naturally, you must be able to come up with strong advertising ideas.

Nancy Temkin, Creative Recruiter at Greenberg Kirschenbaum in New York, advises art directors: "We want to see books where the concept, the idea, is paid off visually. We look for books where the creator takes risks.

"A book full of ads with strong concepts and basically the same layout in each campaign may be okay for a copywriter's book, but not for an art director.

"The books that get me to call my clients are the books where the concepts are smart and each page is a visual treat because it expresses the concept in an unexpected and intelligent way.

"It's better to be smart and gutsy (even if some things don't quite work), than smart and safe."

I couldn't agree more.

Copywriters: You must also think visually and you must be deft with the written word, even if none are called for in every campaign you "write."

People still read. We still think with words.

As always, the big idea is what counts most of all. If you've got a teammate or teammates in school, you'll work with this partner on visualizing your concepts.

If you're working alone, you should be able to create a workable layout on computer. If you don't have a computer, consider paying an art director to work up your ads. We rarely see hand-drawn portfolios anymore.

As a writer, your goals are big ideas and apt, vivid words. As with art directors, smart and gutsy applies to you as well.

Take some risks. Dare to be great. Your headlines are going to have to be terrific – smart, economical, instantly engaging.

In general: Each ad in your campaign should have a new headline. Each word in each headline should be well-chosen.

Grammar and spelling count.

And you really must write body copy. When we look at your book we're hoping to see an impressive use of the English language – fresh writing that makes us think about things in new ways.

In at least one of your campaigns, preferably two or more, write out the first ad completely. The second ad should have a new headline, but might need only a few new lines of copy to re-establish your thought. The third ad might simply have a new headline.

Many areas of the advertising business demand superior writing skills in addition to great ideas. Direct response advertising isn't taking a back seat to general consumer when it comes to quality writing. Take a look at The Sharper Image or the J. Peterman catalog, for instance.

But, even if you're destined to spend your career writing nothing longer than 30 seconds, your first writing portfolio ought to have some great body copy.

Even one terrific long copy ad can make a strong impression.

In sum: A great copy book has big ideas, terrific headlines, well-crafted body copy, and at least one, well-developed, long copy ad.

You're a writer. Writers write.

Writers and art directors:

When recruiters look at books of both writers and art directors, they're looking to see striking visual solutions – then, they'll think the book through again, this time judging your work on the quality and originality of the words and design.

Not long ago, art directors laminated their ads and writers put their samples in glassine-sleeved portfolio cases.

Both formats are now deader than Old King Tut.

For your main book, copy and art, it's good to mount your ads flush on nice, clean illustration board or even on firm stock instead of printing it on soft paper, so that a reviewer can easily flip through your book.

Lauren Slaff, Director of Adhouse, a portfolio school in New York says, *"Art directors should mount their work in such a way that there is no border around their ads because the screener's eye will incorporate that border into the layout."*

Writers have more latitude. Black board is customary, but consider using white board for a cleaner look.

Mounting your ads on illustration board not only keeps them neat, but makes it easy for the person looking at that book to hold the pieces in his or her hand, strew them around on the sofa, put them on the chart rail, or take a few of them out of the book to show to someone in the office next door.

Your goal here is to make your entire book reader-friendly and easy to handle.

Your mini-book should look fresh and "in progress." Lamination or anything permanent-looking in a mini, suggests to the reviewer that you're not open to comments or change, that in your mind, your book is finished. And that could prevent them from giving you a critique you may very well need.

In class, in portfolio review, and in real life in advertising:

Be prepared to have your ideas shot down.

Be prepared to do your ads again and again and to come back with something even better.

Q. How many ads should be in a campaign?

A. In real life there can be hundreds of ads in each campaign.

For your book, three ads per campaign are generally enough, but it's not a rule.
Two good ads are better than two good ads and one bad ad.
Four in a campaign aren't too many if all are really good.

In truth, the number of ads in a campaign and the number of campaigns in your book aren't the point. *The point has to do with the consistency and quality of your ideas.*

Be prepared to have your ideas shot down.

Q. How many pieces should I have in my book? Any special order?

A. There's no right answer to this question but since we're asked this a lot, I'll say your book should contain 20 to 30 pieces that make you proud. That number should probably break down to a book of three or four campaigns – about three ads per campaign, a few one-shot ideas, and *perhaps* some ideas for alternative media that may extend one or more of your campaigns.

May I be blunt?

If you can't sell yourself in 15 ads, 15 more won't help.

So don't pad your book just to bring up the number of pieces.

The order? Just as a good commercial must capture your attention in the first few seconds, so must your book.

Remember that killer sandwich? Put your best ad in first. Close with one that's just as good to reinforce that first impression.

Your book should flow. Let me try to explain what I mean.

On one hand, your book is a collection of different campaigns for different products. On the other, your book is one presentation.

Your reviewers will be adding up all their feelings about your separate campaigns to come up with a single impression of you.

So try to balance your portfolio with an eye to the whole presentation. Seek a rhythm to the order of your campaigns that feels pleasing to you. Weed out campaigns that do you no good.

We'll talk about how to edit your book later on.

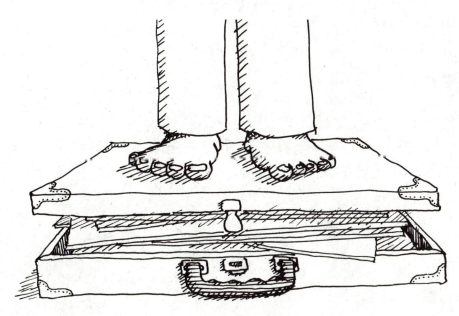

Too many.

39

Q. What kind of alternative media pieces should I include in my book? How many pieces?

A. Some recruiters want to see what they refer to as "smart thinking," advertising problems that are solved in non-ad or nontraditional ways. Store banners, billboards, bumper stickers, and packaging ideas are all examples of "alternative media," and the executions of these non-ads can be thumbnail drawings or brief descriptions of the media, stating the problem and how you've solved it.

Pippa Seichrist, President of Miami Ad School told me that at a recent portfolio review 70 agency people came to see 20 student books. The hands-down favorite was a package design campaign created by a talented young art director for Duracell Batteries.

Tracy came up with an environmental approach for her "client," Duracell. Her concept falls under the heading of "smart thinking." Tracy hit on the notion that old batteries that are sent to landfills are bad for the environment.

Pippa says, "Tracy thought it would be good for Duracell to institute a recycling plan. When their consumer went to a retail store to buy new batteries, they could drop off their old batteries for recycling at the same time.

"Tracy designed packaging around the batteries to convey this environmental theme. Small watch-sized batteries were packaged to look like a ladybug on a leaf. AA batteries were bubble-wrapped to look like caterpillars, and so on.

"Her idea really had legs; it could be spun out into radio, TV, just about any media."

Guerrilla Media.

The term "guerilla media," "guerilla postings," or simply "guerilla" for short, has crept into the advertising vernacular. Referring to jungle fighters, guerilla is a very varied bag of nontraditional, alternative media.

Small companies and creative advertisers have to fight their competition with lower budgets, so while they don't have F-16s, they do have posters and paint.

You'll see guerilla postings stenciled on asphalt streets, stuck to the bottoms of beer mugs, the backs of public restroom stalls, and as Creative Director Giff Crosby says, "Nature abhors a vacuum and blank 8x4 slabs of particle board."

Giff is referring to the plywood sheets that block off construction sites from the street, empty surfaces that are almost instantly covered with About.com posters.

When you're creating a piece of alternative media for your book, you can go with a "one-shot," but if the idea is "campaignable," or if it springs from one of the campaigns already in your book, so much the better.

But do keep this in mind: coming up with ideas for alternative media is not a requirement for a killer book.

Bertrand Garbassi, Creative Director of Euro RSCG MVBMS Partners, has this to say: "I'd rather see a traditional print book of strong, conceptual advertising ideas than a book filled with lame guerilla ideas."

Giff Crosby agrees. "For a beginner, the most compelling stuff, regardless of what form it takes, is really wonderful ideas, hilarious or delightful writing or a fresh approach to the graphic arts and an original use of the various traditional media.

"I simply love to see when a beginner shows a talent for noting special things about our culture, or lines that nobody else has noticed. This shows me so much about what this creative person can do for our clients, as opposed to displaying a particular skill in the new media. We know talent can make the leap from conceptual ads to any kind of problem solving."

Q. What about TV commercials?
Should I do storyboards? How many?

A. A storyboard (also called a *"board"*) is a page containing blank spaces in the shape of television screens on which important frames of a proposed commercial are drawn. There's a space beside or below each frame for copy and visual instructions.

Recruiters haven't expected to find storyboards in portfolios in a long time. Most stopped reading them because they were often just an exercise in creating eight frames of pictures with dialogue, and they simply took up space.

In truth, your ideas pop more quickly in print format. Portfolio reviewers can "get" your conceptual ability more quickly in a headline and visual than by reading the dialogue and camera direction on a storyboard.

But. If you feel especially fluent in the television medium, or if one of your campaigns simply demands to be expressed in moving pictures, do one storyboard and make it a great one.

Or, instead of doing an entire storyboard, do what is often called a *"key frame,"* or *"key visual."* In this shorthand version of a storyboard, you create only one television frame, but make it big, say half your page. Have it represent the most important instant in your commercial.

The only way a key visual will work well for you is if your idea is a big one, clear enough to be expressed in one frame. Put the dialogue (or monologue) underneath the frame. Unless your commercial shifts location, it should not be necessary for you to describe the visual details and camera action.

Done simply, your key visual will read quickly and show off your television idea to its best advantage.

My advice? Only do a television commercial if it really makes your concept come to life.

Keep in mind, your objective is to make your work accessible.

If your campaign is good, people will read the board.

If it's not, they won't.

Keep your book free of clutter.

A storyboard represents the important frames
of a proposed TV commercial.

A key visual can work
if the idea is a big one.

43

Q. Should I do scripts for TV? How about radio? Should I produce a CD of my radio commercials? How about videos?

A. Copywriters, if you want to do one TV script, the same rules apply as for storyboards; it's not necessary to do them, but if your great concept begs to be expanded into TV, a script is an easy way to go.
How to do it:
Your script page will need two columns.
A 30-second TV script usually fits on one page.
On the left, write the visual description, usually in capital letters.
On the right hand column, write the audio. Make sure the action you describe on one side matches up with the dialogue on the other.

Time your commercials with a stopwatch. Read out loud. A 30-second commercial may not slop over to 35. You might also want to make use of a key frame as described previously.

Creative directors, especially those in smaller markets, like to see radio. If you're especially good with dialogue (perhaps humor is your forte) radio can demonstrate your ability.
Write up a script. Time it. But promise me something.
Promise you won't bring your CD player and insist we listen to your homemade radio commercials.
You may ask politely, but please don't get pushy.
Creative people develop short attention spans almost as a survival mechanism. They're quick to "get" it. Quick to get bored. A 60-second commercial can seem endless; five of them, an eternity.
Even if you play a mean harmonica, 40 seconds of "The Boxcar Blues" won't justify the joke at the end of your commercial.

Recently, I visited the Miami Ad School and saw videos made by students as portfolio pieces and for self-promotion.
The spots I saw were delightful; executionally primitive but conceptually sound. It may be that by the time you read this, all portfolios will include videos.
If so, my guess is that the same rules will apply. Doing TV just for the sake of doing it will slow your book down and cost you points. But great video ideas produced in a simple, powerful way will knock people out.
To repeat. If a TV or radio spot will bring your campaign idea to life, do a script, a board, a radio spot, a video. Don't go overboard.
Make it great or stick to print.

Q. I don't have a computer. Am I dead in the water?

A. Pretty much, yes.

Today, speculative ads look like finished ads. Reviewers are used to seeing fabulous visuals, great type, four-color spreads. They aren't often beguiled by a pretty page, but they do expect a professional-looking collection of ads.

If it's just not feasible to generate your ads on a computer at this point, you can still put a book together.

Recently, we saw a wonderful book of ads made with marker pens. Vinny could draw, letter, he was conceptual, and because he didn't have the dazzling array of typefaces and the use of other people's photograpy, his book had an elegant simplicity we don't see often these days. Vinny had a choice of job offers.

At a recent portfolio review, I saw the return of markers – here a storyboard, there a few marker comps – and all of us looking at the books were relieved. Once again we could determine what role the art director played in coming up with an original visual idea rather than simply borrowing other images in the form of scrap.

Leslie Kay, a creative placement specialist and owner of Leslie Kay, Inc., lauds the return of "hand skills." "A kid who can draw may find freelance work while he or she's looking for their first job." And, Leslie adds, being able to draw is still a useful art director skill. A magic marker in hand can make a quick change possible, and that could make the meeting successful.

Sell the campaign. Win the war.

Rick Boyko has more to say on this topic (See his essay in Part III). There's growing concern that the computer can be limiting, not liberating. But, in the larger picture, computers are a way of life.

Recently, an informal poll of 25 creative directors across the country revealed that nearly all expect their junior creative people to be fluent in *several* computer programs. I cannot imagine how a creative person getting into advertising now will succeed without being computer literate.

Q. **Can I put my portfolio on a CD or Zip disk?**
Can I send my work electronically?

A. As of this writing *some* creative recruiters and creative directors will review books on disk. One recruiter I know says that sometimes she'll print out a book on CD and so turn it into a mini-book, but she's the exception.

Most people who look at portfolios still want to hold the work in their hands. They want to be able to see a book when they have a moment to spare, not just when they're at the computer, and even then, they don't want to have to close down other applications in order to view your book.

I spoke with Kathy Primozic, a headhunter at Judy Wald in New York. Kathy specializes in direct response candidates and job openings. It's possible that her people are a slight bit ahead of the rest of us when it comes to computer literacy.

Kathy had a few portfolios on CD, and I could see the magic of it all. For ease and economic feasibility, what could possibly be better than mailing your half-ounce portfolio in living color, complete with sound and animation?

Consistently, recruiters say they want to see what the consumer would see if the ad were running in a magazine.

They say they want to handle the physical work.

Right now, it only makes sense to send your mini-book in tangible form and while you wait for the rest of us to catch up to the electronic age, why not throw up your own Web site and post your ads there.

Note your URL on your résumé or somewhere in your mini-book. While the recruiter wants to handle the ads, a creative director might have their computer up and running and will happily type in your URL.

Then he or she will see every last one of your ads.

Web sites are cheap or free, cool, and cutting edge.

I think you should have one.

Q. With all this talk of integrated marketing, should my book show campaigns in all media: print, sales promotion, Web sites, or what?

A. Speaking in the present, the big agency recruiters look at both copy and art portfolios for great ideas expressed in print campaigns.

They assume that ideas can be translated into any medium and will ask you if you're interested in a direct response opening if they have one.

In large consumer ad agencies, advertising for alternative media is still most often being shunted off to the direct response division of the big shop.

Smaller agencies may apply their creative talent to all the assignments they are executing for their clients, be that free-standing inserts in magazines, interactive advertising, or Web sites.

If you're a designer/techie, you might consider slanting your book toward the collateral areas and getting in on the ground floor of the new media. I recently saw a small, square book with a dozen Web designs inside.

If you want to do general consumer advertising but are open to other ad-related work, do a general consumer book of print campaigns. Direct response people can translate your consumer campaigns into moving billboards, etc., but feel free to extend a campaign or two into other media to give them proof.

For copywriters, there's no actual difference between writers who write for the Web and writers who write for TV. It's your choice whether to gear your book for consumer advertising, direct response, or trade.

Q. We're a team. I wrote his ads. He did my layouts. We collaborated on the ideas. Can we get jobs as a team?

A. Yes. More and more, agencies hire twin sets.

However, be prepared to get separated eventually. Most creative people have many teammates during their careers.

By the way, should you go on interviews without your teammate for a job that is just for one, make sure you credit your partner or partners.

Q. **I've been told to write up the strategy statement with the demographic background, etc., and tape it to the page across from my ad. I hear some agency people don't like to see this kind of thing. What's your opinion?**

A. I'm not a big fan of explaining ads.

When I see these little notes explaining how the product is being positioned and what the strategy is, I don't read them. I want that headline to do the work. And the body copy. And the visual.

If your ads work without the note and you want to keep the notes in anyway – to describe your assignment, for instance, okay. But please excuse me while I play through. I want to see the *ads*.

And while I'm on the subject of demographic background, let me tell you the about the sinking feeling I get when a student who has competed in a national competition presents a bound hundred-page so-called "campaign" created by him and his ad club team.

This body of work comes complete with marketing data, media plans, and a piece of advertising tailored for every conceivable type of media – from matchbooks to bus posters.

Bethany had one of these books. She was president of her ad club, and her team placed second in the finals. She was justifiably proud of her accomplishment; she'd devoted a good portion of her school year to this effort, and it paid off in lots of acclaim and top grades.

So that means Bethany and her group don't need the kind of portfolios all the rest of you folks need, right? Wrong.

Group work doesn't tell me what I need to know about the candidate's talent and originality. Even if the advertising concept and the executions are great, and fundamentally the work of the presenter, is this person with the team presentation a one idea of a lifetime person?

Contests such as the AAF Student Competition can be fun and a good learning experience, so do participate if you get the chance.

But, don't think you can skip putting your book together.

Placing in a national competition is not a substitute for having a portfolio. Period.

48

Q. **If you're applying for a job as an art director, but you are also a good illustrator and photographer, should you include some of those samples too?**

A. Sure. And put in design pieces if you really like them, but be careful not to weight the book too heavily in a non-advertising direction.

The purpose of putting in more "artistic" work should be to show that you're well rounded and talented. But don't confuse the issue for folks who simply want to hire an agency art director.

If you're undecided about possible careers, say between art direction and fashion illustration, you absolutely must have two portfolios. You don't ever want to come off as neither fish nor fowl. With two books, you can see two different sets of people and be two different people.

May the best one win.

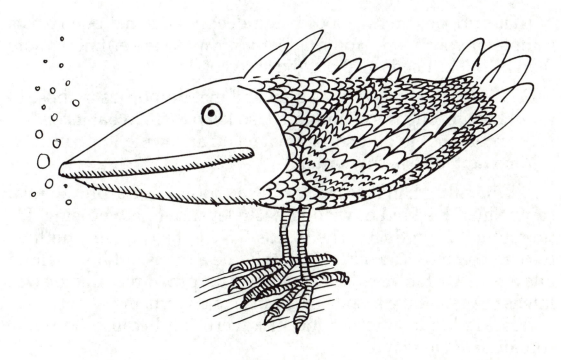

Neither fish nor fowl. If you're interested in two careers, you must have two portfolios.

49

Q. I have slides of my paintings and some package designs. How should I show them?

A. As with everything else we have discussed, you want to make your presentation as easy to access as possible.

Most people don't have slide projectors in their offices. If they are madly in love with the rest of your book, they may make a special effort to have the slides screened, but I wouldn't count on it.

As with the section on homemade radio commercials, slide shows are risky things to force on people.

Probably the best way to display your slides is to put them in one of those plastic pages with the little pockets.

Q. I write short stories. Is there a place in my portfolio for them?

A. Sure. Just as an art director can put in some slides and some design pieces or photographs in his or her main portfolio, a copywriter can add non-advertising writing.

Carol Vick, Placement Director for The Creative Circus says, "Some creative directors like to see that you have 'creative reach' in nontraditional ways because they want to create nontraditional advertising. Those agencies have been very interested in seeing college-written scripts and short stories."

That said, be careful about using deeply personal poetry as a sample of your work: You may let your interviewer know more than he or she needs to about the love you lost.

College newspaper articles aren't all that humorous to those of us who have long since graduated, so keep them in balance.

Be careful not to diffuse the image you are trying to present.

You want to be a copywriter.

On the other hand, Mark wrote soundbites for a presidential campaign. This kind of writing has relevance to advertising. It's promoting a "product." The words have to be concise, and they have to communicate fast. Mark told me a thousand lines would bite the dust before one was chosen, and the pressure in this job was intense. Again there is some relevance to advertising.

Was Mark guaranteed a job in advertising because he wrote soundbites? No way.

He still needed a portfolio of great ads.

Q. **I like to invent new product ideas.**
How many of them can I put in my book?

A. Only great ones and, even then, no more than one or two.

Coming up with new product ideas is the least of what a creative person does. It might come up a couple of times in a person's career, but not every day, so developing new products doesn't tell us what we really want to know about you.

Even so, some professors ask you to develop new products as part of your advertising education, and in limited doses, this kind of "ideation" can demonstrate an intellectual sparkiness that can be a valuable trait in a creative person.

If you come up with new product ideas, be reasonable.
No magic, please. A tire that lasts forever is magic.
A wallet-sized computer that cooks dinner, diapers your baby, and tapes the hockey game may exist some day, but we're not in the science fiction business.

No fair.

51

Products you "invent" should be ones where the technology is already in existence, or at least feasible. They should be products an advertiser might actually market; that an agency might advertise. Appetite-suppressant chewing gum. Calcium-enriched dog biscuits.

We've seen some new product ideas that were hysterical.

A prescription windshield, for instance, so that only the owner could drive his car. "Gun-shoes," a sort of a James Bond idea to protect the wearer in the hazardous New York subway system – though a lot of these things aren't quite as funny post 9/11.

However, sometimes a new product idea can be good enough to move your book away from the pack.

Steven came up with an idea for rubber gloves with scouring strips on the fingers and palms so the consumer could really get at those tough scouring jobs: grills, tiles, nasty pots and pans. "Get a Grip on the Grime," said one headline. He called his product, "Scrubs. The Helpful Handful."

Which reminds me, it's a good idea to name your product while you're at it. That may make your idea twice as good.

Q. **Should I change my portfolio for different agencies? Should I do ads for accounts a specific agency has?**

A. No and no.

If you consider each ad in your book as the only ad in your book, and if you are pleased with that representation of you, you will feel confident on each interview.

You'll be able to discuss and defend your work.

You'll be open to good criticism and will be able to pass off criticism that doesn't ring true.

I think you could get into trouble when you put ads in your book that are there for any reason other than showing the best ads you can do.

Say you do a car ad because you're going after a job on a car account. If you don't love the ad for its own sake, you're going to sound weak defending it should it be challenged – and given that experts on the car account will be looking at your ads, you can be sure you will be challenged.

And if that ad is not as good as you can do, it will dilute the quality of the rest of your book.

Doing ads for actual accounts held by the agency you are approaching is an additional problem.

Most agencies have a policy against reading unsolicited ideas for their clients' products. There is, among other things, a danger of lawsuits from people who see ideas produced and on-the-air similar to ones they dreamed up. In fact, some agencies may make you sign a legal release when you leave your portfolio.

My advice is don't deliberately do ads for a specific agency for their accounts.

Q. **I have some produced work that I did during summer jobs. Should I put it in my book?**

A. How good is it? If you want to put work in your book because you're proud of the piece – and you don't have to be there to explain what you had to do with it – then put it in.

If the work is not totally pleasing to you – say it's a couple of cocktail napkins and a menu, and you were heavily supervised – note the summer job on your résumé and forget the work itself.

If a piece of work isn't terrific, just the fact that it has been produced won't get you a nickel.

But your question leads us to another kind of produced work, and that is freelance work.

As with summer jobs, if you do freelance work basically for pay and to the tightly drawn specifications of your client, then the work may not be as good as speculative work you create yourself without heavy "client" supervision.

If your freelance work isn't as good as your spec work, then it, like summer job work, should be excluded from your portfolio or consigned to a special place in your book, a pocket or envelope.

But what if your freelance work is very good? Can it enhance your book? Give you an edge over your competition?

Dany Lennon, a placement specialist, suggests you go out and solicit freelance accounts for the sole purpose of doing great ads and having them produced.

If your produced work isn't wonderful,
just the fact that it's produced doesn't get you a nickel.

"Forget about money," Dany says. "Go to dry cleaners, retail stores, type shops. Tell the owners you will do ads for them for free if they will run the ads in local papers. Many of these small businesses will be delighted to let you do your best.

"They won't see you as juniors, you'll be advertising people. You'll learn to work with a client, present your work, and get your ads produced virtually as you created them."

Dany backs up her excellent advice with action, by letting juniors do ads for her business.

She chooses the best ads, then runs them in award annuals.

Why should you do these ads for free? Because, presumably, you'll have more say in the creation of the ad.

If your "client" is paying you a fee, he or she may be more inclined to dictate the ad, and you will be obliged to follow directions.

Of course, this doesn't mean you should forget the client's needs and point of view when you're doing the ad *gratis*.

The client will still only run the ad if they like it. Doing the ad for free might give you more creative freedom than you'd have otherwise.

I like this idea, don't you? In a few weeks, you could go from being a starving creative person with a spec book to being a starving creative person with a spec book, produced ads, and a client roster.

Q. **How can I make my book sing?**

A. Good question.

Because the difference between humming and singing is the difference between being told to keep in touch and having a job created for you.

It's all about "singing."

I don't expect to see a portfolio stuffed full of blindly original ideas. (Most of us have seen so many ideas, don't be surprised if some of your "original" ideas have actually aired.)

But one great idea, one killer ad, can be enough to show me I'm looking at a person who's going to make it.

If you've got one great ad, the rest of your ads should be in second and third place to that great ad, not trailing the pack. And obviously, the more killer ads you have, the closer you are to having a killer book.

And a killer book sings.

When you have a book that sings,
you'll have something very special. A job.

56

Editing: Why and How to Do It.

Your book is trying to do two things: sell your products and sell the interviewer on you.

As you work to develop a book that sings, believe this. Every ad counts. Here's why:

• Your judgment of what's good and bad is being evaluated.

• We'd also like to know that your talent is pretty consistent, that you've had more than one flukey great idea in your life.

• Your book is a presentation. The sum of the parts equal the whole. Do you want a smooth, consistent presentation? Or a choppy one full of question marks?

Here's how to get good at editing your own book.

Pretend that the most points you can get for your entire portfolio is 100. Divide the number of pieces in your portfolio into 100 and see what each is worth.

If you have 20 ads, each is worth 5 – even your killer ad.

If you have 10 ads, each is worth 10. So, doesn't it pay to reduce the number of pieces to the ones that work very hard for you? I think 12 wonderful ads say better things about you than 40 okay ones.

Average campaigns can dilute the effect of your very-good-to-great campaigns. Scripts and storyboards in excess may go unread, and that will cut into your 100 points.

Throw out any ads that have to be explained. Watch out for too many "punny" headlines, too many celebrity spokespersons, too many non-advertising pieces, too much public service.

Check yourself.
Do you have heartless ads?
Walking strategy statements?
These items don't sing; they moan. Or at least we do.

When organizing your work, put your best ad(s) first, your next best, last. Start with a Pow. End with a Wow. We hope it's not too mushy in between.

57

Your ads should be clean, neatly presented.

Remember that often your book will be going out without you and that means your book has to represent you in the absence of your charming personality.

An unedited book is like a person who talks too much. Boring. That's why you should edit your book.

Q. **What should a book look like physically?**

A. Today, creative people need several books.

To start with, you'll have a "Main Book," or "Full Book," also called the "Interview Book." This is *your book* – the one that you'll take with you on job interviews, a case filled with life-sized ads mounted on illustration board, printouts rather than photocopies, and maybe some collateral material in a side pocket.

This might be package design, photography, short stories, or other writings in an enclosed envelope.

Your interview book will also contain a bunch of your "mini-books." As previously noted, minis are the scaled-down version of your main book for you to send ahead or leave behind.

More on minis, shortly.

Your main book should look professional. Please use good taste as your guide. The classic rectangular black art case is just that – a classic. But both the huge, forty-pound suitcase-style portfolio and the zip-up case with flippy glassine pages inside are dated.

Yeah.   *Sure.*   *Fine.*   *Whatever.*

Take a look at the clear plastic cases you can find at Sam Flax and other art supply stores. You can go upscale with a burnished metal Zero Haliburton, or even a wooden or leather case. Frankly, we just saw a book that was covered in camouflage material with red piping and had excellent ads inside.

But please keep in mind that the main point of this case is to keep your ads organized, not to call attention to itself.

Most of the time, you and your main book will stick together.

In the rare instance where you'll have to leave it for review by a creative director, that person most likely will have already seen your mini-book, heard about you from the creative recruiter, and won't need be wowed by a hand-stitched pigskin portfolio with a hologram of your pitbull on the side.

For best results, put your creativity inside the case, not outside.
But do put a nametag on the outside.
Books get lost. With good identification, they get found.

Cute. But for the best bet,
put your creativity inside your book, not outside.

Q. **I'm told I should create "a look" with my mini-book. What's cool and what's over the top?**

A. At this writing, mini-books are the calling card for beginning writers and art directors. The mini-book is the perfect *send-ahead* or *leave-behind,* made to be user-friendly, accessible and disposable.

In other words, it's a complete portfolio packaged as a promotional piece. And guess what, it's so good you can use your mini-book for job interviews, too.

Typically, mini-books run from 8.5 x 11" to 11 x 17" in size.

They are generally printouts or photocopies of your ads on decent paper stock, sandwiched between two cardboard covers that can be bound at Kinkos with a spiral or rigid or springy-coiled plastic binding.

We've seen some minis that are hole-punched in one corner, fastened with a key-ring clip and others that are bolted together with rivets. We even saw one that was made of a drapery sample book, an ad pasted to each sheet of fabric.

Generally, mini-books are mailed in plain manila envelopes or dropped off in either plain envelopes or the glassine kind you can get at Staples in jellybean colors.

The actual cover of your mini-book is an advertising opportunity – more on this when we talk about promotional pieces – but I want to say here that it's good to put your name, discipline (art or copy or team), and phone number somewhere on the front cover. That way, when a recruiter reaches into the pile, or file drawer full of minis, she can find yours on the first try.

If your mini-book is bigger than 11 x 17", it's not a mini.

If it shrinks to 6 x 8", the person you're hoping to reach may not be able to read the type. According to recruiters who are your primary audience, the mini-portfolio should fit comfortably on the desk, and the ads inside should be lifesize or close to it.

Michele Daly, Creative Recruiter at Bozell, New York, says, "A lot of minis are black, and some have a clear transparent cover so that you can see the résumé that's affixed to the first page.

"Some people put a small sticker on the cover, like 'Hello, my name is,' or a little drawing of themselves, something to 'brand' their name into my memory.

"Then, when they call to follow up, I associate their names with the little symbol on the book.

"I'm looking now at one mini in the stack that has a bright orange cover – it stands out, and I remember it."

That's what branding is all about.

A recruiter can go through her collection of mini-books and remember at a glance which ones she liked best; the magenta one, the orange one, and the one in a plaid jacket.

Q. **I just got my BA in Communications and Advertising Design, but my book isn't getting me anywhere. What should I do?**

A.   There used to be lots of internship and training programs – those days are gone. Because of downsizing in the agency business, these apprenticeships have been largely scrapped.

And because of the small number of jobs for beginners, the competition is exceedingly fierce. What to do?

Well, there are now a number of "portfolio schools."

These are finishing schools for people who've already graduated, usually with majors in advertising, with portfolios that are not yet of "killer" quality.

These schools provide a very competitive environment, with instructors who are usually working professionals.

The whole purpose of these schools is to help you develop a portfolio that's good enough to get you a job.

And, for the most part, they do what you pay them to do.

There are two reasons these programs work.

First, you focus totally on developing your portfolio.

You don't have the distraction of other courses in school.

In a full-time portfolio program, you are as totally dedicated to doing great work as you'll be after you get that job.

Second, you share this experience with dozens of other young men and women who have exactly the same objective.

It's very competitive, and you learn the kind of work ethic and professional standards you'll need to succeed in the business. When the economy is good, graduates of these two-year programs usually have a pick of jobs.

Some schools of note at the moment are:

Portfolio Center in Atlanta, **800-255-3169** was one of the first of the "new generation" of portfolio schools. They feature courses in art direction, copywriting, design, illustration, and photography. Their Web site is www.portfoliocenter.com

The Creative Circus, also in Atlanta, **800-728-1590**, specializes in advertising copywriting and art direction. www.creativecircus.com

The Miami Ad School in Miami, **800-858-3190**, is a unique program with a network of facilities in major ad centers. They also feature courses in Spanish. www.adschool.edu

Virginia Commonwealth University (VCU) in Richmond takes a grad school approach at **The VCU AdCenter.** Students form teams with account executives, writers, art directors, and account planners. Top advertising professionals are on their Board. You can find out more about the VCU program by calling **804-828-0100**. Or you can go to www.adcenter.vcu.edu

Two programs that have been around for a long time are **School of Visual Arts** (SVA) and **Art Center College of Design.**

SVA in New York City has been offering evening courses for years. Many fine people have come out of SVA, and many fine people have taught there. If you're already in New York, you might call their continuing education program at **212-592-2000.** Or go to www.schoolofvisualarts.edu

On the West Coast, **Art Center College of Design** in Pasadena, has long had one of the top advertising art direction programs. It is not uncommon for someone from a smaller (and less expensive) art school to finish up at "The Art Center." For more information, call **626-396-2200.** Or go to www.artcenter.edu

Two other West Coast programs have been around for quite some time. **The Advertising Arts College** in San Diego has grown into **The Art Institute of California/San Diego** at **858-546-0602.** Their advertising program Web site is www.taac.edu

In San Francisco, the **Academy of Art College** has a growing advertising program for their growing advertising market. They're at **415-274-2200.** Or **1-800-544-ARTS.** Or www.academyart.edu

Other cities have programs – usually of the part-time evening variety. The Boston and Cleveland Ad Clubs had programs. Check with your local ad club to see what's happening in your area.

Chicago has a number of programs. **The Chicago Portfolio School** is at **312-321-9405.** Or www.chicagoportfolio.com

Minneapolis has **BrainCo: Minneapolis School of Advertising** at **612-822-1313** or www.braincomsa.com

And New York now has **Adhouse,** founded by Gary Goldsmith and Lauren Slaff. They're at **212-243-7334.**

CMYK magazine features work from most of these programs. Go to www.cmykmag.com and take a look around.

If your four-year program wasn't quite enough, one of these portfolio schools may be just what you need.

PART II

...AND GET A JOB IN ADVERTISING

RÉSUMÉS.

After you've put your book together, it's time to go out there and get that job in advertising.

Naturally, you must have a résumé.

The primary purpose of this document is to provide a quick summary of what you've learned, what you've done, and what you want to do for a living.

Your résumé should be pasted to the first or last page of your mini-book, and you'll need to bring résumés to portfolio reviews and job interviews, because interviewers like to get a quick fix on your background.

While they're looking at your book and talking to you, they might make notes on your résumé and file it for later use.

Make sure your résumé scans easily. Put your name, address, phone number, and e-mail address on the top with the position sought – copywriter or art director – listed prominently.

If you have a Web site, list your URL here, too.

List your summer jobs even if they're not related to advertising. We know you're not a professional yet, but we're interested in what you've done with yourself up to this point.

Copywriters: We're especially interested in life experience. What other kind is there, you may ask. This is what I mean: *we think unusual and enriching experiences increase your writing range.*

If you've worked in a psychiatric hospital, or on an ocean liner; if you've bagged all-beef patties, or driven a cab, tell us. Don't worry if you didn't graduate from college. It's your copy skills that interest us, and if they show, that's what's important.

Art directors: Put all your art education on your résumé, because for you, it's important, but *you should resist a common tendency to over-art direct your résumé.*

It would be nice if your summer jobs related to advertising or graphic design. You certainly want to list your computer credentials and any other experiences that we may find interesting.

A clean, distinctive logo of your name is fine, but it must be readable. If you make us untangle your name from the design, your logo will hurt rather than help you.

If you want your résumé to fold and fly like a plane, it damn-well better work, or it'll fly right into the trash.

It's a good idea to cite your job objective as the first item on your résumé.

We want to know pretty quickly if you're a copywriter, an art director, or if you've sent your résumé to the wrong department – and we shouldn't have to figure this out according to what school you went to.

Avoid hyping your job objective. "My goal is to become chairman of the board" isn't going to impress us. It's the wrong goal.

Kelly's job objective was phrased as: "What I want out of life: A job as a copywriter and a red Porsche." Okay. A good goal and Kelly's got a sense of humor.

David's objective: "To be the best damned copywriter ever." Way to go, David.

Anonymous's objective: "To use the knowledge that I have acquired from my educational background and job related experiences to become a success in Art and Advertising Design." I think Anonymous should have pruned out all but the last nine words, don't you?

Your résumé doesn't have to be devoid of personality to qualify as a résumé. Some creative directors I know would like to see résumés with a little spark.

Paul had his name printed in big block letters across the top of his résumé. Underneath this huge type in smaller print; "Hoping to be a big-name copywriter," says Paul.

Your résumé should always go out with or as part of your mini-book, but since mini-books can cost you about $25 each to produce, there may be times when it's not practical or affordable to send a mini.

In that case, the résumé can serve as a mini-book by reducing two or three of your ads and putting them somewhere, usually at the bottom of the page.

Or you may use it as a cover for a few photocopies of your ads.

Here's another idea.

Make copies of your best three ads and staple them to your résumé. No one can object to that, and it saves the creative director to whom you've targeted your appeal a heck of a lot of time. Always appreciated.

Check your spelling, or better yet, have someone else check it.

Sometimes the small things count. More than one résumé has been passed to me with misspelled words gleefully circled in red.

Final note: More times than I can count, I've opened the portfolio of a graduating senior at a portfolio review, looked for a résumé, and not found one. "I've been too busy," he or she says. "I've got finals. And I had to finish my ads."

Okay. But after I've seen the résumés of your 40 classmates, how am I going to remember your book? Where am I going to jot down that headline I liked or a note to remind myself that you graduate in December?

If this could be you, and you haven't had a chance to produce your masterpiece résumé, may I suggest you just bang off a simple one on your Mac tonight? Something. Please?

As long as it's neat, it will serve.

Q. **What résumés have you seen that are off-beat and successful?**

A. I'd like to distinguish here between a résumé – a document that's supposed to identify you and your book and summarize your business career – with cover letters and promotional pieces that can be considered advertising. More on this, later.

With the advent of the mini-book and résumés with a couple of photocopied ads attached, more than ever before your résumé should be simple. I'm not ruling anything out, but it would be quite remarkable for an "off-beat" résumé to take the place of a terrific mini-book. Here's my case for the traditional approach.

Bill, an aspiring art director who had one of the best books I ever saw (we all watched him pick up his gold statues a year later), did his résumé on plain white linen paper.

He put his name and address on the top, centered.

His job objective: "to be an art director."

Following this were his educational credentials, his summer job experience, and awards he'd won at school. He listed references.

The only thing that distinguished this résumé on its face was that the type was set entirely in lowercase. And, of course, the résumé was distinguished by the things the young man had done.

Interviewers got into fist-fights over Bill.

Sometimes an off-beat résumé works.   *Sometimes it doesn't.*

But I know this hasn't convinced you.

So, what résumés have I seen that are off-beat and successful?

The rule here, the thing that makes some off-beat résumés work, is that they demonstrate the individual's talent. They are clever in a way that is directly applicable to the discipline the person wants to pursue – and to the business of advertising.

One of my favorite off-beat résumés belongs to Stephen.

The résumé looked ordinary enough. Stephen put his full name, address, phone numbers, and e-mail address across the top of the page, and adjacent to position desired: copywriter.

Here's what Stephen wrote under the "experience" column.

> June – Present – Part-time Chauffeur/Word processor for New York consulting firm specializing in non-profit organizations.
> • Transport president to and from appointments.
> • Edit and type staff associates' fundraising proposals.
> • Deliver and recover Blanche (president's cat) to and from vet.
> • Claim president's fur from furrier.
> • Bring in for repair president's pearls.

> June – Feb. – Mr. B___. New York.
> Live-in Companion/Cook to 90-year-old man.
> • Accompanied Mr. B___ on walks through United Nations Park. Often stopped to see Moon Rock.
> • Coordinated/prepared Sunday lasagna luncheons.
> • Initiated subscription to *New York Times* large print edition.

> Sept. – May – New York. Au pair for divorce lawyer and her 12-year-old son.
> • Laundered their dirty clothing.
> • Washed their filthy dishes.
> • Cleaned their stinking kitchen.
> • Prepared their wretched meals.
> • Never complained once.

Stephen listed his degrees, his work as a playwright and author, and ended his résumé with the traditional closing, "References: Available upon request."

So you can't say the above isn't a regulation résumé. But it's an unusual résumé in that it obeys the time honored rule followed by writers everywhere: "Show, don't tell." And Stephen showed a lot of things. He's funny, literate, irascible, and he can be creative within a prescribed format.

Loren, an art director, did her résumé in a narrative style.

Her name, address, creative discipline, etc., was in large type, centered at the top of the page. In the same large type, this time in bold face, was this copy:

"They tell me that to be in advertising I'll need a big ego. The only thing big about me is my hair. They say it's a dog eat dog world. Too bad I'm a vegetarian.

"All I have is a degree from F_____ University, a faculty award from Portfolio Center, real agency experience, and a vast collection of empty No-Doz boxes.

"As long as you don't make me brag or eat a dog, I may be just the art director you're looking for."

This résumé was well-art directed, well-written, shows that Loren has a sense of humor and that she's willing to work all night! I'd ask to see her book. Wouldn't you?

One style of off-beat is the résumé as an ad.

Bruce used this approach. When he was looking for his first job, he drew a simple line drawing on a regular 8 $^1/_2$" by 11" piece of paper of a male figure holding a portfolio. He ran it off on a copier and added some color with markers.

The headline read, "This is an ad for a product that isn't working." In the place for the body copy he gave his name and stated that he was looking for his first job. I thought this "off-beat" résumé was very effective.

Mia's ad-type résumé was a killer. It was a visual of an Elle MacPherson-type model, soaking wet in her bathing suit. Mia's copy read:

"No way ... This is soooo weird. This girl looks just like me. I mean, she could be my twin sister or something. Freak me out! Oh, by the way, my name is Mia. I'm an art director, just graduated from the University of Blank. And I'm available."

Her phone number and address followed.

This off-beat résumé worked so well, Mia never got to use it. It was tacked on the wall where Mia was taking her portfolio classes, a creative director walked in, looked at her portfolio and hired Mia on the spot.

While Mia had planned to send her résumé out to agencies, she also used it as the first ad in her book. Mark and Bruce did the same.

Here's another example of a narrative style off-beat résumé that began with a phone number, centered at the top of the page.

UPtown 7-3927

I was in the middle of a nightmare when the phone rang. The clock said two-thirty. I reached over and grabbed the receiver.

"Hello."

"Hello, Shelly, this is Bill." The night editor paused. "They caught Son of Sam."

"No kidding."

"You comin' over?"

"Where'd they catch him?"

"Somewhere's in the Bronx."

I got to the paper 10 minutes later. I found the assistant editor poring over a picture. "Who is he?" I asked.

"Look for yourself." He handed me the shot and smiled. "Berkowitz. And Breslin thought 'Sam' was a Catholic just because knew how to use a semi-colon."

I walked into my office and turned on the light. The phone number I needed was taped to the wall for emergencies. I was waking the general manager of WCBS-AM to tell him I needed to buy air time for the morning.

"It's the middle of the night," he whispered.

"I'm writing the copy now."

"You want air time for today? What time is it?"

It was four o'clock, but he sold me three spots starting at six. I delivered the script to the station and heard it on the air going home. "Good morning, New York. The nightmare is over …"

My name is Sheldon G_____ and this is my résumé.

I didn't know if this was a résumé or not, but I loved Shelly's writing. I called him in. I wasn't the only one.

Here's one of the responses Shelly received. It was from the late, respected creative director of Karp, Newton, Van Brunt.

949-1318, 949-1326

I was in the middle of a terrible day – two presentations due in two days with a mad account man slavering outside my door, when I got this funny letter.

Demonstrating my inaccurate reading habits, I had to scan it twice before I discovered it was a résumé, not a short story or a misdirected spy note.

When I finally did understand what it was, I fell into a blue funk, a brown study.

I liked it and, I thought, I'd probably like the guy who wrote it.

But I had no job to offer him and no job was looming. I hoped he wouldn't be discouraged and that he would keep in touch with me. But not at 4 AM.

My name is Howard Karp. I am the Creative Director at Karp, Newton, Van Brunt and this is my reply.

Wow. I'm just standing here in the wings clapping.

Here's what Ed McCabe (co-founder of Scali McCabe Sloves, now doing a lot of interesting things on his own) has to say about a good, off-beat résumé.

"I hired a guy who sent me a résumé, and I was going to hire him even if I didn't like his work when he came in. This guy sent me a résumé called 'A Not-So-Professional Résumé.' And what it was was his life experiences and what he had learned. And it was brilliantly written.

"And I made up my mind on the spot that I wanted to hire this guy. Because he was communicating about the things that he felt were important and that I also felt were important.

"His résumé took me through his jobs as delivery boy, cab driver, parking lot attendant, all qualifications which I think are perfect for the advertising business.

"And every one of them had a social, moral, political, or human message involved in his experience in this thing.

73

"And I said this is a guy that is a sponge. He does something that a lot of people might think would be very boring and very dull and he takes the most interesting things out of it, recalls them, and is able to formulate it into a meaningful experience and get me involved in his meaningful experience.

"And that is what advertising is all about.

"It is taking everything you learn in life, soaking it up, and being able to push a button at the right time and have it come out so that it is meaningful to other people and, just by virtue of its interest and content, turns people on."

Here are some off-beat ideas that don't work very well.

Wanted Posters.
As in "Wanted for Copywriting," complete with a category called "modis operandi" and one called "Reward."

The last category describes how the agency will be changed forever by hiring this person.

Icky Puns.
Icky puns having to do with "new blood."

Icky puns on the person's last name. Carol Flowers decorating her résumé with sweetpeas. Joe Wrench sending a scaled down model of a you-know what.

Icky puns to the tune of "I'm hungry for this job" or "food for thought." These résumés are generally accompanied by perishables that putrify in the file cabinet. (Okay, I confess. Occasionally we have been known to eat the brownies and the popcorn, but we don't think we owe you anything for sending it.)

Icky puns that have nothing to do with anything: A sneaker ("I want to get my foot in the door..."). A box of candy ("I'm sweet on _____ Advertising.").

And More.
Rap résumés on audiotape or CD.
Poetry.
Photos of yourself, especially in your diaper as a child (even then, you knew), studio portraits, life-size blow-ups mounted on styrofoam boards with easel.
Deception of any kind.

To summarize:

Your best bet is to have a great mini-book with a simple résumé bound or glued inside.

Simple résumés with a few of your photocopied ads attached work well as an abbreviated mini-book.

If you use an "off-beat" résumé as a mailing piece, remember that clichéd, self-aggrandizing, "punny" résumés that try to convince the reader that the creator is talented, rarely work.

And lastly:

Résumés that depart from the basic format have to demonstrate your talent in a way that is applicable to the job you will be doing, to the business of advertising.

Show, don't tell.

And by all means, break the rules if you know you can win.

Q. How do you feel about business cards, promotional pieces, stunts, and cover letters?

A. First, about business cards. A few years ago one portfolio school began making mailing pieces part of the course work, and business cards were created as part of a self-promotion campaign. The cards were to be left by the individual in an interview situation, or mailed out, attached to a résumé and cover letter.

For the most part, the ones I saw were clever, well-executed, professional. But a lot of interviewers thought they were stupid. "Why do we need a card, pray tell?" they asked. "We only want your résumé." Because of this, the trend in business cards fell off pretty quickly, and we haven't been seeing them much any more.

Promotional Pieces.

Your mini-book is actually a sales promotion piece.

You are the product, and the cover of your mini-book can be seen as opportunity to advertise.

I've seen mini-books tucked inside handmade paper boxes with interesting quotes and text on the lid, and I've seen other mini-book covers that work as ads for their creators. Now that color printers are almost as cheap as marker pens, it's possible to make up a different mini-book cover for each agency in the world.

Lauren Slaff, Director of AdHouse, says, "The mini-book for an art director and for a writer can be different. I was recently very impressed with a writer's mini-book. It was small enough to fit on my desk, yet I didn't have to struggle to read the body copy. Art directors have to be especially careful not to reduce the ads so far down that the message is diminished.

"A mini-book should be clean, self-contained, easy to look at and easy to read. Shoving ten ads on a page so that you need a magnifying glass to read them, clearly works against you."

So, keep the principle points in mind. The mini-book should be small, light, cheap enough to get into as many prospective employers hands as possible, by mail, by drop-off, as a leave-behind at a portfolio review.

A killer ad for yourself on the cover could move your mini to the top of the stack, but smart-looking covers don't have to be more than basic black with a small, clever logo and your name and phone number. Even raw cardboard brown will do. For me, that beats a mini-book dressed in pink bunny fur with sequins every time.

The outside of your mini is much like what to wear when you meet someone for the first time. Make sure this first meeting makes a good impression.

Promotional Pieces from the Advertising History Channel.

Once upon a time, before the ubiquitous and handy mini-book, some people did send out promotional materials of unique and sometimes questionable value. As with the guidelines for résumés and mini-books, the best promotional pieces are simple, communicative, relevant, and most important, they're good.

Richard Glass (not his real name) sent out glass paperweights with his résumé engraved in miniature on the surface of each. They were fairly nice paperweights as paperweights go, and some people called Richard in for interviews.

Probably out of a sense of obligation. The funny thing about those paperweights was you didn't want one particularly, but you found it hard to give or throw them away.

I suppose if Richard had had a related tag line of some sort, like "Richard Glass really wants to sit on your desk," this item might have made some sense.

As it was, Richard's glass résumé sat around on a few desks for a while as sort of an irritating reminder that someone who could afford to have engraved paperweights made up and shipped was looking for a job. A creative director friend of mine described this promotional idea as "bridging the gap between stupid and 'I'm an aspiring art director.'"

On the other hand entirely is a promotional piece that wowed everyone who saw it – a classic, and most effective, promotional piece was created by Jelly Helm, who has worked at a number of top agencies around the world.

His original promo consisted of a small, shiny black box with this inscription: "I understand the Martin Agency is hiring art directors for $22,000."

Inside the box was an actual check made out to Mike Hughes, the creative director, for $22,000 and the copy line, "When do I start?" Jelly sent five of these promos personalized to the five agencies he wanted to work for. The Martin Agency bit, and Jelly landed his job.

His promo piece also won some awards, and this talented art director became a name in the advertising community before he even began working!

Flinn Dallis, Sr. V.P. Director of Creative Operations for the Leo Burnett Company, tells of a promotion that sent her racing for the phone. "Mary D____ called herself a copy diva," says Flinn.

"Her mailing piece, business card, and résumé all had the same line: 'The Ad's Not Over 'Til the Copy Sings.' And Mary had a logo of a cartoon opera diva with long curly hair, a horned helmet, breastplate and shield, but in the sword arm was a sharpened pencil. This little character was singing her heart out.

"Mary's copy was fantastic. I got her in so fast her curls got straight. We hired Mary in about a minute.

"On the other hand, I had to see about two thousand gross and offensive promotions before I saw this one.

"One guy actually sent me pieces of his résumé, one piece a week for a few months, with little personal objects in the envelope. Once it was a used razor blade complete with scraps of facial hair. I was scared! I don't even think he knew it. He sent flowers as his finale.

"I wish I could just get the kids to understand one thing. We don't want a bunch of junk in the mail. We just want to know they get it."

So. If you're going to spend the time and money on a self-promotion piece, make sure it demonstrates your talent in a relevant way. Okay?

Finally… **Stunts.**

Stunts usually involve sneak attacks on a creative director's office. Half the time the applicant is in costume, the point being to get the target to grant an interview and see the portfolio.

Do you really want to have your first interview while wearing a chicken suit?

If there's not much else going on that day, the portfolio might get seen, but you should understand how this stunt is positioning you; you've become an entertainer, and unless you're a very good entertainer, you'll look and feel ridiculous.

Charles did a number of these stunts, none of which worked very well, but he's had a great career, has a sense of humor about himself, and doesn't mind me using him as an example.

It was Christmas time, so Charles rented a Santa Claus suit.

His sneak attack on a small midwestern agency came just before lunch, and the creative director was looking for some distraction.

Rather than bring Charles back to his office, the creative director thought everyone would enjoy the show, so he asked the staff to gather around in the reception area.

Charles, in full Santa regalia, sang this:

> "Jingle bells, jingle bells, jingle all the way
> I'm a college student who graduates in May
> Jingle bells, jingle bells, jingle all the way
> Oh, what fun it would be to work here every day."

Feeling a little dumb, but it was too late to stop now, Charles took a present out of his pack; it was a basic résumé and a cover letter:

> "Last year I dropped in on hundreds of families, slid down
> thousands of chimneys and delivered millions of Cabbage
> Patch dolls. My magical talent deserves better. Please let me
> put my creative spirit to work with you."

When the laughter stopped and the show was over, Charles got his interview. "I think you need to consider another side of the business," said the CD. "Like media or account work."

Undaunted, Charles announced to other receptionists he was from the IRS to see Mr. Creative Director. He got badly chewed out for this one.

He announced he was from Publishers Clearinghouse.

Presumably the creative director was to infer he had won a prize. No applause for this approach, either.

Most of the time, Charles got his book seen, but he didn't get a job until he took his energy out of stunt work and put it into his portfolio. (Read Charles Hall's essay in Part III.)

My least favorite stunt was disguised as cover letter and a pair of résumés. When I was with Saatchi & Saatchi, I received a note from CEO Ed Wax on "from the desk of" notepaper with Ed's name printed on the top.

> "Maxine, do me a favor," the note read. "There's this great new up-and-coming team. Take a look at their books. The copywriter is _____ and the art director is _____. They're real go-getters. See what you can do for them. I've enclosed their résumés and have asked them to give you a call. They'll really fit in. Please extend them every courtesy and consideration.
> Thanks, (signed) Ed."

I was a touch suspicious. Ed didn't have to do much to get me to see someone. So I called him. And he'd never heard of this wannabe creative team.

Turns out, a similar note had gone out to every creative director in the agency (and to creative directors in other agencies, I'm sure). When it was revealed – inevitably – that the memo was a ruse to get interviews, there were some very put-out creative directors.

I saw one of the lightning bolts that went back to this team, and believe me, it was bad. No interviews from us.

Once I witnessed a junior job applicant push through a crowded restaurant and try to insert his portfolio between an advertising luminary and his shrimp cocktail. I've been assailed by bogus "messengers," fake telegrams, even a visit from an art director in a wet suit.

It's hard to come up with a stunt idea that's relevant to the job of writer or art director, and although advertising is supposed to feel like it is one person talking to another, it doesn't actually work that way.

That said, I leave it up to you.

ORGANIZING THE SEARCH.

This getting a job business can be as hard as the job itself. The competition, as you well know, is fierce.

A battle plan is required.

There's a book you should know about, commonly called "The Red Book." Its real name is *The Standard Directory of Advertising Agencies,* and it's a reference book you can use to get a fix on who's who and who their clients are in the agency business.

This book lists every agency in the United States in alphabetical order. It shows their overall size, names their accounts and the officers of the company. There are also regional lists and other useful subgroupings. Many libraries, advertising agencies, and media companies have this book. Find a copy if you can.

Familiarize yourself with this book. What you're trying to do is get acquainted with the names of the agencies and what kind of accounts they have.

You can also get a feel for the agencies you want to approach by reading the advertising trade publications. They can provide you with fresh information: Who has picked up new accounts, new creative people hired in key positions, and so on.

These publications can help you get to know the business.

Advertising Age, published by Crain Communications in Chicago, can be found on some newsstands and is received by agencies all over the country.

AdWeek has East Coast, Midwest, and West Coast editions, and they publish a directory of ad agencies.

Some city newspapers have an advertising column, and if you're in one of those cities, I'm sure you are already reading it.

Finally, there's the Internet. Of course. Most agencies have Web sites – though you may be surprised at how much is "under construction." Usually you'll find the Net is most helpful *after* you know what you're looking for.

And the next place you should look is…

Award Annuals.

Check out the award annuals. National advertising award annuals are available in most art stores. Find them. Look through them.

What agencies are doing the advertising you admire most? More specifically, what are the names of the people who created your favorite ads? Write to those people. More than one creative person has given extra consideration to a devoted fan.

Most cities have an advertising club and a local advertising awards competition. Many of them also have local annuals, available through the local ad club. It may take a little detective work, but you can track down the people you want to meet. The point here is to create and qualify a list of likely prospects.

Ask yourself: Would you be happy in a mega-agency or would you be more at home in a small one? Find out the difference.

Is location the most important thing? Or will you go anywhere?

Are there only 10 agencies you'd work for – and no other will do? Or will you take any job that gets you in?

At some point, you may want to start jotting down the names of the agencies for whom you feel an affinity, their accounts, and a likely person to approach. That's when the Net can be helpful. Often an agency's Web site will have the e-mail address of the person to contact – but remember, they also hire a lot of clerical people. Don't find yourself standing in line at the wrong entrance.

In selecting your target person, here's a guideline.

In a large agency, you should probably approach a group head, an associate creative director, or a creative director when there are several people in the agency with that title.

That's not to say you shouldn't write to the executive creative director, but he or she will probably pass your résumé along to someone else anyway, and it might go missing.

In a small to medium-sized agency, you may find that *the* creative director is accessible to you.

If an agency lists someone as "creative manager" or a similar title, address your inquiry to this person. He or she is in charge of creative department hiring and knows in a more comprehensive way where the openings are and when others are likely to occur.

Individual creative directors generally don't have the same overview, and most of them don't have much interest in interviewing unless they have an opening in their specific group.

Once you have your "short list," you might start calling by phone. This can work in your favor right away because it's quick.

Be pleasant and direct. Give your name. Say that you're looking for a job as a whatever. Have this conversation with the assistant.

Don't be vague or deceptive.

Specifically, looking for your first job as a copywriter does not qualify as a "personal" call. The fact that you sent in your résumé does not mean that the creative director "knows what this is in reference to and is expecting me to phone."

Determine whether there's a job opening, but ask if you can interview or drop off your mini-book even if there isn't one.

If you want to do a mail campaign at the same time as your phone campaign, you should compose a cover letter to "cover" your mini-book or résumé.

Q. What's the purpose of a cover letter?

A. A cover letter is like a handshake. It's your introduction to a person you want to review your mini-book. It's a letter meant to intrigue that person enough to bring you in for a job interview.

A cover letter should be personal and should feel as though it's a one-of-a-kind letter to the person who is receiving it.

Don't send form letters.

Your résumé can be one of a hundred thousand, but if you can, create a special cover letter just for me.

Your cover letter can be brief, and it doesn't have to make me howl with laughter, but it should convey something special about you or at the very least, convince me to open your mini-book in the middle of a hellacious day.

When Marshall Karp was EVP of Lowe, he received what he calls "The best letter I ever got. It was from John, a 'starving' writer in Cleveland. It asked me to save his cat, Andy. John had eaten all his other pets, and Andy was next in line. The headline on the cover letter was, 'Are you going to just sit there and let me eat my cat?'

"It was adorably illustrated and masterfully written." And even though there were no openings, Marshall gave John his first job.

You can always write a plain vanilla cover letter:

"I'm an art director looking for my first job. Please look at my mini-book, and I'll give you a call next Tuesday to see if I can make an appointment."

But, if you're inspired to write a cover letter that works as an ad for you, go for it. Keep it brief and compelling. A good cover letter could pay off big time – even when "we're not hiring."

Your cover letter is a big opportunity.

Q. How long should I wait to follow up a mailing with a phone call?

A. Give it at least a week. I know that sounds like forever, but if you can imagine how many mini-books land on a recruiter's desk in the course of a week, you'll realize that a week to them is equivalent to a blink of an eye.

If you can get through to a creative manager and make an appointment, great. If your target recruiter won't return your calls and won't return your book, either, this may be simply something you have to accept as a fact of life in this multitasking, hyperventilating experience we call modern life.

Sometimes a kind assistant to the creative manager may be willing to help you by getting you a yes, no, or maybe response, or by leaving your mini for you to pick up at the reception desk.

And if you get turn-downs, take heart, take heart, take heart.

Cathy St. Jean, owner and COO of Judy Wald Partners, a headhunter in New York, says, "You may be talented, but there are so many people looking for creative jobs right now. You have to be persistent (in a nice way), keep striving to make your book better, keep studying, keeping looking at magazines and refining your taste, and if you really want to be in advertising, keep going.

"Work as a bartender or a waitress until you get your break.

"It's the same as when theatrical people go to Hollywood to try and make it in films.

"If you really believe in yourself, go for it and don't give up."

THE JOB INTERVIEW.

At last, the opportunity you've been waiting for. An actual meeting with a real person. Possibly you'll get offered a job and have a chance to realize your parents' expectation and justify the $80,000 they spent on your education. Or was it $120,000?

Whew. No wonder you're nervous.

Hot Tips on How to Take an Interview.

The clothes you wear on an interview give the reviewer clues as to what kind of person you are and how you'll fit into the agency. I'd leave the taped-up running shoes at home and consider carefully: is this really the day to wear your motorcycle helmet?

Some agencies think khakis and a white oxford-cloth shirt are the minimum acceptable interview wear. Others think the same garments tell the world that you should be in account services!

Says Michele Daly of Bozell, "We want people that have a lot of energy, and sometimes you can see that in their wardrobe. If they're dressed funky, if they're stylish, that works in their favor."

A recruiter I know suggests you research the dress code of the agency where you'll be having your interview and then shoot for the high end of that agency's code. They wear jeans? You wear *clean* jeans.

Consider carefully: is this the day to wear your motorcycle helmet?

If the agency is the height of fashion, by all means, be cool.

But as Betsy Yamazaki, EVP Creative Manager at Lowe, suggests, "If your nose isn't already pierced, don't do it just for effect. Be your cool self, not someone else's."

Jennifer came in for an interview recently wearing ripped jeans and her boyfriend's white shirt. "Do you think I ought to have worn a dress?" she asked me halfway through her interview day. I would have said "Yes, why didn't you ask me yesterday?" But instead, I noticed that no one who interviewed her that day cared what she was wearing.

One creative director knew she was the right person for his group when she ripped off a piece of cellophane tape from the dispenser and chewed on it. Everyone who saw Jennifer was knocked out by her killer book and her "do advertising or die" attitude, and we offered her a job, ripped jeans and all.

Know where you're going before you leave home.

No kidding, The agency might have moved since their address was posted in that old Red Book you used. Why not check out the address and floor number on their Web site.

Be on time.

You are too low on the totem pole (wait, you're not even on the totem pole) to keep people waiting. Your interviewer has things to do that are more pressing than gazing out the window waiting for you. He or she may not have allowed more than a few minutes for your meeting, and you might miss your appointment altogether.

Or, as my friend Jean-Claude says, "Ten o'clock is one thing. Ten-thirty is a different matter entirely."

Be flexible.

One creative director I know can give an interview so fast, you might not know it even happened.

He says, "If you can't take an interview in 30 seconds, you don't belong in a 30-second business."

Some people are sweethearts, especially those who don't interview people for a living, and you might be in store for a full-length, hour long, tell-me-all-about-yourself kind of interview plus a tour of the agency. So make sure you've allowed time between interviews if you are doing more than one on a given day.

Be prepared to wait while the person is in a meeting. Sometimes things happen that can't be helped. If you are going to be late for your next appointment, call and say so.

Be prepared for the secretary to come out and say, "Listen, I know you had an appointment, but my boss just can't make it. Will you please leave your book?" As I said, things happen. Ask if there is someone else who can see you. Can you schedule another appointment now? No? Okay. Leave your book. And be nice about it.

Mind your manners.
Don't chew gum.
Don't smoke.
Don't swear.

Please be nice to administrative assistants.
I had an assistant once who used to come in and tell me whenever someone was rude to her or treated her like a dope.

Rudeness says something about you, and when Dianne worked for me, I got the word. That person you perceive as a stone wall is there for a reason.

Someone wants her there. Or him.

Q. If I were having an interview with you, what would you be looking for?

A. In the first few minutes I'd be gathering some early impressions about you as a person. Do you make good eye contact? How's your handshake? How do you look? Do you seem comfortable or ill at ease? (If the latter, I must try to make you the former.)

Do you have a résumé? Is your book with you?

Hard to believe but some people have actually made appointments without having their books available. "I just wanted to talk to you first," he or she might say. "I can drop off my book later in the week." Really? What would you like to talk about? Tennis?

Please do me a favor. If you don't have your book, cancel our interview. I'll understand.

Don't worry about being a little nervous.

We expect that, and in a way it's flattering because we know that nervousness means the interview is important to you.

The early impressions I'll be gathering about you are similar to the ones you'll be gathering about me. Do I seem nice to you? Too busy? What's my office like? Will you feel comfortable here?

Will the phones keep ringing and will I answer them? How many portfolios are lined up against my wall? Anyone you know? Any ads on the wall? Do you think they're good?

Don't worry. Anything that goes wrong in the first few minutes is retrievable, even if you can't make eye contact because you spilled coffee on your pants and you can't shake hands because your portfolio is in it. (A tip: Carry your book in your left hand.)

Because when I've opened your book, that's when the real interview begins.

I look through a portfolio pretty fast.

Possibly disconcertingly so. I'm on a treasure hunt, and I want the treasure to jump out at me. If it doesn't, I may dig for it on the second pass.

I'm looking for advertising ideas, new ways of looking at the same old things.

Your ideas should make me want to read your ads – buy the products. The more your ideas work on my emotions, the more I like them. And I expect to be intellectually satisfied, too.

I want to be pulled in with a great headline, and see that your copy supports the promise you've made.

I don't truly expect to see a portfolio stuffed full of blindingly original ideas. As long as your work is fairly consistent, one great idea and one killer ad can be enough to show me I'm looking at a winner.

After I'm convinced you're a conceptual thinker, I look at technique.

- Are your headlines well crafted?
- Is your body copy logical, persuasive, a joy to read?
- Are the graphic elements innovative, riveting, tasteful?

If I criticize your work, pause before you leap to defend it. Maybe I just didn't get the point of your campaign even though you made it perfectly clear.

That happens sometimes, in which case you can say, "Did you understand I was using cashmere to indicate luxury?" I'm not afraid to say, "Oh. How stupid of me. I missed that completely."

If, however, I'm having problems with more than that one ad, pay attention. Maybe you're about to learn something. Maybe I can tease out the part of your idea that's good and help you reformulate it into a better idea.

Some reviews of your book will be very thorough. Some won't.

Or. Maybe I'm a complete hack and I don't know what I'm talking about, in which case play along with me just a little. Even "hacks" have more experience than you have.

Or. Maybe you're resisting improving your book, because you finally got it looking like you wanted it to look, and because it's too close to graduation for you to think about redoing anything for God's sake!

Hey. Don't lose sight of something important here. *Your portfolio is a means of getting a job. Getting a job is the important thing, not keeping your portfolio intact.* If you are in that last-moment-before-you-graduate panic, and you're getting a lot of "advice," here's what to do…

Take a deep breath. Now exhale. You don't have to chuck out your entire portfolio just because you've gotten criticism.

Just take out the weakest link: the ad or campaign that took the worst blows.

You know which one that is. Now, start thinking about something better to replace it with. Do a killer ad. Then take out your next weakest campaign. And so on. In this way, you'll still have a book to show and it will keep getting better. *All portfolios are works in progress.* Even professionals are constantly weeding out their books, making them better.

But back to our interview.

Most people hate to give criticism.

It's a lot easier for us to say to a young creative person, "Nice book. I'm afraid we just don't have anything right now" than it is to say, "You know, you seem to be playing it too safe with your layouts." Or "You've really got to work on these headlines. I don't know what you're trying to communicate."

Once we've given this kind of criticism, it behooves us to try to help you, and that's a lot of work. If you are very defensive, you let us right off the hook. Why should we invest our feelings and time if you don't want to know?

And another thing. Try not to take criticism too much to heart.

It's your book that's taking the flack, not you. You're still the same tall, freckled, wacko, sci-fi movie buff, hamster breeder, girlfriend-of-the-boy-next-door you were before you came in for the interview. You're trying to become an even better copywriter or art director.

Guess what? Our goals are the same.
We want you to become better, too.

So. I'd recommend you ask for criticism.
Try to use the interview as a learning experience. The process may seem overwhelming sometimes. So many people and so many conflicting (!) opinions. (More on this later.)

Back to the interview once more.
During the interview, I'll be asking you questions. Directly or indirectly, I'm trying to find out several things.
- What area within the creative department might suit you best?
- Are you resilient enough to survive and succeed in advertising?
- Are you willing to work hard?
- Can you take criticism?
- Do you have enough personal confidence to present your ideas and convince others of your point of view?
- Do you seem able to get along well with other people?

Interviewers ask different questions to get at the answers to these and their own particular questions.

One creative director I know wants to know what your parents do for a living. He's trying to discover what might be special in your upbringing that might influence your creativity.

Another creative director wants to know what books you read. And how many. Yet a third creative director is most interested in your feelings about film.

By the way, an interview is a two-way street. You're also allowed to ask questions. Find out who's who in the creative department. How did the creative director get to be king? Every agency is structured a little differently. How will you fit in? What accounts might you work on?

One copy hopeful I know tries to ascertain the interviewer's predisposition to styles of advertising; does he/she hate puns, for instance, or revere elegant prose?

If it seems appropriate, this student sometimes asks to see some of the interviewer's ads. All of this helps him sort out the criticism when he's back at home with his book.

Whether your interviewer is a creative department manager, an agency principal, or a person whose name appears in every award book you've ever opened, try not to feel too intimidated. Know how good you are.

An interview is supposed to be a conversation between two people who are trying to find out if they're right for each other. Be friendly and open. Impress me with your personality, but don't talk your head off. I'd like time to see your book, too.

When the interview is over, I'll probably suggest some kind of action: Leave your book, call some time soon, let me see your book again in six months, take some classes to polish up your work, or, perhaps, I'll set up an interview for you with someone else.

If this last step isn't spontaneously happening as you close up your portfolio, you can initiate this closing yourself by nicely asking the interviewer, "What's the next step from here?" Try to get some kind of answer so you know where you stand.

Last thing.
On the way out, say "thank you," even if every moment of the interview was pure hell. And, if you feel so moved, a thank you note would not be inappropriate.

Don't take criticism too much to heart.

92

Q. Some people hate my book, some people love it. I'm going crazy. How am I supposed to figure out what to believe?

A. The most frustrating experience for a beginner is the mixed review. Usually these conflicting opinions are delivered sequentially. You just got a rave from Person A and when Person B sees the same portfolio, he tears it apart.

What's going on here?

Sometimes unusual, very original thinking polarizes people. If some people love your work and you respect these people, and they offer you a job, don't worry about the folks who hate it. Take the job. You can't please everyone, and you don't want to work for people who hate your work.

When a book is great, there's very little disparity of opinion.
For instance, I could like an individual ad, and Marie Arteca (my partner for many years at Saatchi & Saatchi and now recruiting for JWT/NY) could hate it, *but our opinion of the whole book would probably be very close to the same.*

In most cases, our difference of opinion regarding an *individual* ad will probably be a personal one. Marie is a ski fanatic. I wouldn't know a ski from a toboggan. So your ad for ski-wear just goes by me in my euphoria over your whole book. Marie reads your body copy and she knows you don't know what you're talking about. Or vice versa.

Maybe I think the ad is lousy because I don't get it. She thinks it's great because she does. These simple likes and dislikes are irrelevant when the book is great, and you'll know if your book is great because interviewers, especially the ones who do it for a living, will gush and toss airplane tickets at you.

If your book is terrible, you won't get much criticism.

Most people just don't have the stomach to tell a bright-eyed young thing to get into a different line of work. If you're getting no criticism, and no job offers either, and you've been looking for six months to a year, get tough with your interviewers. Beg us to tell you the truth. We won't enjoy it, but most of us will administer the *coup de grâce* if we must. (I'll deal with this again, later.)

93

The problem is when some people say they love your work and don't offer you a job. And the people who hate your work don't offer you a job, either. This is what we call a mixed review or the Conflicting Opinion Syndrome.

An average book is the hardest one to critique.

The Conflicting Opinion Syndrome mostly happens with the books that are in the passable to very good range.

What happens is this: the interviewer gets an over-all B+ to C- feeling about your book.

Generally, the reason for this lukewarm response is that you picked up your markers or turned on your computer too soon (that biggest mistake I mentioned in Part I).

You started with an execution, and your strategy is faulty. So, what we see is something that is almost good or could have been good, but because the ad is misdirected, we get thrown.

Should we tell you to throw out a whole campaign that is fabulous-looking but off-kilter? Or should we praise the art direction and move on?

If we can help you adjust the headline, will that help the ad, or will it just be a slightly better off-kilter ad?

Sometimes your ads are – sorry – boring.

Aah. The old Conflicting Opinion Syndrome.

You understand the whole process and you've figured out some formulas, but the ads just lie there, staring blankly. "There's no news here," I said recently to a copy hopeful. "No news?" she asked, in a tone that could be interpreted as: "Where did this rule come from? I never heard that one before."

Let me explain.

Boring ads are just another form of ad-like object.

The ads may be technically correct, but you've told us the same old thing in the same old way.

When your ads are boring we may try to motivate you to shake things up. "Get a little wild and crazy," someone might say.

Someone else might suggest, "Try using fewer words in your headline. This is a little too head-y for me." I might say, "There's no news here."

These remarks sound as though they are addressing different problems. But they're not. The problem is in the work.

We see some problems and potential. We want to explain to you where you've gone wrong, but we're having trouble articulating why that particular ad, campaign, or bunch of ads isn't working, so the feedback we give you collectively may be erratic.

Something about your work is loose and wobbly, and we don't know whether to turn you clockwise or counter-clockwise. Maybe either way will work. You get conflicting opinions because I suggest left and Marie suggests right.

We're trying to help.

And believe me, it takes a lot out of us. A full day of interviewing can make me feel as though my blood has been drained by hundreds of little vampire bats. No offense.

Sometimes people have bad days and good days, come from all schools of advertising, all kinds of educational and ethnic groups, and all kinds of disciplines.

I might be offended by something that someone else thinks is a laugh riot. I might pay more attention to your ideas – or lack thereof – and the guy standing next to me (who knows more about art direction than I'll ever know) thinks your layouts are trite.

So you get a thumbs up and a thumbs down.

And we could both be right.

Sometimes this conflict of opinions is based on something as human as this. I'm having a hard time saying, "Yuck, no, phooey," and I want to say, about this one ad at least, "Okay! You've got it here." I want to give you a smidgen of encouragement. And leave it to me, I've just picked the ad that was shredded in your last interview.

This also happens when I've seen your book a couple of times before and it's getting better. But the last guy you saw didn't know that you've improved, so he just sees that average book and he dumps all over it.

Sometimes, in a portfolio review where dozens of books must be reviewed in a couple of hours, the reviewers would like to identify the problem fast enough to help you but can't, so they struggle with what to say.

Their comments may be vague.

Or their attempts to help may be off.

In some cases you may get no comments at all.

I've sometimes felt I can take a book apart in five minutes – even yours. But in that small period of time I can't put you and it back together again. So, I might smile and murmur innocuously rather than start something I can't finish.

Frequently, people who look at books are good advertising people, but not good teachers. While in real life some creative directors are able and willing to nurse you along, many creative directors cannot or will not cosset you.

If you were to bring that heartless ad into your "for real" creative director boss, he or she could reasonably say, "Where's your idea? I don't see it. Go back and work on this ad again." Or, "This is no good." Period. And then that creative director is going to ask someone else to do the ad. Or do it himself or herself.

Now. Put these creative directors in a portfolio review.

They can't and shouldn't redo your ad for you, and phrasing why a thing is wrong is not their style.

Furthermore, it's not their job.

They are at this portfolio review to pick out one kid to hire.

That's it. And there you are, hoping for the perfect, and above all accurate, critique.

Back to interpreting the mixed review.

When your reviewers mostly agree that your book is very good, you're on the right track. Here's what they say as they look at your ads. "Yes, yes, good, I don't know, okay, good!"

But discounting personal likes and dislikes, reviews that are all over the place mean that you're not there yet.

If you're getting mixed reviews, what should you do?

Listen and learn.

Don't tear up your book after every interview.

Let the advice you've gotten steep a little bit. (I've seen some students take notes for later reference.)

Mull it over. Add up the opinions and then weigh them.

Question your professors and your interviewers. You don't have to accept their advice as law, either.

David had this experience once. He had an idea for a plastic kitchen wrap. To demonstrate that it didn't stick to itself, he ran a sheet of it up a flagpole so that it flapped around in the breeze.

One creative director thought David's approach too esoteric. She felt the only place to demonstrate plastic wrap was in the kitchen. David promptly complied and came up with a kitchen demo for the same product.

Naturally, the next person who saw his book told him the demo was too tame; why didn't he bust some boundaries?

My best advice.

If you hear it over and over again, then it's probably true. Try to understand the criticism so you learn from it.

Then, when you upgrade your portfolio again, you'll be working with your own insight and beginning a process called forming your own judgment.

Your long and happy life in advertising depends upon it.

Q. **When I create an ad, I never think it's an ad-like object. I always think I've come up with something that's really good. How can I know the difference before someone shoves it down my throat?**

A. Forming your own judgment isn't easy.

Leora tells about the ad she created for Zippo lighters. Visual: The lighter. Headline: "The Eternal Flame." Without a word, Leora's teacher took out his lighter and turned Leora's layout into warm, gray ash. Leora held up another ad, this one for a brand of men's underwear. Headline: "Eleven Reasons Why You Should Buy Hanes' Underwear."

Leora's teacher took her layout and dropped it out the window. He gave her a cold stare. "Don't do this any more," he said.

Okay, so this was no fun for Leora (although her classmates may have gotten some nervous pleasure out of it), but this is how Leora learned to do ads with heart. In fact, she's lucky, and so are you if you are learning from a tough teacher.

*Cultivate the opinion of the person
whose opinion matters most. You.*

98

Making mistakes is how we all learn. So suffer the humiliation because you must. It's part of the process. Go back and read about ads with heart. Check your ads for killerhood. Keep yourself wide open to the learning process so that you'll have a basis for forming your own style and judgment.

And if you want to find out how it worked out for Leora, read her essay in Part III.

Q. Should you go on an interview when there is no job?

A. Absolutely.

There are two kinds of job interviews. One is a job interview for a specific job. There's also a type of interview called an "exploratory" interview where there is no job. You should go on any interview you can get.

It's great practice and a chance to learn. And, maybe you can talk or charm somebody into creating a job for you.

Use every opportunity you have to go on a job interview. If your father knows somebody in the business, use that entree. If you're related to someone who is a client of the agency, that's fine. Don't be embarrassed. Everybody does it. Exploit every source you have because it's very tough to get interviews when you're looking for that first job.

By the way, look up the agency before you go on any interview. You'll sound better to us if you know who we are.

Person-like organism with ad-like object.

99

Now, let's say you've had a great interview and there are no openings, but you think the interviewer genuinely likes you. That's your cue to say, "I really want to get into advertising, and I'd love to work here. Do you know someone who's looking for a junior writer at some other agency or someone who'll see me even if they aren't looking?" People have been known to give out a list of names. Lisa, a junior art director, parlayed two names into 30 before she was hired – just by asking that question.

Q. **If you have a decent book, but you're not a salesperson, will you have less of a chance getting a job than the good salesperson with the bad book?**

A. I won't say personality doesn't count. It can and does. But let's not conclude so quickly that you don't have one.

If you have a very good book, not just a decent one, someone will hire you for your talent.

A great part of salesmanship is *confidence,* and once you've been hired for your talent, the confidence should come. Sales is the whole point of advertising, but you don't have to be a razzle-dazzle presenter to get a job and to succeed.

I've never even heard of a someone with a good personality being hired with a bad book. Lose no more sleep over this.

No contest.

Q. When I'm asked to leave my book, should I do it? How long must I leave it?

A. When you're asked to leave your main book, it generally means that your mini-book has gotten high marks by the creative manager or someone else in the agency, things are heating up, and you're being actively considered for a job. Good for you!

You shouldn't allow an agency to tie up your interview book for an unreasonable length of time. But be fair. Don't expect someone to look at your book right away.

When you leave your book, ask how long they're likely to keep it. Give them a week if they need it that long, more if it's a real job and you're in the running.

Some kids we know have *two* main books, so that they'll have a spare if they are up for two job interviews at the same time.

When you have to pick up your book, give the agency a "heads-up" the day before. Then, call again as a reminder on the morning you're coming to get it.

This way, your book won't be locked in a closet when you arrive, and also, the person who has been keeping your book knows that it is "active." In most cases, if he or she hasn't seen it yet, they'll do it right away.

Leaving your book is a fact of life,
but don't allow an agency to tie it up too long.

By the way, make sure you have your name somewhere on or inside your portfolio. It's not even a bad idea to put your name on the back of each ad. People sometimes take ads out of the case and strew them all over their sofa. You don't want your ads to get mixed up with someone else's. Label – why not be safe?

Q. **If you know you've got spark, how do you make a dumb, inanimate portfolio reflect the wonderfulness that is you?**

A. Sorry. If it's not in the book, the wonderfulness that is you will have to be applied to some other profession. Or, don't give up until you've learned how to make the transfusion from you to it. Your question makes me think you can do it.

Q. **When the person across from you says, "I really like your book, but there aren't any openings right now. Keep in touch because that could change," does that mean keep in touch or something else?**

A. It means keep in touch. But don't be a pest. Figure out how to be persistent in a pleasant way. Ask if you can keep in touch via e-mail – it's not as intrusive as the telephone. Take your cues from the interviewer. If he or she calls you back to see how you're doing, the invitation was quite sincere.

Ditto if an encouraging message is relayed from the interviewer to the secretary to you. If the secretary is pleasant to you when you call, ask her if a call from you to check in every three or four weeks would be okay with her. Perhaps you might send a note every now and then with a new ad attached.

Don't call your target at home. Don't drop by unannounced.

If you follow up with me in six months, please don't act like I loved your book if I didn't actually tell you I loved it. If I really loved it, I'll remember you, and if I didn't, I'll look you up in my database where I noted exactly what was in your book and exactly what I thought.

And do keep working on your book so that if you get another appointment, your book will be even better than before.

Q. **How kindly disposed are those who look at portfolios to looking at people's books again?**

A. Everyone is different, but let's be optimistic. Let's not assume that you had your one chance with Cliff Freeman or Gary Goldsmith (or, insert your hero's name here) and that was it.

Call and ask if you can resubmit your mini-book. If enough time has elapsed for improvement to be plausible, I'll bet three out of four people will say, "Okay, you can drop it off again."

But this question leads me to an important point. When you start approaching the people on your list of prospects, you should launch your attack in "flights" of four or five agencies.

Then, stop and analyze the results.

Did your mini-book result in any interviews or encouragement? If not, you could send out another flight, or take this opportunity to redo your book before sending it out again.

Pull a questionable campaign and replace it with a better one. Reorganize. Rethink. Rewrite. Redesign.

It's okay to stop and regroup before charging ahead again.

Q. **Is it helpful to go to an employment agency in the advertising field, or should I just go directly to the advertising agencies?**

A. An employment agent can help you – maybe. If they're impressed with your book, great, they'll try to place you. They'll occasionally call personal friends and will sometimes waive their fee to the ad agency if a job is created for you, just for the satisfaction of getting you a first job and in the hope that when you're looking for your second job, you'll call them.

But if an agent doesn't fall in love with your book, you may not get an interview. No interview, no feedback.

You also have to understand, employment agencies don't get many requests for juniors. Most advertising agencies are deluged with beginner books and résumés and don't want to pay a fee for someone they can hire for free.

Also, it takes time for an agent to place a junior, and they don't have the time to work with and develop all the juniors who call them.

A friend at a placement agency in New York: "I have a number of clients who every so often ask, 'Have you seen any great juniors?' When that happens, I'm delighted to send along a few exceptional people. But they do have to be exceptional."

That response is the rule rather than the exception for most employment agents, although some individuals and a rare agency do more work with juniors than others.

Check with your peers or last year's graduates before you. They may know of some kindly headhunter who loves juniors and would love to see you.

HOW YOU FIT INTO THE PICTURE.

I would think it must be difficult from where you're sitting to imagine how you'll fit in and function in an advertising agency.

You know that life in a company is bound to be different than life in school. And you're right.

Because in the real world advertising is a collaborative effort, you'll find that ad-making is no longer solely concentrated on you and your idea.

You'll have a teammate with his or her individual point of view, supervisors in layers above you with their points of view, layers of account people with their points of view, and strategies developed when you were nowhere around.

And there will be a client – actually the "client" may be dozens of people with varying objectives, personality, biases.

There will also be market research testing, the results of which may alter your brilliant ideas. And there will be air dates and executional restrictions of all kinds.

The good news is: you'll never be alone on a project again.
When you get that job, you'll be joining a team.
You'll have backup, support, leadership, and resources to tap into beyond your imagining.
And there will be people who will be depending on you.

Excited? I would be, too.

Q. **How are creative groups organized? Do you have one teammate on every project or do you get changed around?**

A. The basic organization chart looks like a pyramid.

There's a creative director at the top of the heap, a small clutch of supervisors below the creative director, and a bunch of copy and art folks under each supervisor.

The size of the agency and capacities of the creative directors determine the dimensions of the creative group. And, naturally, titles and responsibilities vary from agency to agency.

Generally, the creative director is responsible for all the people and the advertising on his or her accounts in his or her division.

The supervisor-types below the creative director are responsible for the work on their accounts, with less responsibility for people management.

Copy and art people are responsible for the assignments they've been given.

In some organizations, you could work with one teammate on one account, another teammate on a different account. In some agencies, you two are joined at the hip until otherwise informed. Sometimes one or the other of you might be asked to help out on a piece of business in another creative group, for or with another person.

Q. What kind of beginning jobs are there for art directors and writers?

A. It's more and more common for junior art directors to land a job with their copywriter teammates and find themselves in the thick of a major advertising push on day one. Others may come up through the time-honored studio job route. These days, it's a digital studio.

Everything's electronic. Everything's on a computer.

In some agencies an art studio job is an end to itself. In others, it's a promotable position – after you've spent a certain amount of time there, you'll be moving into the creative department.

The equivalent of the art studio job for copywriters is to be a creative assistant; that is, assisting the creative people by answering phones and typing scripts with the occasional opportunity to write an ad or a script under the supervision of a more senior creative talent. But most often these days, juniors are assigned to a creative group and given responsibility right away.

Your typical copywriter-art director team.

Perhaps that responsibility is for collateral material or package copy, but at least it's their collateral or package copy. Or, a junior may be asked to work on a Web site. You will, of course, have a copywriter or supervisor above you, and this person will be responsible for helping you grow.

Young creatives paired with each other, or with someone slightly more senior, are soon working on their own ads, sometimes their own accounts, coming up with ideas, not only assisting other people with their ideas.

Here's how Greg, an art director in his first year at Hal Riney, Chicago, describes a day in his life.

> September 25th. 9:15 a.m. A very good start for a Monday. My writer and I just found out that the print campaign we've been working on for the Chicago Symphony has been approved by the client. But the celebration has been cut short by my associate creative director. He's in a crunch and needs my help mounting some ads for a meeting.
>
> When I finish mounting the ads, I start working on the design of the symphony ads. Just before lunch, my creative director calls a meeting to discuss a hot assignment. TV. Two 30-second spots.
>
> But they have to be presented to the client first thing Thursday morning.
>
> We break for lunch, and my writer and I start to discuss the new assignment. When we return from lunch we barricade ourselves in his office and begin brainstorming.
>
> Six hours and one layout pad later, we come up empty. But we'll try again tomorrow, and sooner or later, the big idea will come to us. It better. If it doesn't, I may be needing another copy of this book.

Somehow, I don't think Greg and his teammate need to worry.

In your first job, no matter what it might be, you can impress people by demonstrating your untiring energy and your desire to learn. Try to get someone who's involved in TV to let you tag along to an after-hours recording or editing session. (Many of these sessions go on late into the night and over the weekend.)

Volunteer to help other team members in a crunch. Creative directors would rather you come to them than have to go looking for you.

Make yourself someone who can be counted on. Volunteer and make sure to follow through. I'm not talking brownie points here. I'm talking about putting yourself in a position to learn so that you can contribute sooner, give a lot back, and in the process get to more of the places you want to go.

It's impossible to overstate how much good you will do your future if you work extra hard at this time in your career.

Q. **What's a typical working environment like? Lots of open offices? Working in groups? Fairly informal?**

A. It could be a Dilbert cubicle, an office with a door, or even an office with a window. The Virtual Office may be coming, and many top freelancers may be able to create their own unique work siutations, but for your first few jobs, you pretty much have to take whatever they happen to have. Now most agencies are fairly informal. "Casual Day" now lasts all week, except for the occasional presentation.

Work extra hard at this time in your career.

Q. Should I care how much my first job pays?

A. I wouldn't. If you're getting lots of bites from agencies of relative merit, and you like the people who want you equally, then by all means go for the most money. If, however, you get more offers from other agencies – one of which might prove more fruitful for your career than the other – disregard the money and take the job with the most growth and learning opportunity. You'll make up the dollar difference some other year, and by then a couple of thousand dollars one way or the other won't make a difference.

Q. If the agency that offered me the job wants me to relocate, who should pay the expenses?

A. The general rule on this is based on who made the approach. If you go out to San Francisco and knock on doors and land a job, you'll probably be asked to pick up your own moving expenses.

If, however, you are going to school in Atlanta, and a recruiter comes to your school from San Francisco, they may be prepared to pay for your relocation. But don't count on it.

Some protocol.

If you are flown in for an interview, fly coach. Don't pig out on champagne and oysters via room service and charge the agency. Don't take the subway and charge the agency for a cab.

If you want to take the subway, take it. If you want to take a cab, take that. Don't fly out on Friday and expect the agency to pick up the tab for your weekend.

Good manners would dictate that you fly home Friday night, or if it's a cross country journey, the following morning.

If you want to spend the weekend in a city you've never seen before, do so, but at your own expense. Or stay with a friend.

But don't cheat, and don't take advantage.

It's okay to set up interviews for yourself with other agencies since you happen to be in town, but don't flaunt it. And make the schedule of the agency that is paying your way your top priority.

If you end up getting an offer from someone else, you really owe it to the agency that flew you in to tell them. Don't expect your "flying-in" agency to be pleased, but if you don't want an enemy for life, do give them the courtesy of telling them about your offer, and a chance to match it.

If you get an offer from the agency that paid your expenses, but don't wish to take it, be extra gracious when you turn them down. Flowers. Notes of appreciation. You get the drift.

In closing, any time an agency pays your expenses, whether it be for interview purposes or a relocation, save your receipts. No padding. Ever. Promise?

Q. **Does it make sense to take an administrative job if there are no copywriter jobs right away?**

A. Yes, it can make lots of sense. It's probably better for you to be an assistant in an advertising agency, especially if you are an assistant in the creative department, than to drive a cab or waitress at a diner (although people from both of these professions have done very well in advertising).

You'll be exposed to people in the business. You'll hear the way they talk about their work, and you'll become familiar with the process of doing advertising and with the experience of working in a company. And, you'll make friends who can help you with your book.

Frequently, assistants, file room clerks, A.V., and stat machine technicians are given a chance to write or to assist an art director, and many are promoted.

Carin, formerly a creative assistant, now a creative supervisor, offers this advice on "how to climb out of the secretarial pool." She says:

> You've literally got to advertise. Tell the people you work for that you want to be a copywriter and beg for assignments. Take copywriting courses and ask your bosses to critique your book. Set your goal and work toward it with perseverance.
>
> If you just sit around waiting for some group head to read your mind and magically drop a coupon assignment on your desk, you could end up waiting an awfully long time.

John was a studio assistant who asked for an opportunity to work as an art director in the agency's hottest group, and he got his chance. He knew this opportunity would be pass/fail and if he didn't make his mark he would be out of work pretty fast.

111

John had a wife and child, but he took the risk.

Today, that risk has paid off in a superior reel of commercials, a vice presidency, and a long row of metal statues on his window sill.

Laura was an assistant in creative management. She also answered telephones for seven television producers. Laura went to school at night, worked on her book, and was promoted to junior copywriter within a year.

Two years later, Laura has a fat book of produced ads, a few good pay hikes, and has gone on location to the Far East.

The business is filled with people who have stories like these to tell. But remember, the job you are being paid to do must be done diligently and with a good attitude.

What the "boss" really wants is an assistant who does the job he or she was hired to do. They don't want someone who is above getting the coffee or who makes it all too obvious to others in the assisting tier that they are just "passing through."

This kind of attitude can be very disruptive, and it devalues jobs that are necessary to keep an agency running smoothly.

For these and other reasons, don't expect every boss to be patient with a hopeful creative person's ambitions, especially if that person is forgetful, sullen or, how shall I put this, a little distracted.

My advice.

If you can't get a copy or art job right away, take an agency job that's not copy or art if one is offered.

Do your "crummy" job very well. Make friends.

Make your boss want to offer you a good reference should you need it later. Work on your book on your own time. And when it's good enough, try to get a promotion. If you can't get promoted, try to get a job in another agency.

Q. I'm a writer in my 30s. Am I going to have trouble breaking in as a junior?

A. I think you'll be pleasantly surprised to hear this. No problem. Diana, now an EVP, Creative Director, raised her two children before she got into advertising at the age of 39. These are far from isolated cases.

Creative people aren't too particular about things like age, background or education. They only care about how good you are at what you do. Your age may even act in your favor.

After a year or two of junior-level work, people may simply see a 30-year-old writer and forget that, in terms of experience, you're just a "kid." After all, you have the poise and sophistication most 23-year-olds haven't yet acquired.

After a career as a waiter in some of New York's best restaurants, Ray got his first copy job at the age of 34. I don't think I'll ever forget the look on his face when a creative group head, who started working at the agency a week after Ray started his first job, handed him and his art director a full-sized assignment. She never questioned Ray's length of time in the business, she just gave him a deadline.

A week earlier, Ray had been standing in front of customers reciting the specials of the day! After a few moments of sputtering, he jumped right in. Jumping right in is kind of a trademark of Ray's, and he's considered a very valuable member of the agency team.

So, if your cap and gown went into mothballs long ago, or if you never graduated, don't worry. In fact, you may find that you'll get raises faster than your younger associates because your superiors recognize and reward your maturity.

Q. When do you get to do television commercials?

A. It depends on the size of the agency, the accounts, the luck of the draw. Could be immediately; could be in two years.

The larger packaged goods agencies, the ones who do 80 percent or more of their work in television, are more likely to let you do a commercial sooner than a small agency that only does a few commercials a year.

In a large agency, you could find yourself coming up with a TV idea for an account before you get your I.D. card from personnel. You may or may not get to go on the shoot if the commercial is approved, but you'll get your name on it, and you'll feel great.

In a small agency, it's more likely the top teams are going to do all the television, but you may get a stronger grounding in print than your large agency counterparts.

Whatever the size of the agency you join, you can prepare for the time when you will do TV by learning as much as you can about the process. Ask to go on local shoots. See if you can attach yourself to a producer or two when your schedule and theirs permit. Many shoots and recording sessions go on at night.

If you find yourself in a job where the prospects of ever doing television are close to zero, learn what you can, and then, unless you've decided on a career in print, consider finding another job.

You may get to do television in a couple of years.

114

Q. Can you tell me what my career and salary objectives should be?

A. Your first five years should be spent working hard at learning your craft and working with as many good creative people as you can. Your starting job could pay from an average of $30,000 to $35,000, depending on the city, state of the job market, and how fabulous your book is. Star hires from portfolio schools may get much more.

After that, anything goes. You could be making six figures with lots of perks, or you could wash out of the business.

Many people would tell you that this is not the stuff you should be worrying about right now; that you should be worrying about learning, growing, coming up with big ideas that become successful, and even award-winning campaigns.

You know something? They're right.

Q. Is advertising really as fast-paced, life-on-the-razor's-edge, laugh-in-the-face-of-death job that I've always heard it was? Is there a high stress factor? Why do they call it a "cut-throat" business?

A. Um, well. There are some aspects of the business which may seem a little cut-throat. For example, advertising agencies are suppliers to their advertiser clients; if the agency gets fired, so can you – whether you did anything to deserve it or not. One reason advertising people make so much money is to offset this risk.

Competition is the essense of advertising. It's one of the ways businesses compete in the marketplace. Suppliers compete for jobs with agencies, creative groups in agencies often compete against each other, and agencies compete against one another to "pitch" accounts or to keep them.

The result of all that competitiveness seems to result in a tough, straightforward, to-the-point attitude, to the effect that people in advertising work harder to cut through the b.s. than they do to cut anyone's throat.

Advertising is a business that seems to work well for nimble people. The quick, the bright, those who are adept at walking on quicksand can make big money at a fairly young age – so advertising does encourage a certain amount of aggressiveness and self-promotion.

I've also noticed that the young people who acquire additional skills – such as the ability to make presentations, for instance, or those who get into television right away – can move ahead rather quickly. And so this doesn't go unsaid, great ads are like money in the bank. Those "kids" who have genuine talent are in demand and will always be in demand.

The more you dig in and learn, the better the quality of the work you do, the more useful you are to the people you report to, the sooner they can send you out to a meeting or a print shoot without them, the more appreciated you will be.

I'm talking about legitimate skills acquired by hard work, now. Buttering up bosses will earn you antagonism from your peers and may catch up with you later.

Bluffing your way in over your head could be a learning experience, or it could cost your agency thousands in ruined film footage, excess talent fees, or even lawsuits. In some agencies you might get forgiven once. In others, it's back to you and your book. And the street.

As for stress, I won't say that good creative people thrive on stress. But I won't say they don't.

I won't say that good creative people thrive on stress.
But I won't say they don't.

My advice.

Work hard. Do good. Put the team's interests before yours. And – this is not a contradiction – keep your eye on your career. Those "kids" who have the earmarks of potential leaders are watched by those in a position to make it happen.

Promoting from within is desirable in all phases of American business, not just advertising. Advertising is simply a faster track than many businesses.

So don't let this talk of bloodletting scare you off. If you get into advertising, you'll make friends that will last a lifetime. You'll have fun. You'll mingle with smart people who will mingle with you because you're smart. You'll be in a field that is quite small and quite hard to crack – and you got in! You'll be able to show the fruits of your labors to your friends and your children.

And, if you know your job and do it well, you can have a long and rewarding career.

Q. **I'm in my junior year at school. I have an offer to drop out now and take a job with a good local agency. Should I get my degree, or should I take the job?**

A. Are you enthusiastic about the job? Will your parents kill you if you don't get your degree? Sorry to ask questions, but there are many factors involved here.

If you're good enough to get a job offer before you graduate, I don't think this job offer will be the last you'll ever get. In fact, these exact people might offer you a job again when you graduate.

If you're close to that degree that your parents have been paying for, why not finish what you started? If you're working nights to pay for that last year of art school, getting a good job is why you went to school and you don't need to graduate.

Either way, as far as your résumé is concerned, your degree doesn't mean a whole lot to us. I mean, it could be interesting if you get a degree in law from Columbia, but, as I've said 200 times before, what we care about is your book.

Q. How much bearing does one's GPA have on hiring? Can a wonderful book make up for a less than wonderful GPA? Can coming out of a good school give me an edge?

A. The best schools are making sure their copy graduates can think visually and their art graduates can think verbally. These ambidextrous creative people can have very sharp-looking books.

The schools that consistently turn out graduates who have great books get the most attention from the agencies. And in this way, coming out of a good school can give you an edge. But only in this way. Your diploma is not a license to get a job.

We don't care about your grade point average.
We care about your book.

Q. What's expected of a first year employee? What are the major reasons that juniors fail?

A. Junior-level creative people are expected to show up earlier and stay later than anyone. Be willing to do any kind of work. Learn, learn, learn.

Failing in the first year is hard to do, but here's how to do it.

Bad-mouth other people's work.
Especially if you're not so hot yet yourself.

Act like you're too good to work on certain assignments.
Make faces, roll your eyes, and throw deep sighs.

Be lazy.
Hide when your supervisor comes looking for you or make your supervisor nag you to get assignments finished on schedule.

Contradict your boss in a client meeting.

Keep coming back with that same old ad your boss has killed.
(You know it's great even if he doesn't get it.)

Play big-shot with a supplier.
Do this especially if it looks like there's something shady going on like kickbacks or favors like producing ads for your book in exchange for giving the supplier a job, etc.

Don't live up to the promise in your book.

As in, did you really do those spec ads? Yes, this happens. And, sad to say, it happens at many levels, from beginner to long-timer.

If you lift someone else's ads and are found out, you will find this is one area where retribution is swift. No agency wants a thief in their house. Period.

Actually, hardly any people lose their job in their first year except for reasons that are outside their control.

Namely, the agency has a cutback and the extra junior art director is seen as an unaffordable luxury.

If you should happen to lose your job because you made some mistakes, own up and learn from them.

If you lose your job because of agency finances, there is no stigma attached, believe me. And you now have an edge on all those inexperienced people looking for their first job.

Q. How long of a commitment does an agency expect from you?

A. Two years sounds about right. But I'd still call that a minimum.

If you're doing well and are appreciated, why leave? If you hit a rough patch, before you bail out, talk to someone who's in a position to make things better for you and see if they can.

Jumping around doesn't look as glamorous as it used to.

If you've had a lot of jobs these days, people want to know why.

Q. Is it better to be a small fish in a big pond? Or stay in a small pond until I learn how to swim? Or should I go to NYC?

A. I guess I'd advise you to determine which is more important.

A career in the big time? Or a good job in your home state?

One thing does not lead to the other, nor does it necessarily obstruct it. If you like Santa Fe, don't force yourself to go to New York. If you think you'd like the intensity of the big city, go for it now.

Two years in an agency in Santa Fe isn't going to help you get a job by itself. But what will help you get a job in New York is if you did very good ads in Santa Fe. Otherwise, you'll have to rely on your spec book.

You won't quite be going back to zero, but you won't quite be in the same place as someone else who's been getting good work produced during his or her first two years.

119

Q. **Is it true New York is no longer the center of advertising?**

A. The center of advertising has been a moving target for years. Chicago, Minneapolis, Dallas, San Francisco, Los Angeles and other cities have long been featured in the advertising news of the world. Richmond, Portland, and Austin are also homes to agencies with national stature.

These days, you don't have to work in "the Big Apple" to make it, and right now the odds of getting a job in New York are tougher than ever. Headhunters and creative managers suggest that you take a job offer wherever you find it, and if your heart is set on New York, send out your mini-book again at a later time.

And, by the way, New York City isn't everyone's idea of fun. Don't move to New York unless you've really checked out what it's like to live there.

You might be happier being a star in Dallas instead.

Today, if you can make it in Portland, you can make it anywhere.

Q. **What are the odds of survival for a single, unemployed male with no friends or contacts who just happens to show up in New York?**

A. A lot depends on how flexible you are about the kind of work you may have to do until you get an agency job. And are you willing to live with someone or sometwo or three until you can afford a decent apartment?

You might not be able to afford Manhattan. For years, Steve, Rick, and Brian tripled-up out by the airport in Queens.

Before you pack your trunk, sell your car, and kiss your sweetheart goodbye, try to pave the way. Make calls, send letters to schedule appointments. Do a two-week foray before you move.

Network around a little. Who do you know who knows someone living in New York? Are there any friends from school who might let you sleep on their floor for a few weeks? Or friends of friends?

Now, take a trip. See how things go. See if you even like New York. If you do, and if your interviews have given you reason to hope, get a fix on the housing and interim job markets while you are in town. In a two-week, pre-move visit, your status can be altered from friendless, contactless, unemployed male to unemployed person with friends, a bed, and prospects.

Maybe you've got friends in New York who'll let you sleep on their floor for a while.

121

Q. What about internships? What are they about? And how can I get one?

A. Agencies of all sizes hire interns.

Sometimes there is a formal training aspect to the program, contact with interns from other disciplines, a mentor, a rotation through the agency.

Sometimes "intern" is just another way to spell "go-fer."

Since internships are usually offered to students, they usually only last for the summer.

From the agencies' perspective, internships can be a way of acquiring inexpensive assistance in return for the experience such an opportunity affords.

An internship can be a favor granted because someone you know has sufficient pull to get you in somewhere.

Or it can be a way for an agency to brand a promising junior so that person can be harvested after graduation.

In any case, internships are valuable, and I'd urge you to spend your summers in the employ of an advertising agency if you can.

You may be lucky enough to go to a school that actively promotes internships in the surrounding area.

If not, why not prepare a list of prospects and write them letters?

See what you can cook up.

Q. If I can't afford to go to New York to knock on doors, is it okay to mail my book?

A. Yes, of course. Mini-books are the perfect mailing piece, so send them out in flights of five or so and follow up with phone calls.

Calls from out-of-towners asking for appointments generally get a higher rate of response than local requests, so give it a try.

Make some appointments with creative recruiters, if you can.

Then, ask your folks to break out some frequent flyer miles for you. If you've got a buddy in New York who'll let you sleep on the sofa, your trip to New York may suddenly be more affordable than you thought.

122

Q. **If I've been looking for a while and it's not going so well, how do I know when to give up?**

A. If you're getting interviews, get feedback. As I've stated earlier, most people are loathe to be so honest that they cause some adorable stranger in front of them to cry.

If you suspect the worst, that your book is too average to compete, and you've done the best work you think you can do, you've got to ask for the famous "brutal" honesty.

Ask more than one person.

Tell them you really need to know the truth.

If you're given some encouragement, by all means continue. I have a theory about the learning-to-do-advertising process. I think it's like learning a new sport – like tennis or golf.

You're told that you are supposed to stand a certain way, put your weight on this or that foot, hold your wrist straight, or flexed, your head up or down. And you want to learn this sport and are trying hard to achieve what you can't really see or feel. One day you take a swing at a particular ball and everything you've learned falls into place automatically. The ball goes exactly where you want it, and beautifully. I think this is called muscle memory.

I've seen a similar thing happen with people who are learning advertising. Bad, boring ad follows bad, boring ad. The student, meanwhile, is working, analyzing, re-working, studying. Forming his or her own judgment. One day, seemingly effortlessly, this person creates his or her first killer ad.

It's a wonderful moment. To be clear, there's no substitute for talent. But some talent and lots of very hard work should pay off. Eventually.

So, should you quit if you are advised to quit?

I believe you should weigh what you've been told, then decide for yourself whether to give up or to press on regardless.

Here's a true story.

A couple of years ago I met a young man at an ad club portfolio review. His name was Joey, he wanted to be an art director, and he wasn't having a good time.

"Please tell me what's wrong with my book," he said. "I know something's really wrong.

"I'm taking classes and working on my ads day and night, but it's been two years since I started looking, and I'm still unemployed.

"I used to think I was the victim of bad luck and bad timing, but now when I drop off my book, I get calls saying 'Thank you. Please pick up your book.' Then one of my friends from class gets the job. Lately, my classmates are telling me to go back to my old book. Like I'm getting worse."

I looked at Joey's book. He had some ideas in there, although not startling ones, and these frail things were buried beneath labored constructions of words and images so that it took a long time to get the messages Joey was trying to convey.

When I did "get" them, it was too late to feel anything except relief that I had figured it out.

And, as for the art direction, no magic there either. Joey either had average talent or he had yet to develop an original graphic point of view. I asked Joey, reasonably, I thought, if he'd considered getting into some other line of work.

He said, "If I could think of something that turns me on as much as advertising, I would do it, because I feel so whipped. But I can't."

So, okay. I tried to help.

I noticed that Joey spoke colorfully when he was discussing his ad concepts. He was also a bit of a wise guy and words came out of his mouth in an interesting way. But somehow he seemed incapable of listening to himself and setting down his own words. He said he knew he would freeze up if he tape recorded himself, as I suggested he do.

I talked to Joey about getting back to basics – concentrating on products he knows and considering how a consumer might feel about those products, instead of striving for clever headlines that had tied him in knots and resulted in a collection of heartless executions.

Joey called me a day later. He wanted to talk to me about a hair gel he liked to use.

He said, "I have hair that's a different kind of problem every day." And I said, "I think you've got an idea there."

I wouldn't make up a happy ending just to close this story.

But it has a happy middle. Joey improved his book and got a job.

I saw his portfolio not long ago and I can only say, he was right to stick it out.

It's interesting how, upon occasion, a brave interviewer will say to an applicant, "You're really a nice person, but your book isn't too good. Why don't you go into another line of work?" At that point the would-be creative makes getting that creative job the focal point of his or her life. A commitment is made.

John tells this story about getting his first job.

John's first book had a lot of fun in it. People smiled a lot, in fact, he generally had great interviews – but no job offers. One day he interviewed at an agency, and a creative supervisor told John his book was awful and why – out of 20 ads, only one had a glimmering of an idea.

John, to his credit, absorbed the blow and realized what had been going wrong for him.

He went back to school. At night. He really toiled over his book.

His work became very solid, and his sense of humor began working for the products he had chosen.

A year later, when he took this new book around, he had his pick of job offers. And the agency that gave him that "brutal" critique created a job for him.

There's a lot to be learned from John's story. If you keep hearing "good book, but no openings," and you don't get any substantive criticism, you may be getting the fast shuffle because nobody wants to level with you.

Which do you want? More pleasant interviews? Or the truth?

Take the truth. As with John, Joey, and countless others, you don't have to give up just because someone gives you a damning critique.

In fact, it may be just the push you need.

Another story.

A macho friend of mine admits that a particularly rough ad giant made him cry. Lee, who was an account executive at the time, dying to make the switch to creative, managed to hold back his tears until he was in the elevator. "He told me I should be selling shoes," Lee says, with a certain pleasure.

Over a number of years, Lee had two more fairly devastating interviews with this man, and then, lo and behold, a job offer was made.

Lee turned the job down – not on principle, but because he had a better job by then – and now, a dozen years since that first traumatic interview, Lee is an executive creative director holding down one of those fancy salaries I was telling you about.

Yet another story.

Giff wanted to be a copywriter.

He was in fact, working in sales for a rivet company in New Jersey. He quit his job, took a $5,000 pay cut, and got his first copy job in a small agency.

Three weeks later, he was fired. The creative director told him to forget it. Said he was in the wrong business.

Giff didn't take no for an answer.

One week later, he had his second job at a top agency for more money. Today, Giff is Creative Director at Wolf in New York, a winner of two Gold Lions from the Cannes Film Festival (among other awards), and he illustrated this book! Giff credits the creative director who fired him for getting him where he is today.

Last story.

An advertising superstar was invited to visit an advertising class at a university. He gave the class an assignment on one day and came back a couple of weeks later to review the work.

On that day, the ads were proudly tacked up on the wall. With his back to the class and his hands clasped behind his back, the superstar went from ad to ad, silently appraising for many long minutes each and every one.

Just as silently, the class awaited the critique of their efforts.

The moment came at last.

The superstar turned to face the assemblage. He spoke. "Every-thing on this wall is s--t," he said.

What happened?

My guess is Ad-like Objects struck again.

Did the entire class drop their majors and transfer to biology?

Of course not. As a group, they and their professor used the critique as a learning experience. They worked even harder, and although I can't swear to it, I suspect that experience with that superstar was a turning point for a few.

So. As far as giving up is concerned – don't – not just because you can't find a job right away. Sometimes not finding a job has nothing to do with you.

Timing is important. Summer and the Christmas season can be bad times to look for work. Occasionally, the whole industry goes into a hiring slump.

I'd give your search a solid year if you are sure you're learning and your folks are willing to support your habit. Give it more time, up to two years, if you've found a job and are working on your book at night.

An informal poll taken at the Leo Burnett / Medill School Symposium "Teaching Creativity" a few years back revealed this interesting fact: Most hires in the creative area interviewed between 35 and 70 advertising agencies to get one offer. Seventy! That's one interview a week for almost a year and a half.

Does this depress you? Does this process seem too long, too tough, too uncertain?

Well, as my friend Renata says, "Pressure makes diamonds."

On the other hand, not everybody is meant to get into the creative side of advertising. If you've tried your best but the wall won't budge, there's no shame in saying "enough."

And just because ads aren't your thing, doesn't mean your creativity can't find another successful and satisfying outlet.

We all have to find what's right for us. Sometimes that means a few false starts on the road to a happy life.

Eric, a former copywriting aspirant I know, gave up his advertising agency job search after whatever he considered an appropriate amount of time. He opened a shoe store.

And not just any shoe store. It was a wonderful shoe store full of luscious Italian shoes. Two stores followed the first, for a chain of three, and Eric began designing his own brand of shoes, which were made up for him in Italy. Today, Eric is happy, rich, exercising his creative abilities, and I think it's safe to say, when he started his shoe business, he never looked back.

The hard truth is there are far fewer jobs at this level than the number of people who want them, so I guess that what's at work here is some Darwinian principal. Like natural selection.

The people with the best books, the people most suited to the rigors of the agency business will be hired, and the others will turn their talents to something else.

Q. What if I'm really not cut out for advertising? Should I jump off the Brooklyn Bridge?

A. What? And waste all that talent? Of course not!

Don't jump!

If you're a writer, start investigating public relations, journalism, publishing, sales promotion, retail. And don't consider these fields second best. They're all exciting, vital industries and may be the very best for you.

Look into other occupations altogether, and keep your writing alive by writing on your home time. Many novelists, playwrights, and poets have rent-paying work which gives them the financial support they need until their writing pays off.

If you're an art director, think about all the areas of graphic arts to be explored.

The burgeoning electronic universe is your playground. There are design studios and worlds of in-house graphics operations that involve many phases of packaging and promotion.

If you think your strength is illustration, check that out – maybe you can get started in retail, for instance, and work up a freelance business.

Or, for now, you can choose a field completely unrelated to art and exercise your artistic talents painting, drawing, and designing in your free time. Art for art's sake.

If you, like Joey from the previous question, feel it's do advertising or die, keep in mind that your first job need not determine your life's work. You may want to get a job now and think about getting into advertising again next year.

Mark's first job was a package designer. Today he directs television commercials. In between these two careers Mark was an agency art director/producer and wrote commercials, too.

Gary's first job was in retail. His second was writing ads for a company that sold ad space on the inside of public toilet stalls.

Gary finally got that agency copy job and created a career for himself from copywriter all the way up to creative director on the West Coast.

He's now in Hollywood – a famous head-writer and producer of a fantastically successful TV show. He met the show's star when he was a copywriter and the star did commercials for his account.

Q. **I'm a senior, about to graduate. Our final critique is coming up soon. Could you go over the most common portfolio mistakes one more time? How about a list?**

A. My pleasure.

The 10 Most Commonly Made Portfolio Mistakes.

1. Heartless ads. Slick headlines, puns for the sake of making wordplays, ads that seem to be ads, but there's nothing inside.

Heartless ads are the result of using the computer to make ad-like objects before you've come up with an original concept. You didn't spend enough time getting to know your product and your consumer. Instead, you jumped to a seemingly clever execution.

2. Walking strategy statements. These are also called "ad-like objects." They have their roots in research, their creators understand their product and the marketplace, but the resulting work has no zing.

Heartless ads, walking strategy statements, and boring, unoriginal un-advertising turns interviewers into gibbering, inarticulate fools. They want to help you, but they can't figure out where to start. We want to see original ideas that make us feel something.

3. The casual use of celebrity spokespersons. We want to see selling ideas, and grafting a celebrity artist or pitchman onto your campaign is not an idea. It's an execution, and generally, an easy way out.

4. Too much clutter. Storyboards and radio scripts that your reviewers may not take time to read. Filler ads to round out a campaign. Filler campaigns to fluff up a book. Miscellaneous freelance projects that simply take up space.

When in doubt, take it out.

5. Too much public service advertising. One or two poignant ads to spotlight a worthy cause is fine, but more than a few and we know you're taking the easy course.

6. A sloppy looking presentation. Make your book look professional. Sure roughs are okay, but not with food stains.

It's okay to put in last night's brilliant idea before you've had a chance to work it up.

Otherwise, make your book look as good as you do.

7. Crude, rude, sexist, racist, or vulgar advertising.
Bad taste is bad news.

8. Too many ads. You can't edit your work, and that's too bad.
If you can't tell your good ads from your bad ones, you've got a long way to go.
But everyone tells you something different, you say.
You're confused. Of course you are. Listen to the critics, stand back, and make some judgment calls yourself.
Some confusion is understandable, but you'll feel dumb standing up for ads you don't like if you're only keeping them in your book because someone else liked them.
Start editing your own work, now.
Take out your worst campaigns.
It's okay if your book is a little thin.
Replace your worst ads with killers as you get better.

9. "Faddy" topics and a book full of class assignments.
This says you haven't taken the job of getting a job seriously.

10. No résumé. So who are you, anyway? And how are we supposed to call you and offer you a job if we don't have your phone number? We know you're in a state of panic right now, but take 10 minutes and bang out something simple on your Mac.
This could be the most worthwhile 10 minutes you ever spent.

What's next? Something a little special.

The next section is titled "A Little Help From Some Friends."

You'll meet creative directors, executive creative directors, CEOs, and people who just got started.

In this section, you'll hear a few things you've heard before – that it's essential to start with the product and the consumer, and that your ads must make people feel something.

But you'll also hear a few things you never heard before.

Like why, if you wove green snakes in the spokes of your bicycle wheels and rode very fast, that was cool. Why life inside the crystal palace can dry up your brain. Why you should kill all your darlings. Or how to make $500,000 a year before you're 30.

And lots more. Each and every one of the following essays is a rare treat, so get ready to enjoy yourself.

Now you know everything I can tell you. I loved writing this book and hope that it's helpful. If it is, we'd like to hear from you.

We'll be updating this book again in the future and your tales from the job market might be part of it.

Just as those before you have contributed to this book, your comments could help those who come after you.

Send me an e-mail to thecopyworkshop@aol.com when you get your first job in advertising.

I've got my fingers crossed for you.

We knew you could do it all along.

PART III
A LITTLE HELP
FROM SOME FRIENDS

Advice on how to make it from some people who made it

HERE'S WHY

by Bruce Bendinger
Friendly Neighborhood Creative Person

As you figure out your future, you also need to figure out the world you live in. This may help.

First, the world really is going faster. Here's why.

It took a few thousand years to grow from the Agricultural Revolution to the Industrial Revolution. It only took a few hundred years to go from the Industrial to the Post-Industrial Revolution. Then, it seemed to change by decades – '60s, '70s, etc. Now, it's about every 18 months.

Here's why – marketing.

Every year, marketers look at last year. And they try to figure out how to do it better. The result? "Harderfastercheapermore."

The flat-out fact is you live in a world that dials it up every year.

It's real world as video game. Soon as you learn to play at one level, they boot you up to the next one.

That's the new reality. Deal with it.

Second, everything in advertising is less effective. Here's why.

All those harderfastercheapermore marketers keep adding messages – cool new commercials on cable, scratch and win at the convenience store, and a big inflatable floating over the beach during Spring Break. There's more everything.

And the more everything there is, the less effective each one is. Got it? OK. Time for some good news.

Third, there's more stuff to do, more ways to do it, and more places to do it. Here's why.

It's the two previous reasons. Rapidly improving technology and an expanding number of media opportunities equals more ways to do more stuff. Cool.

So if you think about all the different stuff there is to do – and all the different groups that need it done – well, I think I see the dim beginnings of your bright future.

Whether you write the commercial, or the Web site, or produce the limited-edition CD that they're handing out right over there near the Spring Break inflatable, there's more to do – and they need you to help them do it.

The trick is going be figuring out who it is that needs you and what it is they need you for. And, since it's all moving faster (see "Here's Why" #1), don't be too surprised if you have to do a little work to make that right place/right time thing happen.

Fourth, care about people.
Connect with them in ways that matter. Here's why.

If you start thinking too much in terms of Target Consumers – who exist to be manipulated by Clever You – that sows the seeds of cynicism and indifference.

My guess is you probably have little use for some clever phony who merely wants to talk you out of your hard-earned money.

Well, the rest of the world feels the same way.

All those Target Consumers are hip to the game – just like you.

You have to connect with them in a way that's real.

Caring about them and respecting them is a good way to get your head in the right place.

You'll be more effective. Who knows, you might even become a better person. Finally…

Don't confuse all that harderfastercheapermore with other parts of your life.

Maybe you have to be smart, tough, clever, hard-working, and quick-witted to succeed in the business world we live in, but you don't have to be all those things all the time.

Enjoy life. Help people. Relax.

Make the world a better place.

Hey, I bet I don't have to tell you why.

Bruce Bendinger (and Lorelei) publish this book (and others). Bruce is a minor Chicago advertising legend with a résumé that has become a bit of a blur… JWT/Chicago… Boutique. Awards. Leo Burnett. VP CD at 27… CD for President of the United States… Artist in Residence/Group CD @ FCB… Love That Chicken from Popeyes… The Copy Workshop Workbook… The Book of Gossage… *www.adbuzz.com*
If you'd like to know what Bruce thinks about something other than advertising, you can find some of those thoughts in three of Studs Terkel's books: American Dreams Lost and Found, The Great Divide, *and* Will the Circle Be Unbroken.
He is now becoming better known as "Jessica's Dad." (She wrote the teen hit movie Bring It On!)

WHAT'S THE "IDEA" BEHIND TODAY'S TECHNOLOGY?

by Rick Boyko, Chief Creative Officer,
Ogilvy & Mather North America

About 20 years ago, I was standing outside Chiat/Day's sunny Venice office with the agency's head of print production and a vendor who handled our color separations.

The vendor was telling us that someday we'd be able to send all our files digitally, with no further need for preprints and reprints.

He predicted that in this brave new world of the future, agency art directors would be able to approve ads from the desktop.

My first reaction was "There's no way in hell that art directors are going to allow that to happen." No way they would want the process to get so streamlined and so digitized that they would lose the experience of actually sitting over the mechanical board, of playing with the type and kerning it just a little tighter – the whole experience of "owning the page."

So much for my ability to predict the future.

Dazzled.

Obviously, every thing that vendor was talking about came to pass, sooner and more extensively than even he thought it would. And even though I'd had those concerns beforehand, I quickly changed my tune and was dazzled – like almost every other art director in the business – by the unlimited capabilities that technology brought to our craft.

All that playing with layout, all that kerning of type, could now be done on the computer. And it could be done faster and with more assurance that it would come out right.

The beauty of this (which I hadn't anticipated) was that the technology could be so liberating.

It simplified and quickened your ability to play with layout and type, which meant you could try many more approaches, even harebrained ones. You could try anything – and if you didn't like it, instantly go right back to what you had.

You could readily use special effects that weren't as available before, manipulating images, retouching photos – all those formerly painstaking processes were now at your fingertips.

Or at least they were at the fingertips of someone in your department. It freed all of us to experiment in ways that just weren't possible before.

And, of course, the same things the computer was doing with print production, the Avid was doing with TV production. It's now almost hard to believe the fumbling process we used to go through, not very long ago, when editing.

You'd hand cut the film on a Movicola or flatbed, with the trims hanging in a trim basket. You'd tape the pieces together, and synch up the sound, and if it wasn't just right, you'd have to pull it all apart and start over.

Special effects were extremely difficult, and usually you didn't even think about something like that until after you had the cut.

But with the Avid, suddenly you could do repositioning, and color correcting and special effects, all on the rough cut (in fact, there's nothing "rough" about rough cuts anymore). Again, this was all very liberating: By freeing us from the mundane cut-and-paste aspects of the creative process, we could try more things.

And just about anything you could think of or visualize you could get done.

All of that represented the positive side of technology's impact on the day-to-day creative process at agencies – and it really has been a huge upside. But there's a substantial downside to it, as well.

And I think many art directors and creative directors are starting to acknowledge this.

State of the art without art training.

One problem is that agencies are now finding themselves increasingly staffed with a new generation of young art directors who were weaned on the computer.

And while it's great to have people who are so computer literate and up-to-speed on the latest software applications, it's also becoming evident that many of them lack certain basic skills – such as the ability to put an idea down on a piece of paper.

Many of today's art directors are coming out of school with no training in the art of drawing, human anatomy, and perspective.

Consequently, they're almost illiterate when you take them off the computer.

You may ask, "Why does this matter?" Since the computer dominates the production process, what difference does it make if someone is unable to draw a picture on a scrap of paper?

The answer is that it can have a surprisingly profound effect on the process of generating ideas.

Here's why: A classically trained art director is able to instantly convey visual ideas and perspectives. If I'm thinking of a particular shot or photographic angle – say, a low angle looking up at the subject – that creates a certain distortion and visual emphasis – I could sketch that out in rough layout or storyboard form. And I could then show that rough drawing to a photographer or commercial director and say, "Here's the dramatic perspective I'm thinking of." That becomes a starting point for my collaboration with that artist, and who knows where we go from there.

Scrapping good ideas.

Now contrast that with an art director who is totally computer-dependent. They also start with an idea in their head, but instead of sketching something, they're more apt to go right to the computer. And the first thing they do is look for scrap to convey their idea.

This is where the problem begins. For starters, their imagination is limited by the scrap that is available – which is, by the way, the same scrap every other art director is scanning into their rough layouts. In other words, it's generic.

Once they've found this generic scrap, they scan it in. And then they go ahead and start tinkering with the layout (because you're on the computer already and it's easy, so why not?). And they end up with something that looks almost like a finished ad – except that it's not really original, it's borrowed from other sources.

By the time the photographer sees this layout, it's practically a done deal. Because the client has probably already seen it and signed off on it – which means you really can't change it all that much now, even if you wanted to.

So instead of being a starting point, this is more like a dead end.

By relying so much on computer scrap, art directors end up limiting not only themselves, but also the photographers they work with.

138

By opting for that more polished, computer-generated layout instead of the rough sketch on paper, you've lost the creative freedom and the magic that happens when you simply show a drawing to a photographer and begin to really explore things together.

Wait. It gets worse.

In some ways, the problem is even worse with television. Because now instead of sketching storyboards, we can go down there on the Avid and cut together a "rip-omatic" that pulls together the best scenes out of 15 award-winning, million-dollar commercials shot by star directors, and jam them into a rough cut for one ad.

And once you've shown this to the client and he's signed off on it, now you've really set yourself up for a fall. To actually replicate all the great stuff in the rip-o-matic would probably cost you $15 million to shoot, and your budget is $500,000.

And worse.

There's a second problem related to the tech explosion, and it has to do with time. More and more these days, I'm hearing creative people talk about the pressures of having to generate ideas at "dot-com speed."

Of course, this is partly a reflection of the pressured times we're living in and the hyper-competitive business environment. But it's also a direct result of technology having obliterated the accepted timetables for producing advertising.

There used to be a set amount of time available to creatives, after the strategy was agreed upon, to generate ideas and get them approved – and it was more or less tied to time built in for the production process.

But then technology came along and collapsed the production schedules – since we were doing all these things digitally we could do them faster, of course. And it was just assumed, by clients, that we could speed up the idea-generation part of the process accordingly.

Of course, that was a completely faulty assumption.

The dot-com world may have made lots of things faster, but coming up with a great idea wasn't one of those things. We can't change the way that an idea comes to us. Sometimes the lightning strikes right away, but sometimes it takes a while.

A growing realization.

I think there's a growing realization now that we can't just keep saying to clients, "Sure, we'll get that done by tomorrow."

We all need to start re-educating clients about the time required to generate ideas, assuring them that, yes, we will use technology to expedite things wherever possible – but there are some things you can't speed up without compromising quality.

As an industry, we're starting to take a more balanced approach to technology, making sure that it serves us instead of dictating or constraining what we do.

One encouraging sign is that the creative community – after an initial period of infatuation with highly cluttered computer-driven design – has lately moved back toward work that is simpler and shows more craftsmanship.

If you look at what's doing well at awards shows these days, it's simple, and it recognizes a basic truism that has been unchanged by technology – that in the end, it's all about the idea.

We've been trying to drive home that principle within our own agency, and we've set up a couple of programs with that in mind.

In our Young Guns program, which mentors creative teams straight out of school, we're actually training people to put their ideas down on paper before going to the computer (though I do wish we could get some support from the ad schools in this regard; it would be easier to encourage people to sketch ideas if their schooling included some basic courses in drawing and perspective). And we've also set up a typographic program, to help teach some of the basics of type.

Rhymes with scrap.

At the same time, we're trying to break some of the bad habits of computer design – such as the tendency to spend more time on execution than on concepting.

Too often, I see people come up with a mediocre idea and then spend hours polishing it on the computer.

They find the perfect scrap, they scan it in, they play with the type – and they fall in love with it. But even after all that polishing, there's a word for what they end up with. (It rhymes with scrap.)

The frustrating part is that in the same amount of time they probably could've come up with five ideas – if they'd been working in rough form.

Ideas first.

Obviously, technology has been a huge asset in terms of helping with the creation of ads and, of course, there's no way we're going back to the days of being hunched over the mechanical board.

Nevertheless, I think we need to look for ways to evolve the creative process so that it takes full advantage of technology – yet always puts the idea first.

And we should remember that just because we've got state-of-the-art desktop equipment that doesn't mean there isn't still a place for the simple idea scribbled on a napkin.

Just think of Fallon McElligott's famous "Perception / Reality" campaign for *Rolling Stone* – the original concept, with those juxtaposed images, was jotted down on a napkin in a restaurant.

And that concept lived on, and was incredibly successful, for the next 15 years.

That's a pretty long while, especially in "dot-com time."

Rick Boyko, Co-President/Chief Creative Officer, Ogilvy & Mather Worldwide, Inc. Rick is a graduate of the Art Center College of Design. He began his career at Leo Burnett, working on United Airlines. In the '80s, he made his mark at Chiat/Day LA and then joined O&M in 1989, where he worked on DuraCell and American Express. In 1997 he was named Chief Creative Officer of the flagship New York office. He sits on the boards of the VCU AdCenter, the One Club, Creative Circus, and he is on the steering committee for the Art Center College of Design.

A PHONE OF YOUR OWN

by Leora Brayer
Copywriter, New York

Dear Secretaries/Would-Be Copywriters of America,

Don't throw in the towel! It can be done... I'm living proof!

We know, we know...you went to college and you can't believe you're sitting behind a desk saying, "Mr. Bosseroli's office" 47 times an hour. We know you hate it when everyone else is cc'd on memos and you're not because you're "just a secretary." Well, all that doesn't matter as long as you're working hard on your book, and you believe in yourself.

Actually, if you're serious about copywriting, then being a secretary (especially in the creative department of an ad agency) is much better than you think. That's what I did.

I guess I had a lot of gumption, gall, chutzpah (call it what you will), but I used to sprawl magic markers, magazine cut-outs, and headlines all over my desk. It was nice to have a lot of creatives roaming around so I could get their feedback – which is a blessing and a curse. When you show an ad to one person who loves it, feedback is great! However... one person's favorite campaign is another person's nightmare. After about 10 months I decided if I really like the ad, it stayed in my book (like my Dustbuster ad, which read, "This product really sucks.")

So where was I? Oh yeah... I was working on my book for a good eight months at Young & Rubicam. I made four-color copies of it and sent it out all over Manhattan.

What was nice about getting into the job search was that I learned something. After listening to all the hotshots in the industry, I realized my opinion really did count for something. This field is quite subjective, so at some point I had to follow my heart. Eventually it paid off.

After a year and a half at Y&R, David Metcalf (of Lowe Tucker Metcalf) called me and told me he liked my book. Considering that I considered him the best copywriter in town, I was considered at the time to be "thrilled to holy high heaven!" I met with him. He didn't want to hire a junior. I wept. He had no time to train. No money to spend. I convinced him it wouldn't cost him much. He wanted more experience.

I'll end this letter by telling you how I got the job (it may also be a juicy piece of advice). Are you ready? The reason I think I got my first copywriting job is because David liked my book. Period. He just needed that extra Push! I returned to work after our meeting and messengered him a thank-you letter that afternoon. I told him I would commit homicide to work at his agency. He hired me the next day. I was making the secretarial salary, but I was now a copywriter.

Six months later, a woman at McCann-Erickson called and asked if I'd be interested in writing radio and TV commercials for Coca-Cola. Does Dolly Parton sleep on her back?

Needless to say, I've been here for 16 months and I'm enjoying myself. I get to be creative and use my musical ability, as well. Besides, I have a great secretary!

He wants to be a copywriter.

Ms. Brayer wrote ads and jingles for Coca-Cola and is now in the midst of what she hopes will be a long and distinguished career in advertising.

HAVE YOU DOWNLOADED A FORD, LATELY?

by Tom Cunniff
Chief Creative Officer, Fry Multimedia

You are hurtling at 900 mph toward a career in advertising.

The awards book your eyes are glued to is the rearview mirror.

The brick wall you're about to encounter is interactivity.

Interactivity is in the process of changing advertising, forever.

A seismic shift, from one-way (broadcast) to two-way (interactive) communication, is taking place. It's a shift from what Professor Nicholas Negroponte at MIT's Media Lab calls "advertising as noise" (ads you don't want to see for products you don't want to buy) to "advertising as news" (ads you ask to see for products you want to buy!).

Have you downloaded a Ford lately? Today, Lexus, Saturn, Honda, Saab, and other car manufacturers advertise their cars interactively using online services. People can, and do, download information about these cars everyday because they're interested.

On the Internet's World Wide Web, car enthusiasts have created home pages for BMW, Acura, and Porsche. This, if you can imagine it, is like building your own TV station to broadcast ads for a product you love. These people are the best advertisers these car manufacturers will ever have, because they are zealots for their brands!

Advertising is shifting from a monologue ("Try new Yummo!") to dialogue ("I did. It tastes like crappo."). Amazingly, some agencies don't, or won't, understand this new future. Avoid taking a job at these agencies. Like booking a trip on the *Titanic*, it may seem glamorous at first, but ultimately, you'll wish you weren't on board. And, ultimately, you won't be.

The changes will be rough; some agencies will not survive. Many of the old solutions won't work anymore, and entirely new ones will have to be invented.

It will be challenging, but exhilarating.

Who's more fun to advertise to – someone who wants to run off to the bathroom during your commercial or someone who wants to talk with you?

What's more fun – doing ads with no idea if they work or getting real-time feedback that tells you whether or not you've broken the bank?

Over time, this feedback will prove what you already know: Better creative sells better. As a result, clients will not only want more creative work, they'll demand it.

You have picked the best time in the last 25 years to get into advertising. Now more than ever, advertising needs muscular, adventurous minds. People capable of not just creating commercials, but of creating the future.

You know what advertising was. Now it's up to you to reinvent it.

What can you do to get ready for this new, interactive age?

1. Read *The Media Lab*, by Stewart Brand. This is the ideal foundation of understanding what's happening to media and why it's important. Also read *The One-to-One Future*, by Don Peppers and Martha Rogers. If you read these two books carefully, you'll know more about the future of advertising than 90% of the people you'll be working for.

2. Subscribe to *WIRED* magazine. Go the library and devour past issues of this essential resource. *Advertising Age* now does a good job of covering interactive advertising.

3. Buy a computer and modem. Sign up with America Online or some other online service.

4. Next, get a SLIP or PPP account from an Internet service provider. (Note: While exploring the Internet, you will often feel hopelessly stupid. Don't worry. Feeling like an idiot is a clear signal that you are learning something new.)

5. Stop thinking like Darren Stevens. Start thinking like George Jetson. New technologies mean new ways of selling.

At the same time, it means a return to the one-to-one ways of seeing as conducted in a General Store circa 1800. A contradiction? Not at all. F. Scott Fitzgerald once wrote,"The test of a first-rate intelligence is the ability to hold two opposed ideas in mind at the same time and still retain the ability to function." Mr. Fitzgerald would do very well indeed in interactive advertising.

6. Question everything. Creativity is often the result of a willingness to contemplate the impossible.

7. Interact with people who share your interests. You can begin with me. You can send me e-mail via the Internet at tom@fasterforward.com – or on America Online as TJCNYC.

A few ground rules: Cover letters, résumés, and other self-promotional pieces will earn you a place in the trash. Intelligent questions and insights will earn you respect and prompt replies.

One final thought.

Advertising is undergoing radical change, so it favors people with guts now more than ever before. Don't be afraid to be creative.

As the famous jazz pianist Thelonious Monk once said…
"The only cats worth anything are the cats who take chances. Sometimes, I play things I never heard myself."

Tom's career spans advertising, interactive, e-commerce, and direct. You can find out more about Tom on his Web site and online office – fasterforward.com He has helped companies like AT&T, Unilever, GM, and H-P move ahead faster, and he helped build the award-winning internet development firm Brandscape.

CONTROLLING PAIN

by Greg DiNoto
Creative Director, DiNoto Lee, New York

I remember putting my book together and getting my first job in advertising. It was like being beaten by a cat-o-nine tails made from piano wire and porcelain clown figurines. In the interest of offsetting the sensations you are about to experience, I humbly offer some various thoughts and items and such that might be of use.

1. Be an animal. This business rewards the hungry and relentless.

2. Conceive with the heart, defend with the head. The creatives I hire are two-channel people. The first channel is about talent. The second channel is about maturity. It's the ability to become coldly rational when it's time to assess your own work and ultimately defend it. This ability to separate yourself emotionally from your work leads to better work. It gives you credibility with your partner, your creative director, and your clients. And it means a better chance of keeping great work intact despite the incessant onslaught of opinion that goes with the business. Be passionately dispassionate. Mr. Spock never lost an argument.

3. Bitch later. Whether it's putting your book together, getting an appointment with that great agency, or struggling to keep a great campaign alive, put your head down and make things happen before you indulge in an orgy of complaint. The reason is simple. Complaining is a mindset. The more you hear yourself do it, the easier it becomes to blame external forces when things don't go your way. You become your excuses. You forgive yourself. You compromise. You lose. You die. So don't talk about putting the book together. Put the book together. It's the hardest assignment you'll ever have. But when it's done you'll have reason to celebrate instead of bitch.

4. Don't be a writer or an art director. Those terms tend to stultify your thinking. Great advertising is not about coming up with headlines and visuals. It's about coming up with campaign ideas. So approach your assignment by thinking about a unique interplay of visual and verbal components. The great "If it's out there, it's in here" campaign for Nynex is a good example.

The relationship between words and visuals makes me understand the point of the campaign immediately. And it's ownable. So think of yourself as a conceptual engineer or an idea architect. It will make you a better writer or art director.

5. Don't cover your book in pink fur. Or sequins. Or staves of baleen. It makes you seem breathless and desperate for attention. Your portfolio isn't an arts and crafts project. It's the best evidence that you can intuit and argue and persuade with great campaign ideas. Like many things in life, it's what's inside that counts. Don't decorate. Fortify.

6. Feed your head. Go to a bullfight. Sing at Wigstock. Subscribe to the ballet. Read. It will keep you stimulated now and sane later.

7. Don't do ads for the following: Hot sauce. Topless bars. Lingerie. Homeless shelters. Or anything with the word "extreme" in it. These subjects are easy. They have built-in excitement or emotional equity. And they're done to death – especially in junior books.

8. Don't present what you're not proud of. I'd rather see a book with three great campaigns than one with three great campaigns and two mediocre ones. It says you're discriminating. That you can edit yourself. And it should remain law once you land a job. Never present a campaign that you don't want to produce – it will be the one that gets produced.

9. Don't be a backslapper or an a--kisser. Stay focused on the work. It's what makes money for your boss.

10. All important work is great work, but not all great work is important work. Important work moves the business forward. It becomes part of the culture. It's new. It's challenging. Maybe a little frightening. Strive for important work.

Prior to starting his own agency in 1997, Mr. DiNoto was Executive Creative Director at Deutsch Advertising where he spearheaded award-winning campaigns on accounts including Tanqueray Gin, Promoflor and Ikea. He's been recognized with numerous industry awards and has been named to AdWeek's Creative All-Star list.

THE RIGHT WORD

by Jim Durfee
Partner & Copywriter
Messner Vetere Berger McNamee Schmetterer Euro RSCG,
New York

"The difference between the right word and almost the right right word is the difference between lightning and a lightning bug."

Mark Twain said that. And if you don't have a comparable reverence for aptness I suggest you forget about being a copywriter right now. Account work would be nice.

Mark Twain also said, *"Kill your darlings."* In other words, beware of those cutesy phrases that are written to show off one's cleverness.

And don't try to be funny. Above all, don't try to be funny. Try to be interesting. If it turns out to be funny, great. You'll have humor without strain. The only kind that really works.

(So you think being a copywriter is fun, or something?)

Here's something to think about.

The difference between a weak headline and a strong headline is more a matter of perseverance than talent. Like the miner panning for gold – keep sifting the sand until at last (!), there's a bright shining nugget worth its weight in sales.

Another way you'll know you have a strong headline is when you've written one that doesn't require a subhead to support it. Never use subheads except to break up long body copy.

Never write to masses, because advertising does not appear before the masses. Not on TV. Only one or two (or three or four) people see a TV commercial at a time. And only one person reads a magazine at a time. So write to that one person.

Get a picture in your mind of who he/she is and write to that person only. You'll be surprised at how much more intelligent you'll sound, and how much more effective you'll be.

There's a tiresome, endless argument that people don't read long copy. Nonsense. People will read what interests them. No matter how long it is. Which means there's only "too long" copy. And that can be a mere few words if they aren't the right words.

Here's another piece of advertising nonsense that won't die: "Don't write negative headlines, because people react better to positive things." Would you call the following statement negative or positive: "Don't step back or you'll fall off the cliff."

When you have your copy honed to the point where you think it's ready, suck in your breath and cut it by 20 - 30 percent and you'll have stronger copy.

Use little words rather than big words. Say it as simply and directly as possible. Trust your gut as much as your head.

And above all, never forget that an ad can never be good enough.

Uh...good luck.

"The Faulkner of body copy," Mr. Durfee has trained and nurtured some of the top talents in the business. He was a co-founder of Carl Ally Inc. and a partner in Durfee Solo Advertising. Voted one of the 10 best copywriters in America by AdDay, featured in How the World's Best Advertising Writers Write Their Ads, *Mr. Durfee was inducted into The One Club Creative Hall of Fame in 1997.*

GETTING STARTED

by Phil Dusenberry
Vice Chairman–Creative, BBDO Worldwide/
Chairman of the Board, BBDO NYC

I think most creative directors would agree: there just aren't enough young people coming into the business these days.

Maybe it's because they've been turned off by all the mergers and take-overs or the sense that advertising just isn't as much fun anymore. Or maybe it's just the lure of other vocations.

Agencies today are hungrier than **ever** for fresh new talent and are willing to attract and cultivate entire farm systems of youngsters – rather than pay exorbitant star-system wages.

With this in mind, if you have a passion for writing or art directing, here are a few things you might want to remember.

No assignment is too trivial. Kids today want to start at the top and work their way up. They want to cut their teeth on Pepsi, Levi's and other glamour accounts. Forget it – it doesn't happen. Take everything – *everything* – they throw at you. (My first assignment was writing in-flight announcements for an airline. It wasn't glamorous, but it was a start.)

Learn the basics. The fundamentals are critical. And the better you learn them, the more they'll serve you throughout your career.

Learn to write a good, strong piece of radio copy. (A forgotten art.)

Learn to structure and craft body text.

Learn to write and lay-out small space ads.

And most important: *Learn to write great theme lines.*

Nothing makes a creative person more marketable than the ability to write the "phrase that pays."

Get comfortable with the idea of collaboration. It's an old cliché but nonetheless still true: Two heads *are* better than one. Two heads make the sparks fly and stir the imaginings that shape great ideas.

Neatness counts. It's not all that important for creative people to be organized (most good ones aren't). But it is important when you're putting your book together.

An attractive, well-organized portfolio shows a special effort. It says you care; that you take pride in what you do.

A good book has a good attitude written all over it, and it's your book that will ultimately decide whether or not you get the job.

Seek out opinions. You can learn a lot by the way others respond to your ideas. Try them out on the copywriter next door. Or your friend, the account guy. Or anyone who'll listen.

The playback will be helpful. It may give you new things to think about. It might even dimensionalize your idea. But if five out of six – including your mom – say your ad is lousy, chances are, it is.

Never quit. It's 10 p.m., and you haven't the vaguest notion where your idea is. You're ready to call it quits and turn in that half-baked campaign you came up with at 9:45. (Do not do this.) Believe it or not, you could be a half-hour away from a Clio winner. Just when you feel like bagging it for the night is when you're likely to hit on your best stuff. There are no shortcuts in creating advertising.

And there is no such thing as an advertising genius. No one spins off one sensational idea after another. The real stars – the ones you admire most – are the ones who sweat it until they get it.

A few quick Dusenberryisms...

Never copy someone else's idea. It's not honest and it's not worth it. Imitation is the sincerest form of plagiarism.

Don't be a politician. In most good agencies, it's performance that matters. If you're good, people will know it. Just make sure you get credit for what you do.

Take an account person to lunch. Account people are under-rated. The good ones will run interference for you, keep you on the right track and out of trouble. And usually they'll give you the same reaction to your work that you're likely to get from the client.

Learn how to present. I've seen great ideas slip between the cracks just because they were poorly presented. If you have a flair for the dramatic, use it. If you don't, get one.

Make sure you have more friends than enemies. No one succeeds in advertising without a lot of people rooting for them.

Mr. Dusenberry grew up at BBDO as a writer, spending a significant part of his time on Pepsi. He was a member of "The Tuesday Team," the ad-hoc agency for one of the biggest Presidential landslides in history. He also co-authored the screenplay for The Natural. *He recently retired.*

SHOPPING FOR ADS

by Jeffrey Epstein
Director of the Chicago Portfolio School

I have a friend who is a major-league shopper. I'm not talking about a *Consumer Reports* shopper – someone dedicated to all the gory details about specs, prices, ratings, etc. I'm talking more along the lines of power shopping, in which tough marketing and sales decisions are made quickly based on feel and instinct.

Want proof? OK. She owns nine pairs of Diesel jeans.
Remarkable as that might be, that's not what impresses me.
What's truly wonderful is that she can tell you why she owns nine pairs of Diesel jeans. Better yet, she can tell you why she needs nine pairs of Diesel jeans.
Go ahead. Ask her. She'll tell you all about the wash, the fit, the style, the color, the cut, the best place to buy them (new and used) – maybe even the history of the brand.
And it's not just about jeans, either. She also happens to be an extraordinarily acute buyer of lots of other stuff, including watches, cheese, sushi, cars and sneakers.

1970s ad god George Lois once said, *"Americans may be stupid about a lot of things, but advertising is not one of them."*

So it occurred to me: What runs through the mind of a shopping ninja like my friend is the same thing that a good ad maker is thinking. Like any expert on a subject, she knows her s---.
And even though she hasn't taken the factory tour and can't recite the specs, she knows exactly what time it is.
She knows the details, the fits and the finishes. She knows prices and what seems fair to her. She knows her target market (her) and has an innate sense of what's right or wrong about a purchase. She knows what feels right. There's no wishy-washiness about the decision. She's sold.
Most importantly, she genuinely respects the products she buys.

Which is exactly the kind of resolute thinking you should engage in when making ads, especially when you're doing spec ads for your book, where there's no mandated brand, let alone direction or strategy.

By the way, in the big agency world, there's a word for thinking like a customer. It's called "planning," and it's a much-revered market-research discipline that has helped to produce many great creative campaigns. But regardless of what you call it, caring a lot about the product ultimately will lead to a purchase.

Here's what doesn't work: distancing yourself from the product or the buying experience. When you distance yourself, you end up with the kind of patronizing, tongue-in-cheek smugness that is seen all too often in ad-school books.

Ads that make fun of the product take the cynical low road and suggest the customers are the ignorant ones for actually liking the product.

Ads like that remind me of mother-in-law jokes, and they're about as tired. Sure, it's an easy laugh, but so what? When the humor of the ad is simply a put-down of the product, the category, or the customers, you've produced nothing but a smug nod and wink to the other ad-school smart asses.

By the way, I hope that the people who make ads never start thinking they are cooler than the people who buy the products. Just because you eat only organic, whole-wheat, gluten-free bread stuffs, does that mean it's OK to make fun of Wonder bread?

Presumably, people who buy Wonder bread (and according to the latest official statistics, the approximate number of Wonder bread consumers is three trillion) buy it because they like it. And there's nothing wrong with that.

Maybe the smarter way to make a good ad is to actually like and respect the product you're selling, whether it's Wonder bread, Gluten-free bread, or Diesel jeans. By doing that, you'll be able to find a rationale for buying the product, which will make a great focus for your ads (a.k.a. a concept).

Don't actually buy the product you're advertising? So what? Pretend that you do. Never liked the product? Who cares? Learn to like it. A lot. Like it, love it, enjoy it, buy it, recommend it to friends, buy one as a gift, whatever. When you're able to do that, you'll have found the place where good ads come from.

Or maybe you think good ads don't sell products any better than bad ones. So why try so hard to be conceptual? What's the big deal?

If you feel like that – and it would appear that you're not the only one – then I have some bad news: You're trying (very hard) to get into the wrong business.

Make no mistake. Good ads sell products. (Good ads also win awards. But remember they win because they're good; they're not good merely because they win.)

And good ads help you get a good job.

You want to make good ads?
Think like a great shopper.
And do an ad that will convince my friend.

Jeffrey Epstein, Director of the Chicago Portfolio School (www.chicagoportfolio.com), has previously worked at agencies in New York (TBWA, Scali McCabe Sloves) and Chicago (Doner, Leo Burnett) as a copywriter and creative director.

MY ART CENTER CLASS IN 800 WORDS OR LESS

by Mark Fenske, Malibu, CA

I've taught at Art Center College of Design in Pasadena, CA, for about eight years. If you've been in my class, I offer my sympathy that you had to put up with my arrogance, slothfulness and curmudgeonly ways, and I hope that you have managed to go on to greatness despite the standard set before you.

If you've been lucky enough to avoid my class, I offer here the chance to dig for free through the scraps it usually costs people a heck of a lot of money to have thrown at them. Not many people could distill everything they know into so few words, but I've had the advantage of not genuinely knowing all that much.

1. How well you can write has little to do with your success as a copywriter. Clients don't care what the words mean. No great campaign was ever bought because the client loved the sentences.

Great campaigns happen when a creative sees the product differently than it has been perceived before.

2. Never do what you're told. There are times when this is a bad idea, but I don't know when they are; nobody does.

You'll have to feel your way through the same way Einstein and David Letterman have. The important thing is to not spend your energy and passion (your only true assets as a creative) trying to give birth to something someone else conceived.

3. Love the process. Most of your work will be for naught. And when I say naught, I mean nobody will ever see it. And when I say nobody, I mean not one single person on earth.

4. Becoming a 25-year-old wonderkid is the worst thing that can happen to you. Real people are fat, muff fly balls, have jobs that demand actual work, go to sleep before Leno and do their own laundry, and the idea that eating at McDonald's is très uncool would make them laugh and snort through their noses. Who knows less about real life than a 25-year-old advertising wonderkid?

5. Honor before celebrity.

6. Skip the plant tour. Stay as stupid as you can.
Advertising is a young person's business.

The older you get, the less elastic you become in your ability and enthusiasm to throw away what you've got and stay up all night to do something completely different and unasked-for to replace it.

7. Your fear of exposing what seems embarrassingly ordinary about your life denies your audience the only real story it wants. If two files were laid on your desk, one marked "confidential" and the other one "unconfidential," which would you read?

8. Watashi-wa tensai des. This is Japanese for "I am a genius." Whenever someone criticizes your work to your face, mutter this under your breath. Not because it's new-age crapola but because it's true. You make something up out of nothing; that's creation. Other people don't like it; that's just dumb-ass business.

9. Drink from your own well. Start with yourself every time. What do you think of the product? How would you use it?

10. Money doesn't bring happiness.
Happiness doesn't bring money.

11. You don't have to love the business to say you love the business. If a job in advertising is just a way to make money until you write a screenplay, don't ever tell a creative director that.

12. Award shows are what keep your job worth having. Without award shows, there's no record of who has done what.

If somebody rips off your great idea for a small client and runs it all over television for a big client, who will ever know it was your idea? Award shows, over time, illumine the work of the best and expose the pretenders. Without award shows reaffirming the importance of beauty and truth every year, marketers might take over with their soulless "ads that sell."

13. Don't watch TV unless you want to do the kind of work you mostly see on TV. Whatever you fill your mind with is what's going to come out of it.

14. Everyone is your teacher. In order to teach something, you have to discover how you came to know it in the first place.

It's not a stretch at all to say I've learned a great deal more than I was ever able to give to students.

Mark Fenske is a copywriter, voice talent (you'd recognize his voice), commercial and music video director, creative director, and teacher living in Malibu, CA. This article first appeared in CMYK *magazine.*

CLIFF'S NOTES

by Cliff Freeman
Chairman & Chief Creative Officer
Cliff Freeman & Partners

Thoughts about making it big in Advertising:

Don't kid yourself.

You know great advertising when you see or hear it (if you don't, get out of the business immediately. But let's assume you do).

Great advertising is probably fresh and surprising in some way. It sounds different. It looks different. It has a different rhythm.

Apply these *exact* standards to evaluating your *own work*. If it doesn't cut it, give it the raspberry the way you would someone else's work.

Keep digging until you come up with something unique. And if you can't, tell your boss your work or ideas aren't great. At least not yet. That way you know that he knows that you know.

Write about the product.

In the greatest, soundest, most creative advertising, the theater always revolves around the product.

Ask yourself what makes the product "tick."

How does it fit into people's lives?

How does the competition fail or disappoint? What's its "personality" in the marketplace?

Advertising that isn't really about the product is almost always self-indulgent crap.

Don't be afraid to collaborate.

No one can do it alone.

There's a lot of talent out there.

Use it.

In the final analysis, the important thing is to be part of a great body of work.

Everybody's in the same boat.

Everybody – no matter how long they've been in the business, has those private moments of panic when they think they will never again come up with something great.

Everybody is constantly learning how to do it.

Every time you do a job, you learn something new – particularly in the area of film, when you're always confronting and (hopefully) conquering a new problem.

Stand for something.

This is a business where most clients are approving your work on faith. They must believe in you, so be consistent – never let your standards waver.

The power of advertising is awesome. More people will see your work than saw *Gone with the Wind*. You can shape society with it. It's a mind-boggling feeling. Enjoy it and good luck.

Mr. Freeman is the Chairman and Chief Creative Officer of Cliff Freeman Partners, winner of seven Agency of the Year awards and the 2001 Grand Prix at the Cannes Film Festival. Mr. Freeman was the writer of "Where's the Beef?" and "Russian Fashion Show" for Wendy's and many of the commercials from the Little Caesar's "Pizza Pizza" campaigns. (He also wrote one of the editor's favorite campaigns, "Sometimes You Feel Like a Nut, Sometimes You Don't" for Peter Paul/Cadbury.)

GETTING THE JOB YOU WANT

by Roz Goldfarb
Roz Goldfarb Associates

Being in art school is the best time. It might seem like the worst time as you attempt to survive balancing your class load, work load, and private life. But, be assured, you will look back at this time in wonder at how much you knew and how little you knew.

Professionals are here to tell you what is awaiting you "out there." I, for one, had zero career counseling, and the only five-year plan I'd ever heard of was the one in Russia to grow wheat. Then again, I was a fine-arts major who couldn't spell or type, and a job wasn't in the plan.

Life doesn't always work on five-year plans. So here I am, the abstract expressionist sculptor, dealing on a daily basis with literally hundreds of design firms and agencies clamoring for talent. What do they really want? And what do you want? Is there a match? Let's see.

What does it take?

Simply put, a passion for perfection and the recognition that the visual must have content and must respond to the marketing demands of the business climate.

You have to really, really want to do this and do it right, and you have to become pretty savvy about business.

Too many students and professionals try to get by through coasting. They rely on easy software solutions, swipe art, and other people's ideas. Taste is a factor, and a lot can be done with taste, smoke, and mirrors. But being eclectic is not the same as having a vision and being able to present it verbally. It takes a very special person who has the creative spark, who can visualize conceptual ideas and has the personal drive to sell the ideas.

The trap in this hyper-media culture is the speed with which new or trendy visual icons and images become average. Often it is the more experimental world of fine arts that can point the way toward new expressions, though newness is not always what drives something to be great.

I've always believed designers are the arbiters of taste, as they distill so much of our history and culture into a format widely distributed to the public.

You have a terrific responsibility to our society.

What do they want?

"They," of course, are the enigmatic employers who make the big decisions on whom they are going to hire. What are they looking for? Mostly it can be summed up as issues of perceived talent, commitment, and "chemistry."

The talent issue is very subjective but does rely on "vision" or having a point of view. It is amazing how a portfolio takes on the personality of the designer.

Students from the same school and same class projects do not have the same portfolios. It is that hard-to-define personality that creates the separations and makes the differences. Content in design and advertising is a major factor.

One's ability to communicate the substance of the message – not to simply make something pretty – is a prerequisite. The creative use of typography not solely dependent on current software programs is very important. And, of course, everybody wants someone who can work hard.

Who gets the jobs?

I've just outlined some critical creative and human factors that employers throughout the country are seeking. However, it is the "chemistry" factor that often clinches the deal.

The individuals who get the most sought-after positions in top firms are those who can communicate energy and enthusiasm for their chosen professions. You have to be articulate and well read, not only about the latest advertising and design buzz but about politics, business, and cultural issues.

You have to be a "people person," a team player who has the potential to lead the team some day. You also have to do your homework before an interview so you know as much about the firm as possible. Your portfolio got you this far, but now you have to sell yourself.

How is the job market?

Even in today's economy, the job market is full of new opportunities for creative people in all varieties of media. Global business expansion has driven companies to grow at an amazing rate.

Large firms are growing through developing satellite offices and acquiring offices in other countries.

In some cases, there are still more jobs than qualified people.

Our clients complain that the people are not good enough.

What is good enough?

Creative freshness and innate intelligence.

The potential to manage and present to clients.

I hope you will recognize these demanding criteria and truly be the future talent we all so definitely need.

Roz Goldfarb is President of Roz Goldfarb Associates, a New York-based management consulting and recruiting firm specializing in placement of creative, marketing, and executive personnel for design, new media, and advertising. This article first appeared in CMYK magazine.

NURTURING OUR YOUNG

by Gary Goldsmith
Chairman, Chief Creative Officer, Lowe/USA

Are schools today producing students who can do great ads? Or are they producing students who can put together great books?

This question has become increasingly important as more and more young people with good student portfolios fail to produce great "real" work.

First, some historical perspective.

The percentage of creatives who do great work and consistently win awards always has been small, even at the best agencies.

Many players. Few stars. A fact of life in any business.

But what's troubling now is that while the overall quality of student books continues to improve, the percentage of those who live up to the potential of those books continues to go down.

Why are people who are so seemingly well prepared finding it so difficult to make the transition from school to work?

In my opinion, there are several reasons. Some have to do with the environments they're leaving, and some have to do with the environments they're walking into.

My problem with the schools can be broken down into two areas: (1) what they're teaching and (2) the expectations they create.

The current emphasis on slickness and computer-generated comp perfection has served to disguise weak or flawed ideas. Technique over substance.

And I have bad news: The machines aren't to blame. They are there to make great ideas better. Not to decorate bad ideas.

And what about the assignments? How valuable is it, really, to spend months working on campaigns for museums, diners, or products that don't even exist? And who can't do at least one reasonably funny condom ad?

Shouldn't we be training people to be able to find ways to separate parity products and services from each other and to position or re-position companies in an environment that's changing faster than ever? Isn't that what they'll spend most of their careers doing?

Another problem is quantity. How many ads, how many varied campaigns, how many different kinds of assignments are students doing during their portfolio-building years?

I see far too much "perfecting" of ads done two semesters before.

Presumably you are at your best at the end of your last term.

Shouldn't you be using that knowledge and experience to generate new ideas, better ideas? The mission has become less about experimenting, building skills, and gaining confidence through repetition and more about cobbling together 12 good ads over a three-year period in order to get a job.

While that is no doubt a pragmatic goal, should it be the overriding aim or just the result of becoming good?

As for the expectations created, I can summarize them as follows. Too large. Too quick.

Ours is a difficult business. Many factors contribute to creating, selling, and producing great work. You might not do it your first year. You might not have a One Show pencil by the time you're 30.

It doesn't matter.

If you're good and work intensely hard, you'll succeed.

Never before have I seen more disappointment and disillusionment at such an early stage of people's careers. They obviously have been led to believe that success will come early and often.

While I realize that our culture in general propagates this illusion, we owe it to our students to present the challenges they face in a way that gives them an accurate framework.

There is a startling lack of resilience, hunger, and mental toughness. Students have to be made to understand that without those attributes their talent will be wasted.

As for the agencies that hire these recent graduates, there are several things we could improve.

The first is altering our own expectations. Because student books now are so much more professional-looking than our own were, we tend to forget the transition to the real world is still a big one.

New hires now have days to do what they did in weeks or months before. They now have very specific briefs and executional restrictions. They now have group heads and creative directors and junior and senior account executives and planners and clients and focus groups to find every logic flaw in every ad and lavish contradictory opinions on them.

They are entering a business where the staffing is leaner and the deadlines shorter than ever before. A business that has less and less time for the necessary teaching and mentoring that is required more than ever before.

We need to keep this in mind when we're critiquing work and spend the time teaching so the next assignment will be a little bit less painful.

We need to involve new hires in strategic and brand development discussions to broaden their perspectives as communicators.

And we need to dish out more encouragement and tough (sometimes brutal) love.

All this being said, we still never will reach a point where a great student book will always translate into a great career.

In the end, it comes down to who has the most talent and who wants it the most.

The more those of us teaching and in the business can to do to increase their chances, the better.

After taking one class in advertising his senior year at the University of Texas, Gary decided to go into advertising. He then went to Art Center in Pasadena and had to "work like a dog" for another two years and eight months to get ready. Gary is now Chairman and Chief Creative Officer of Lowe/USA, part of Lowe & Partners Worldwide. He is also co-founder of Adhouse, a creative training program in Manhattan. Gary has won more than 150 creative awards and was recently featured in the Wall Street Journal *"Creative Leaders" series.*

HOW TO CONVINCE A CLIENT THAT THE WORK IS RIGHT

by Jeff Goodby
Co-Chairman, Goodby Silverstein & Partners

An agency is only as good as its finest work. No one sees or remembers the meetings, memos, and phone conversations that may have resulted in the denigration of a brilliant piece. By the same token, bad agencies often possess a file of solid work that they were simply unable to convince a client to run.

At Goodby, Silverstein & Partners, we are above all committed to the creation of great work. Therefore, when we are convinced that something is right, that it is truly a uniquely correct solution, we will do just about anything to explain and sell it.

We feel this way not for egotistical reasons, but for the benefit of our clients and their businesses. In the end, our clients retain us to guard the integrity of their marketing and advertising, to guide it intact through sometimes rocky political and legal waters.

It is in their interests that we hold strong opinions, that we push ourselves and the people around us because, as Pat Fallon says, *"The biggest mistake you can make is to spend all that money and find that no one even noticed."*

That said, it is important to add two things.

First, we are also deeply committed to the belief that a healthy advertising agency remains healthy and does its best work in the context of long, trusting client relationships.

This is a financial consideration, to be sure – but it is also a creative consideration.

Great campaigns don't just run for a month or two.

They acquire their depth and dimension over time. They prove their correctness in the marketplace and earn widespread respect, not just among creative people, but in the business community and in the public at large.

The trust that develops between agency and client can allow the advertising to take more chances, to truly stand for something, to obliterate the competition.

Second, we believe that work forced upon a client under great duress is a time bomb.

166

Such experiences greatly lessen the chances that we will be able to sell that client more, equally challenging work in the future. They lead to resentments that can bring a client to secretly hope that we – and the work we have forced upon them – will somehow fail.

Indeed, there are agencies that succeed through a succession of very short, stormy relationships that never really result in lasting, effective work for the client. For business and moral reasons, however, we don't intend to become one of them.

How, then, do we reconcile the need to sell great work with the demands of building long relationships? It is never clear and easy, but the following guidelines are key:

1. See things through the eyes of the client.

Look at yourself and your work from the client's standpoint, taking into account their business goals and personality. Is this the right work for them? If they are uncomfortable, is that discomfort something that can be overcome in time? Have you really addressed and discussed their needs? What have you done to earn or merit their respect?

2. Use trust, not force.

Trust results in an atmosphere in which you can do more, even better work in the future. You will have a client who roots for the advertising to succeed, even to the point of favorably interpreting research. Moreover, your life will be simpler, your stress lessened.

3. The client can be right.

Always remember that clients have thought about their businesses 24 hours a day for years on end. They are sometimes liable to know something you won't. Appropriate their instincts and knowledge as a solid starting point and don't be too quick to dismiss their perspective or ideas. In fact, don't be proud about adopting them whole cloth. Until you announce otherwise, the world will think the client's best ideas were really yours.

4. Avoid arrogance.

You probably have every reason to believe in your talent and perspective or you wouldn't be working here in the first place.

Yet there is a fine line that divides confidence and strength from arrogance. Confidence and strength make for long relationships in which severe differences of opinion can be constructively hashed out. Arrogance results in short term, often temporary gains, at best.

5. Create a partnership with the client.

If the client always sees you as an antagonist, you start every discussion with a disadvantage that must be made up in order to be successful. If the client sees you as a partner, half the job is done when you walk into the room.

Ed McCabe is one of the most cantankerous, opinionated, argumentative guys you'd ever want to meet. The clients he's done great work for are all well aware of this. Yet they to a person consider him a friend with their best interests at heart.

6. Start over.

This may be the most important point here. The greatest enemy of brilliant work is the loss of perspective. As a piece of work undergoes long changes and revisions, it can often be transformed beyond recognition.

Before any of the participants know it, the very things that made it worth revising are dulled or gone. Be honest with yourself throughout this inevitable process. Is this still great work? If not, make your best appeal and then throw it away. (Sometimes the very act of offering this will galvanize a client to see the merit of your point of view.) It will be better for your work and the relationship. Besides, if there were only one way to do this stuff, it wouldn't be nearly as interesting.

Jeff Goodby is Co-Chairman, Creative Director of Goodby Silverstein & Partners. He is a writer and thinker who happens to work in advertising. With partner Rich Silverstein, he has won just about every advertising prize imaginable. AdWeek called him America's best television copywriter, and he has been chosen three times (along with Rich Silverstein) as AdWeek's Creative Director of the Year. In 1995 he was also named AdWeek's Most Valuable Player. He has won the Howard Gossage Award for best copywriter four times.

His spot for the California Milk Processors was selected by Ad Age as their best commercial for 1995. He directed two of 30 commercials The One Club selected as best of the nineties.

He lives in Oakland with his wife Jan, their three children, two dogs, a cat, a rabbit, and probably some other things they don't know about.

THE GOODMAN VARIATIONS

by Rod Goodman
Copy Chief
Italia/Gal Advertising, Los Angeles

Today I'm going to take you on a brief tour through the world of computers as used in advertising.

To the inexperienced, the computer may seem like a complicated tool, and as usual, the inexperienced are correct. However, any random doofus can use a computer. With a little practice, you will soon be producing ads that look exactly like everything you've ever seen in an awards annual – only less original.

The first rule of computing is to learn basic hand skills. The best advice I've ever received about the computer is this: *don't turn it on until you've done at least 50 thumbnail sketches.* Then you'll know if you have an idea.

There is nothing worse than seeing some hot-shot pseudo art director trying to brainstorm on a computer. Jerk. I really think there is a connection between the movement of your hand across the paper and the thought process in you head.

It's also a good idea to read *Writing Down the Bones* by Natalie Goldberg. It's mainly for poetry writers and the like, but it gives good insight into freeing up your mind to the creative process.

Anyway, once you're sure you've got the idea (and a bunch of thumbnails taped to the wall), get yourself some Cheez-Its and a case of Yoo-Hoo and strap yourself to a chair. It takes about 10 hours a day, six days a week until you're proficient enough to produce an ad without your eyes bleeding, but in the end there's no substitute for the satisfaction that comes from watching scrap photography turn into an honest-to-God book piece.

Before the computer came along, you'd have to spend several hours inking perfectly straight lines and cutting pictures (not to mention your fingertips) with an X-acto knife.

Now you can produce a slick, professional-looking portfolio in exactly the same amount of time – only at a much higher cost.

Learning how to use the computer is not only essential for producing a book that is competitive, it is also what you will be using in the "real world."

You can add a lot to your résumé by listing the programs you're familiar with, which translates into less training time for the agency and possibly more money for you. This is good.

Next, you must learn to think as a computer thinks.

Guys become more attached to their computers than women do. We see them as a physical extension of our manhood, like the remote control. To a man, a computer is one more toy that he can make bigger, faster, and hang fuzzy dice from. Guys need things like huge engines and 1,436-piece Craftsman ratchet sets.

Here is a typical example of a male conversation:

"289?"

"350."

"Duals?"

"4 barrel 650."

"389?"

"411."

"60s?"

"70/SR-15s."

And so on...

This communication is based solely on numbers, similar to binary codes, the same way computers talk. It's also why guys name things. We think it makes them run better.

I recommend you pick up *Macintosh for Dummies*, if you are just starting out. The Mac is very obliging and will try to do whatever you ask of it, even if it causes itself to crash. If you tell it to erase all its memory, it'll do just that. Smiling and humming the whole time. So figuring out how it thinks will be of a great advantage to you.

My first encounter with the Macintosh was at the Portfolio Center. It sucked. I was technically challenged. I thought I'd slit my throat with a pizza wheel. But I knew one day I'd be able to manipulate pictures like they do on the cover of *The National Enquirer*. But that's not why we're here, we are here to... well actually that could be why we're here.

Let's say you want to put someone's head on someone else's body. The first thing you would do is get far, far away from me.

You will then put them on what is called a flatbed scanner. You can use a scanner to turn any two dimensional image, photograph, or drawing into pixel information, although I did once successfully scan a sneaker.

Once you have collected the pictures, you will take them into a photo-manipulation program, such as Photoshop. You can use Photoshop to do color corrections, add textures, take out unwanted items, such as scratches, dust, and background stuff, and add desired items such as a new face. Photoshop also has painting, drawing, and limited typing capabilities. You can also buy a set of filters called Kai's Power Tools, and check into a program called Aldus Gallery Effects. Pretty cool. There are so many things in Photoshop it would take an entire book to contain them all, so go buy it later, when I'm finished.

When you have finished constructing this vision of beauty, you will need a place to put it. Quark XPress is that place. Quark is a desktop publishing program that lets you compress or expand type, stretch or squash any visuals you put into it (although, for any major tweaking I'd use Photoshop). Some of its more useful functions are Master Pages and Style Sheets, which allow you to make a master layout page for you to follow should you choose to run a campaign or write a book or something. It also has several available extensions such as spelling checkers, dictionaries, and thesauruses.

Now, for creating a cool logo for your product there are equally cool programs. Illustrator and FreeHand. Some shops use one or both of these. If you're interested in graphic design, these are definitely programs to learn. You can use them to paint, draw, create and manipulate type. You can also do some killer illustrations if you have an electronic drawing pad. It's a little tricky at first, then it gets harder, so get a book for this one, too.

So now you have a little info on the various methods at your disposal to get your book finished and land a job. Let me briefly wax philosophical. If you want advertising enough, it wants you. ENJOY THE STRUGGLE.

I was one of about three married guys in school. My wife and I both lost our jobs within two weeks of each other. We drove a couple of feeble VW Beetles that sucked up every penny we made. No insurance. No upward mobility. Very few trips to Disneyland. But we made it – with the help of a lot of good people that wouldn't let me give up, and sometimes helped us pay our rent.

These are the kind of people who work in advertising.

Of course, there are also a lot of narcissists and wannabes who'll steal your work when your back is turned, but basically, they are good people, probably a lot like those you're hanging with right now.

Now, you're probably saying, "Okay, I've got all this computer junk and enough paper taped to my walls to wipe out a small forest, so now what?" Well, don't ask me, read the rest of this book! I've already got a job.

Final thoughts:
Remember, it's not how slick and ad-like your book is or how you pinched the type in a computer that counts.

Be big and simple and get the idea across.

Let your personality show through.

That's what they're buying.

Rod Goodman studied at the Portfolio Center and received the Ron Seichrist Scholarship for Merit to the Miami Ad School. He is an active writer of and about advertising.

to the blacks browns reds and yellows periwinkles teals and fuchsias

by Charles Hall

if you want to be in advertising,
there's only one thing to remember.

don't be afraid.

of hard work. rejection. racism. responsibility. sexism.

don't be afraid of being the only one in the room.

don't be afraid to ask questions. find answers. listen. hear. trust.

don't be afraid to follow. don't be afraid to lead.

don't be afraid to learn. to grow. to mature. to change.

don't be afraid to try. to fail. to try again. fail again. try again. and fail again. don't be afraid to ask for help.

don't be afraid to be smart. clever. witty. funky. hard. street. elegant. beautiful. you.

don't be afraid to be fired.

don't be afraid when you hear the word nigger.

don't be afraid to remind them that right after the black jokes come the jewish jokes the polish jokes and the fat jokes.

don't be afraid to master the craft. to master the game.

don't be afraid when they don't understand your accent, dialect, or slang. your heroes. your sex symbols. your style. your music. your people. your culture. your you.

don't be afraid to take criticism.

don't be afraid to be wrong. to be right.

don't be afraid to speak your mind. stand up for what you believe and pay the consequences.

don't be afraid to be a team player. don't be afraid to be the peon. the rookie. the junior. the helper. the pair of hands. the intern. the student.

don't be afraid not to be the victim. don't be afraid to not take it personally. don't be afraid to call a spade a spade.

don't be afraid to have a personality. an opinion. a point of view. a perspective. an objective. a positive attitude.

don't be afraid of those who are threatened by your presence. or feel you don't belong. or those who need you to fail for them to succeed.

don't be afraid to understand the difference between racism and insecurity. between racism and power. between sexism and chauvinism.

don't be afraid to forgive. to apologize. to be humble.

don't be afraid to surrender. to win. to lose. to fight.

don't be afraid of titles. awards. salaries. egos. offices. windows. ponytails. clothes. jewelry. degrees. backgrounds. lifestyles. cars. beach houses.

don't be afraid to compete.

don't be afraid of not being popular.

don't be afraid to work weekends. holidays. birthdays. sick days. personal days.

don't be afraid to work twice as hard. twice as long. twice as good.

don't be afraid when the odds are against you.

don't be afraid to get more out of this business than this business ever intended on giving.

p.s. and under no circumstances whatsoever are you to be intimidated. because some will try.

Charles Hall's short film Are You Cinderella? *recently won top honors at numerous film festivals around the world. He is also most recognized for the L.A. Commission on Assaults Against Women campaign, Benetton Sportsystem "Do You Play Life?" campaign, and Reebok's "You Gotta Love It" work. He has served as creative director on Infiniti cars and Pepsi International. After starting at Saatchi & Saatchi, Charles drew experience at some great agencies; including Spike DDB, New York.*

CREATIVE PEOPLE I HAVE KNOWN

by Ron Hoff

I have known creative people who couldn't get through a simple, declarative sentence without stuttering.

I have known creative people so shy and retiring they wouldn't say a word during a meeting of far less interesting people.

I have known creative people of towering egos and lingering neuroses. But the truly exceptional creative people – the *great* ones – all share four things.

1. They are compulsive observers of human condition. Human behavior baffles them, intrigues them, challenges them – like some irresistible puzzle. They are like playwrights compiling mental notes for an epic drama. They get a kick out of watching people make mistakes, make fools out of themselves, regain their dignity, explain themselves, rationalize their behavior – and then do the whole damn thing over again.

If you're going to communicate with people, you have to be a lifelong student of their behavior. You'll never graduate. But you'll turn out better and better advertising.

2. They enjoy building a case. They like to bring people around to their point of view. I'm not sure why this is so – but something inside a creative mind compels the creative person to want to sway people, guide them, cajole them into a fresh perspective. It is the urge of the great storyteller, the great poet, the great attorney, and the great copywriter and art director. There is a kind of arrogance in this desire – but it is a vital component if you want to succeed in advertising.

3. They see things a bit differently than other people. David Ogilvy pointed this out to me at least 20 years ago, and I have never forgotten it. An economist would say, "Merrill Lynch is confident about the resilience of our economy." The creative person says, "Merrill Lynch is Bullish on America."

The guard at the abbey says, "Please folks – keep it quiet as you go past the monuments." The creative person says, "Tread softly past the long, long sleep of kings."

The clerk at the drugstore says, "Dial is a good deodorant soap – people seem to like it." The creative person says, "Aren't you glad you use Dial? Don't you wish everyone did?"

The creative person takes a thought of universal interest and turns it into a phrase of stunning singularity. Creative people have the common touch, but express it uncommonly.

4. At the end of the creative process, they have a huge need to hold up their work to the light of day and say, "See, world, I did it. Bet you thought I couldn't do it. But I did. And it's mine. All mine." Again, the instinct and drive of the pure artist come surging to the surface. Creative people need to believe in themselves – and this need is most fully satisfied by showing their work – holding it high – and having it acclaimed. A sign of insecurity? Yes, probably.

How do you fit into these four characteristics?

If you can honestly say, "Yes, that's me," I'd say you'll probably do well in advertising.

If you only hit on two out of four, I'd advise you to look for less tumultuous trades.

You'll go home earlier. And you'll certainly have fewer ulcers.

The late Ron Hoff was a top creative exec at a number of agencies in New York and Chicago and a well-known speaker on the subject of presentations.

His wonderful book I Can See You Naked – A Fearless Guide to Making Great Presentations *is still available through Andrews and McMeel.*

NEVER STOP

by Jhames Holley, Art Director

Not too long ago, I was hunting for my first job as an art director. I remember the anxiety of planning trips that would present the best chance of meeting the people I needed to see.

Stressing over how to be myself without appearing to be too comfortable. Trying to decide what pieces stay in the book and what pieces come out.

These are some of the challenges many face at the pivotal point of graduating from an ad school and finding a job.

For you as a future creative star facing the same challenges, I offer advice. Not an answer, just advice. Once you've prepared yourself for the hunt, there is no formula.

You've studied advertising, crafted your skills, prepared a book, and targeted several agencies.

There are many ways to open closed doors.

Some are obvious, others require persistence and wit.

Calvin Coolidge had this to say: *"Nothing in the world can take the place of persistence. Talent will not; nothing is more common than unrewarded talent. Education alone will not; the world is full of educated failures. Persistence alone is omnipotent."*

Being persistent is necessary in shopping your talent.

Two, maybe three, things make an impact on recruiters and creative directors. The first is your book.

Second is impressing them with your attitude.

Third is by someone recommending you. You'll miss opportunities for the second and third impact if you're not persistent.

What is in your favor is that there are few people with good attitudes who are persistent and have excellent books.

What do I mean by persistence?

When you keep getting the secretary and she doesn't put you through, do you argue with her until she changes her mind?

When you wait in the reception area for an hour to be told to reschedule, do you burst into an office?

177

When someone says they have your book but they haven't looked at it, do you threaten to take it back?

No, no, and no.

With persistence there must be wit and tact.

Be nice to everyone, starting with the receptionist. If people think you deserve more courtesy, they will use their influence in your favor. Be persistently nice, not kissing up, but positive at all times. If you talk to agency personnel and they're in a bad mood, you have the chance to be the bright spot in their day.

Optimism in the face of adversity is underrated.

Accepting disappointment without being bitter can change people's opinion of you.

I'll share a story with you. I wanted to work at this one agency sooo bad. It was "THE agency" for me. The recruiter liked my book, but they weren't hiring.

How often is anyone hiring when you need a job?

Well, I asked one of my professors for his contacts at this agency. He gave me a name of a former student. I called the guy and set up an appointment. He looked at my book and was impressed. So I asked if he knew their creative recruiter. He said, *"Yeah she's right down the hall, let's see if she has a minute."*

In that situation she couldn't help but spend some time with me.

The meeting went well. My tactful path to her office amused her.

It is tough just getting someone to return your phone calls.

Things go wrong, and at times life is a roller coaster ride.

With determination, you'll get through the low points.

I remember the mix of emotions I felt when news circulated around school about classmates getting hired.

I was happy for them, yet at the same time reminded that I must continue my search. This may happen to you.

If it does, use the success of others as inspiration.

Know that if there's a place in this business for them, there's a place for you. Persistence will lead you to that opportunity.

Being nice to everyone doesn't end with the agencies on your wish list. Yes, we all have a wish list.

Unfortunately everyone's list is often the same. What you're seeking is a position in advertising where you can gain experience and be mentored, not your dream job.

Many second- or third-tier agencies can be your key to opening a door at a first-tier agency.

Find your way to the ideal situation for yourself by establishing contacts. In my case, I made good contacts while freelancing at an agency that wasn't on anyone's wish list.

In fact, I met this agency's recruiter at a portfolio review.

Everyone else was battling in line to see people from the so-called "hot" shops. This recruiter was at a table by herself reading a magazine, and I was eager to show my book to anyone.

That meeting led to my freelance job, which paid for my trip to New York to interview. The experience and friends I gained from that assignment opened doors at other agencies. This was a result of my respect for all levels of advertising, and persistence.

I remember what it was like to thirst for an opportunity to prove myself. It wasn't too long ago. You're asked to come back for one more person to look at your book before a decision is made.

You're told to wait a few weeks and see if they need to hire some people. Maybe a creative director tells you that your book is two campaigns away from "being there."

Still, no matter what ups and downs you face, be persistent.

Never stop making that extra phone call or visiting one more agency before you go home.

Never stop working on that one campaign that pushes your book to another level.

Never stop greeting interviewers with a smile and leaving their office with optimism.

Never stop, and remember that "nothing in the world can take the place of persistence."

Since earning his master's from the VCU AdCenter, Jhames Holley has produced award-winning work at Leo Burnett for Altoids and Art.com. He has worked on General Mills and Toys 'R Us and is currently producing more great work at a Chicago advertising agency.

EXPECTATIONS

by Wayne Johnson
former Vice President & Manager, Creative Recruitment
Leo Burnett, Chicago

"No squeaky clean, portfolio-carrying, Mac-literate, over-laminated, Sketcher-footed, pierced, joke-telling junior creative is going to come in and sell every new ad around here."

Welcome to your first job in the ad business, where you should expect some level of "junior" treatment. Your goal: Rise above the perception that you are too green by doing great work and proving the skeptics wrong.

What else can you expect?

Well, aside from confusion about the quickest route to the vending machine or the bathroom, expect phenomenal opportunities to make your mark in this industry. You were hired because your employers looked at your book and liked what they saw. They believe you can help make their business better.

To prove them right, you have to produce. Soak up as much information as you can about everything related to your company, its resources, associates, clients, and the competition.

Expect many opportunities to present your work.

If your presentation skills aren't strong now, start practicing. Pick up tips, then develop your own style. Work that dog and pony. But first make sure the work is good.

Expect to learn team work.

Collaborate with your partner, your boss, other departments in your company, outside suppliers, and your secretary.

Expect professionalism.

It's not what you wear: it's how you carry yourself – even when you stroll into work with a backpack, overalls, and the baseball cap du jour. Be mature. Be respectful. Be on time. You represent your company when you're meeting with clients or suppliers, and while on production. Do it well.

Expect criticism.

If it's constructive criticism, take it openly.

Don't ever be afraid to ask for clarification or to defend your position, but do that constructively, as well. Respect other people's opinion. Learn from their insights and experiences.

Some people may expect you to hit the ground running and assume you already know how the entire production process works. Be prepared, but don't be shy about asking for help. People actually like to be asked.

Find an ally or mentor whose work you respect and say, "Hey, I'm not sure about the next steps. I'd love your opinion." Making assumptions in order to seem knowledgeable is a big mistake. Then all hell breaks loose when a project falls apart. And when it falls, guess who it lands on?

Expect big and not-so-big assignments.

Remember that no project is too small. Take on simple assignments, like inserts or small space ads, with enthusiasm. Make them great.

Expect to learn about salesmanship.

You think you're an art director, copywriter, graphic designer, illustrator, or photographer, right? Wrong. Above all else, you've got to be a salesman. You must sell yourself through the quality of your work, confidence, straightforwardness, and professionalism.

Expect much more than you've read here.

No two days are alike in this business. And, certainly, no two agencies are alike.

Oh yeah. One final tip: Expect to be the best.

If you don't, you won't.

Mr. Johnson was Vice President, Manager of Creative Recruitment at Leo Burnett Company. He currently runs Wayne Johnson Design in Chicago.

His valuable advice was first printed in CMYK *magazine, Fall 1996. We are grateful to both Wayne and* CMYK *for their permission to offer it to you here.*

THE ART TO GETTING A START

by Richard Kirshenbaum
Co-Chairman, Chief Creative Officer & Founder
Kirshenbaum Bond & Partners, New York

"Like your new job, Sammy?"
"It's a damn good job – this year."
"What do you mean – this year?"
"If I have it next year, it'll stink."
   (from *What Makes Sammy Run,* by Bud Schulberg)

How does one get started in advertising?
How do you break in as a hot creative?
It's a question I hear all the time.
Unfortunately, there are no easy answers; I can't give you a panacea. I can only give you the benefit of my experience.
It goes something like this.

I went to college.
I studied advertising.
I put together a portfolio.
I graduated.
I couldn't get arrested.
I was a creative leper. I sulked. I pouted.
I decided to go to South America.

One muggy day after graduation, I was sitting at my parents' house (now a holding tank for pent-up unemployed frustration). My father says, "So how's the job search going?" After knocking on doors, or, more appropriately, having them slammed in my face, I answered rather enthusiastically "I'll never get a job. I don't even know who I'd want to work for."

My father proceeded to hand me a copy of the *Wall Street Journal.* "How about working for her?" On the cover was a story about Lois Korey and Allen Kay of Korey, Kay and Partners.

I read it with interest. I knew I'd found the person I wanted to work for. She obviously had a sense of humor (her bio included writing for the *Tonight Show*).

I pondered what to do next. How does one go about securing a mentor? Large bribes would do, but that was obviously not in the picture. How about my looks, charm, and fabulous personality?

"Nah!" I decided. "I'm not going to write her. Who am I to her?" I sat there, dejected. Then I heard a little voice, you know the one in your head you try to ignore but, every once in a while, is too annoying not to listen to. "Richard" it said, "Don't be a jerk. Get off your butt and write the dame a letter." (He tends to be vulgar but humorous.) "Have a little confidence. It's time for (I heard music at this point) STUPID PET TRICKS."

I decided right then and there to write Lois Korey a comedy monologue on what it was like to be unemployed. I would lead her on a journey and supply her with two endings.

Both endings would involve my future, and she would be gloomy and dismal and reveal herself to be the type of woman who shopped for underwear in leather boutiques.

The other ending would involve, in short, hiring me and proving what an upstanding pillar of the community she was.

My father said, "You can't send a woman like *that* something like *this*." My mother thought five pages was too long and perhaps I should take out the reference to underwear. My little voice said, "Send it the way it is, you fool!"

Now, you might be saying to yourself, a comedy monologue – that's not so original. Well, if there's one thing I do know after receiving 110 foot-in-the-door promotions from potential employees, 60 champagne glass promotions to 'toast' my success, and résumés in green, black, or grey to play off the names of Miss Green, Mr. Black, and Mrs. Grey – it's not so much a question of what you do, but the style in which you do it.

Sometimes less is more. (P.S., the letter was funny.)

Anyway, back to the story. As if by some magical hand, after I'd mailed the letter, the next day – yes the next day – I was sitting at my parents' house, when I hear the phone ring. "Oh, I bet it's Lois Korey," I sarcastically said to my Mom. My mother peeked her head out the screen door and said, "It's Lois Korey."

She said, "How about coming in for an interview?" Early the next morning I put on my one and only suit and marched into the city. The moment I walked into the elegant townhouse on 75th Street (they were just starting out), I knew I wanted to work there. Badly.

Lois and Allen seemed like giants to my pea-sized sense of self. They sat at adjoining desks, facing each other in the parlor. The Ultimate Creative Team.

Lois flipped through my book without Allen as much as glancing up or saying a word. She flipped through my scanty portfolio and then handed it to Allen. Allen picked up the poor, mistreated portfolio and said, "Now this has to pass my 'who gives a s--t' test."

After looking at every page he said, "Who gives a s--t." Flip. "Who gives a s--t." I felt very low. Curbfeeler Material. Lois got quite angry at his antics and said "Allen, you're not even looking at his book." (God bless her.) She then proceeded to take me on a tour of the small agency and pointed out some of the funny, innovative work hanging on the walls.

"How would you like to work here, Richard?" she asked.

My heart stopped. "I'd love to."

"It'll be a fabulous experience for you," she said.

"There's only one slight drawback to this position," she stated.

"Oh, I'm sure it's no problem," I said emphatically.

"We can't afford to pay you," she answered.

"Oh."

Well folks, like the old saying goes, "If life gives you lemons, make lemonade."

I never thought that after having my parents scrape and help send me to school I'd graduate and work for (should I say it?) FREE! You got it, no money. Lack of cash. *Pas d'argent*. No deposits.

Think what you'd do in this situation. I talked it over with the "rents" and after careful inspection we all came to the overwhelming conclusion that in the initial phases money was not as important as the valuable experience I'd be gaining.

In fact, I'd often tell people I was getting my M.E., my Masters of Experience. I was just thankful I had parents who were understanding and supportive.

Not to say the next year wasn't difficult. You try sleeping on your sister's couch (especially one who has PMS every day [sorry, Booker, but it's true]). I dodged clock radios aimed at my head for eight months. That wasn't the only frustrating thing.

Not only was I working for free, but I was also competing against a very talented Harvard grad who was also working for free (they had some operation going!) who, ironically, is now one of my associate creative directors.

Of course, I had the privilege, and I say privilege, of working around Lois and Allen, two of the best people in the industry. At times I felt like I should be paying them.

At times I felt otherwise, but I always tried to keep a smile on my face and have a positive attitude.

Example: One day I was asked to do phone duty. But I'm a writer, I thought, and I'm not even getting paid! "No, answering the phones is part of the job." The very next day, Lois asked me to bring coffee to some new clients. But I'm a writer, I thought, and I'm not even getting paid! And I thought, this isn't a man's job.

Well, I bit my lip and answered the phones and served the coffee and plastered a big smile on my lips because you can't tell the woman who runs the company that getting coffee isn't a man's job.

Besides writing, I also moved furniture, rolled carpets, stuffed press kits, parked and retrieved cars in the rain, picked up checks, made bank deposits, ordered lunch, and honestly loved it.

You see, I learned a great lesson that not only did I have to start at the bottom, but I had to re-educate the way I was socialized.

I truly believe this helped me when I started my own business because I'd broken down all the useless stereotypes about sex, and age and race, and all the other "stuff" we're taught from an early age that usually holds us back.

All in all, I learned a few essentials about breaking into the business. I share these with you in the following 10-point summary (I always wanted to give my very own 10-point summary).

Here it goes.

1. **The Ad Biz is a personality business.**
   Worry more about putting a smile on your face than putting something on your résumé.

2. **Get off your butt. It's all in the doing.**

3. **Find a mentor. (Learn from the best.)**

4. **Don't be limited by age, sex, religion, or race.**
   Have confidence in yourself. Cream rises.

5. **Don't be creative for creative's sake.**
   What's more important than what you do is how you do it.

6. **Realize you have to start at the bottom.**

7. **Money isn't the most important thing.**
   If it is, work on Wall Street.

8. **Read, watch, and observe everything.**
   Ideas come from the strangest places.

9. **It's hard work.**
   Just when you feel like throwing in the towel, the hard work really begins. This separates those who will make it from those who won't.

10. **America is a wonderful place to be.**
    I started out answering phones.
    Now, I'm running a multi-million dollar ad agency.
    But that's another story all together...

With virtually no money and little recognition, Mr. Kirshenbaum and his partner built a $25 million agency, Kirshenbaum Bond & Partners in two-and-a-half years.

He is coauthor (with partner Jonathon Bond) of Under the Radar: Talking to Today's Cynical Consumer, *published by AdWeek Books.*

His agency now bills more than $450 million.

DO THE OBVIOUS

by Lee Kovel
Chief Creative Officer
Kovel/Fuller, Culver City, CA

Quite a few years ago, I was looking through some boxes in the back of a dust-filled antique shop and unearthed a small paperback booklet that was written around 1920. Obvious Adams.

It was the story of an advertising guy named "Obvious Adams." As the story unfolded, Obvious got his start by meeting an ad biggie. At the time, Obvious was a clerk in a grocery store.

Now this ad biggie was quite preoccupied with one of his client's problems. Apparently, this client made biscuits. They were very good biscuits, too. They were sold by the pound right out of barrels. But sales, despite all the advertising, were not very good.

Obvious got into a discussion with the ad biggie and told him how the women he saw buying groceries always picked through the biscuit bin because many of the biscuits were broken. And he went on to suggest that maybe it would be a good idea if the biscuits were wrapped in their own containers.

The ad biggie thought this was a great idea (even though it was obvious) and immediately hired Obvious as a copywriter. And the client sold a hell of a lot of biscuits in the new packaging.

Now all through Obvious's career he did things that everybody looked at and said, "That's so obvious...why didn't I think of that?" But the catch was, nobody but Obvious thought of these things.

When you put your book together, there are often truths about products that other people miss. And if you look closely enough, you'll find them and the ad will come.

Unfortunately, most books contain the same recycled ideas over and over and over. (Which is why you should go back to work on your book.)

For example, if you create an ad for eyedrops, or toothpaste, or bug spray, look for the idea. Is there a relevant appeal that you can make that will coerce me into reading your ad or at least relate to what you're saying?

If you can't explain what the idea is, your ad isn't working.

For writers, this is especially important. Headlines and layouts have to work together, too.

If you're an art director, your design skills may get you by in some remote cases, even if you get a B on the idea part. (Which is why you should go back to work on your book.)

I think two of the best ads that illustrate ideas in print are for Parker Pens: "If the pen is mightier than the sword, then some pens are mightier than others." The visuals are a photo of Eisenhower holding the Parker pen used to sign the German surrender in 1945, one of MacArthur signing the Japanese surrender, and one of Warren Christopher signing the formal agreement with Iran to free 52 U.S. hostages.

The other ad shows a Range Rover going through a river with water up to its fenders. The headline: "We brake for fish."

The point is, there is a visual and verbal connection that makes these ads particularly good. And in most entry-level books there is rarely a connection like this.

If anything, there is simply a "punny" headline over a picture of the product. Don't do this. Fill your book with ideas...but remember, it is far from easy.

Now suppose you're talented enough to put together a collection of ads that can stand up to the best, which is highly improbable. (Which is why you should go back to work on your book.)

My next suggestion is to include some ads that are controversial. Almost every creative director you meet will tell you to take risks.

Now, don't be stupid about this. Take smart risks. Your objective is to come up with advertising that makes people remember your book. That's right, the purpose is to make your book ever more distinctive. How long ago did Howard Stern appear at the MTV Music Awards as Fartman? People remember the incident.

You see, every creative director worth his or her title is looking for young talent that can create the unexpected. Even if it's unsellable to a real client, a smattering of this in your book will help.

OK, so let's say your book is as good as you can make it...which is doubtful. (So go back and work on your book.)

The probability that you'll get a job is still slim. You simply have a great deal of competition for very few jobs.

As a result, you're going to have to go to work. You'll have to write letters and follow up with every contact you make.

A great letter can be a powerful tool for getting a foot in the door. If you can't figure out what makes a great letter, advertising isn't for you. After all, direct mail is one of the purest forms of advertising.

But don't forget... 99% of all creative directors will want to hire you because you have a great book. The interview is a small, final hurdle. If your book is good enough, the interview is pro forma.

I'd suggest you pay attention in the interview because you may learn quite a bit.

First, you'll find most executive creative directors love to be intimidating in these situations to test your mettle. Take it easy.

Your book was good enough to get you face to face with the boss. Interview the interviewer. See what he likes (and hates) about your book. Listen carefully, because experienced people can help you make your book better.

You'll discover a lot about the way an agency operates by looking closely at the creative director. Should you get an offer, this is the person who sets the tone for the product and can make your life wonderful or miserable.

Keep your eyes open. Listen and learn. Don't ask stupid questions. (Then go back to work on your book.)

Finally, remember your book also reflects and brings your entire life experiences onto the page. The bits, facets, information, and all kinds of experiences you've had get stored subconsciously and reassembled into advertising.

Therefore, the more you know about a lot of things and the more you've experienced, the better your depth of bringing new ideas to bear. If you think this is a suggestion to work on a steamship bound for Tahiti, you're right.

Or you could work as a clerk in a grocery store. Both are relevant.

The vocabulary that makes great advertising stems from being able to arrange the right thoughts and images at the perfect time – so that people will respond. It's that simple.

Right now, you want to arrange your ads and ideas to appeal to the people who will hire you: a dose of real world ads – a selection of off-the-wall "risk taking" ads.

You want that creative director to know you can sell mouthwash, hamburgers, snowboards, or bug spray better, smarter, and more creatively than the hundreds of other people who are trying to sell mouthwash, hamburgers, snowboards, or bug spray.

It's obvious, right?

Good luck.

And now, go back to work on your book.

Mr. Kovel "held out for the out of the ordinary" for Dr. Pepper, did the Cannes-winning Godzilla spot, did "chicken right" for Kentucky Fried Chicken, and created many "less filling tastes great" spots for Miller Lite. Lee is partner, CCO of Kovel/Fuller, a $120 million California ad agency.

STAYING FRESH
IN A TOUGH BUSINESS

by Alex Kroll
Chairman, Chief Executive Officer
Young & Rubicam

There's a fallacy in the business that there's no life after 40, and, in the creative area, no life after 35.

The myth goes that you have to make it fast because the clock runs out fast.

I was particularly amused by that notion when I talked to some young people recently, because I'd just come from a screening where we had looked at some advertising for Frito-Lay potato chips. We'd been running the same campaign for 24 years, with the same theme line: "No one can eat just one."

At the moment, I was thinking of the man who was the primary force behind this campaign and probably wrote the theme line. He was about 70 years old back in 1964.

If you look at the advertising, it's almost childlike in its simplicity, its innocence, its ability to interest people from five years of age to 85. But people do burn out young, and I think that one reason they do is they let themselves.

There is no divinely ordained lifecycle in advertising that says you're born at the age of 24, you reach maturity at 29, you go into a long slow decline to 33 and you die at 47. But one of the reasons that it happens when it does happen is that people, particularly creative people, become beguiled or wooed by the *interiors* of the advertising business, the life inside the crystal palace, and lose touch with their prospects on the outside.

There's a lot to woo them. There are scrumptious restaurants and elegant hotels and opulent conference rooms and the opportunity to meet very interesting and exciting people who run major businesses.

People can make a fairly significant amount of money in the advertising business fairly fast.

I'll give you an example. It's 1963. I climb out of bed in Newark, New Jersey, to get on the Lackawana Railroad train with straw seats, no air conditioning, and trundle over to New York and walk 12 blocks to Y&R.

191

I'm an apprentice copywriter. I weigh 245 pounds, with a bullet shaved head. I look more like a moving man than I look like a copywriter, even in a suit, because the suit looks dreadful.

I'm not making very much money. The people that I deal with on an everyday level are like Mr. Latero, the delicatessen man across the street. My wife and I have a child on the way.

For some reason, I have a Mercedes in the parking lot, which is almost costing me more than I'm making every week. I am very much my own consumer. I'm borderline hungry.

Assuming a certain amount of talent, I or anyone else will learn this trade and develop skills that can allow me to translate my own particular visions, ideas, selling thoughts into concrete form – like a commercial or a print ad, or something that communicates with people.

Then the lines cross. You begin to make more money and you begin to insulate yourself against things which are painful. You begin to accumulate the things which make life more comfortable.

Why not? Who wants to live in Newark in the 1960s?

Now, the problem is, sooner or later, the comforts (or the interiors of the advertising business) can blunt the sounds and the direct perceptions of the people you're trying to communicate with.

This is slow death. Because we are fundamentally in the business of communicating and *touching other people*. Fundamental to that is understanding the reality of other people.

What really moves them? What are they worried about? What do they dread? What concerns them right now?

Now, you can get a certain amount of that from secondhand sources through the tube of research – abstract information, dished up in numbers, filtered through the screen of your research department or your media department.

That's helpful. But unless it is balanced by tactile understanding – I mean a tactile sense of people – then the advertising communication that you give back to those people becomes abstract.

It also begins to feed off good work that you did in the past.

In advertising, effective solutions tend to be present-tense solutions – very specific to a specific client in a specific time.

What worked in the past may be useful general information, but it is unlikely to work in the present.

That doesn't mean you can't learn from experience.

But if you are constantly harkening back to a specific executional answer that worked five years ago or three years ago – that got you fame or a better job – then you will deliver a derivative or second-class solution.

"Yesterday's hero is today's cold sandwich."

Meeting strange people, inviting strange experiences, being eclectic in your life is difficult – particularly for creative people who tend to have a certain amount of social insecurity to start with.

But the great trap in advertising is to become beguiled by secondhand information – to give in to the siren song of the suburbs and the country club and fail to go back and rub elbows or arms or noses with the people who are really consumers of the majority of products that you try to sell.

These folks will catch you by surprise if you're not alert to them. And creative people have such wonderful antennae.

But their antennae can droop year by year – like lowering the antenna in your car and finding the reception is garbled, so you plug in the antiseptic stereo tape.

You're not receiving anything anymore from the outside. You're just playing the same old tunes.

If there's no life after 40, losing touch with your customer is one of the reasons why. The work becomes acceptable, probably strategically sound. Sound, but never brilliant.

If I can go back a bit, I think that strategic work is often a group effort. It takes a lot of people and a lot of hard thinking to lay the groundwork.

However, when it comes to communicating a promise to consumers, I think there has to be a good deal of individual expression. The communication itself can't be generalized.

The best advertising I've seen springs from the most individual perception. The idea that finally appears in the commercial, in print or television, leans heavily on a direct experience of one individual.

When we want to communicate well, provocatively, most productively, we need one-to-one communication.

If I can draw upon an image, a perception, a dream, an emotion that I've felt very deeply, I can communicate it very well to you. You can almost feel it. If I feel it, you feel it.

When it becomes generalized, when I am speaking for a group or distilling a large number of facts, it becomes somewhat muffled – and you feel it less deeply.

You can accept it intellectually, but nothing happens.

You're not moved.

"I am moved." That's what advertising's all about.

And unless your communication is personal enough to accomplish this, you might as well not advertise at all.

It comes down to a really hard-nosed business problem: People who cannot move other people, who cannot motivate other people, cannot touch other people, are bad for our business.

And that's what the creator who allows himself to go down that long curve – that slide towards abstractionism – is letting himself in for.

We are in the midst of an eclectic pattern of life today with a barrage of other influences – fashion, theater, graphic arts, broadcasting, publishing, and so on – that can be extra stimulants to creative people if they use them.

But don't allow yourself to be funneled into that tube which goes from here to the restaurant, to the hotel, to the bar.

You've got to break out of that pattern. You've got to get into the discount store on a Saturday night and see those women for whom shopping is a primary diversion in life.

Go through those stores. It's antithetical to most people to do it or talk to those shoppers, but you've got to somehow.

I don't mean you have to live there all the time.

I am not against country clubs, and I'm not against lovely people. They buy things, too.

There's a lot to be said for them. But you've got to break out.

Everyone must devise their own tricks, their own stunts for breaking out.

Unless you break out of your comfortable life, you will dry up. Before 40?

I've seen gray brains who were under 30.

Mr. Kroll, now retired, was a Y&R "lifer" who left pro football (he played for the original AFL New York Titans), started as a copy trainee, and successfully made the trip to become chairman and CEO of one of the world's largest advertising agencies.

IT'S A VISUAL WORLD

by Bob Kuperman
Chairman, CEO, and President, DDB New York

"There may be an excuse for a bad ad, but there's no excuse for an ad looking bad." A copywriter said that – his name was Bill Bernbach. He was a man who had an incredible understanding of communication and the power that visuals play in it.

Today we live in an ever-increasing world of the eye. TV, of course, magazines – where photos have replaced copy – even plays and movies which move along not so much by dialogue as they do by film technique and stage production – e.g., *Flashdance, Cats.*

In politics, a picture of a presidential candidate in a tank has a far more telling impact than any speech he may have given.

It's a visual world – an art director's world. But where are the art directors? Where are the people who can understand and tailor strong conceptual images?

This may be getting a little philosophical when all you really want to know is how to get a job. But I want you to understand that there is a void waiting to be filled by someone who can demonstrate the ability to create fresh and interesting images.

Not graphics for the sake of graphics, but visual images that form and advance communication. I rarely see work that reflects this in portfolios, whether they be a student's or a professional's.

So let's start at the beginning. Why is art direction (and the art director) so important in advertising?

Every product seeks to develop its own personality, its own brand image. A large part of that on the most basic level is how it is presented to the viewer. Not only how it speaks to them but how it looks.

Look at most TV and especially print advertising. You'll find that most of it looks the same, and because of that, doesn't reflect any particular personality about the product. There is a very good reason why Helmut Krone (probably the best print art director there ever was) made a VW ad look one way and a Porsche ad another.

195

It's because the look of the ad grew out of the product and the personality that was trying to be communicated about that product.

Think about your work along these lines. Look at your book. Does all the work look relatively the same?

In most advertising today, visuals are used only as an illustration of what has already been said by the headline – when they can have so much more of an impact if they are used as a tool of the expression itself.

If you can cover up the visual and the ad still makes just as much sense, why have the visual (other than a product shot)?

Remember that the most effective use of visuals is when they advance and give added meaning to the ad.

I love having the line and the visual being interdependent. To make a visual that has come to symbolize one thing, and give it new meaning by attaching an unexpected visual image to it.

Thinking conceptually through pictures is what art direction is all about. And that goes for typography, too.

To understand type and its effect on the expression of an idea is an important part of being an art director.

"I love you" set in Caslon 540 12 pt. has a completely different message than if it were set in Futura Demi Bold 72 pt. Is the concept of the ad to whisper about love or to shout about it?

Here are some principles to use as a guide:

Think visually from the beginning. Don't write a line and say, "What am I going to show?" Conceive visually. After all, you are an art director.

Concept leads graphics. All graphics grow from and are defined by the concept. The stronger the concept, the more it dictates how the ad should be handled, how film should be edited, how the ad itself should be laid out.

Have a reason for everything you put into an ad. Why that picture? Why that layout? Why that type? Pictures and words must be totally controlled to communicate the exact message intended.

Never let the layout or editing distort, confuse, or generally screw up what you're trying to communicate. This is not arts and crafts.

Realize that ads must have a dominant design factor. It's either headline-driven or visual-driven. Both are great, but as an art director, recognize it should be one or the other in terms of layout.

Concept is only the beginning – execution brings it alive. When you don't have an understanding of type, photography, layout, or editing, you limit not only your ability as an art director to express a concept – more critically, you limit your ability to conceive it in the first place.

When in doubt, use Caslon and never eat fried foods.

Bob Kuperman, better known as "Kupe," has played an important part in the growth of one of America's most exciting and dynamic agencies. He started his career as an art director in 1963 at DDB, where he worked on many of their landmark ads for Volkswagen – a collection of them hangs at the Smithsonian Institute. He also created the total marketing concept – name, package design, and all advertising – for Meow Mix Cat Food, a phenomenally successful new product introduction.

Bob is consistently cited as one of the Top 100 Advertising People in the U.S. and has received more than 500 awards from every major advertising show. He is one of those rare advertising people known and respected not only for his creative talent, but for his expertise on the account side, as well as his ability as a manager and agency principal. "Kupe" spent 14 years of his advertising career at TBWA Worldwide, most recently as President and CEO of the Americas. In January 2001 he returned to DDB New York.

Kupe has taught at ArtCenter, Pratt, and the School of Visual Arts. Just like his Energizer Bunny campaign, he keeps going and going.

TWO CREATIVES OF EQUAL TALENT – ONE GOES ON TO BE AWESOME, ONE GOES ON TO SUCK. WHY?

by David Lubars
President & Executive Creative Director,
Fallon Minneapolis

You and your buddy are just starting out. You're a couple of juniors from ad school, or wherever. You both have killer books; maybe you've scored in The One Show college competition. You're excited and juiced. You have tons of potential.

Flash forward fifteen years. One of you has become the creative director of a brilliant agency. The other is brain dead in Punxsutawney.

A fascinating scenario, and one I've tried to make sense of in the twenty years I've been at this. If you're a kid, this is written to try to avoid the mistakes some of your talented but misguided predecessors have made. Here, then, are nine attempts at understanding why some people fall off the face of the earth:

First, it seems that these people somehow get it in their heads they're *artistes* and poets. A wrongheaded and dopey notion.

We're business people who use creativity as a vehicle to deliver brand messages. This is different from being someone who uses advertising as a vehicle to deliver pretentious crap.

Second, some people speak about their clients with condescension and loathing. Again, dumb. Not to mention counterproductive. Think about what it's like to be a client for a second. You worry that you're paying the agency big money to help, knowing it's your ass if they don't. You worry about whether they'll create work everyone inside and outside your agency can feel good about. You worry about whether they'll penetrate the issues as solvers of business problems or just ad makers.

But then when the agency people come through for you, you become less worried. You begin to see them as a secret weapon. As time goes on, you allow them to guide you into new territory because you trust them.

The point being, it's hard work to earn and maintain client trust, but it's been the foundation of every great campaign ever created.

Third, some people don't seem to recover well when their first or second batch of work is killed. After a couple of rounds, they decide the assignment isn't good anymore and return with garbage. Bob Moore, our Fallon Minneapolis creative director, points out, *"This is a sure way of becoming a hack. Five years down the road you've got no book and you're bitching about how lousy your agency is. Who made it lousy? You did."*

This is an important point. You should know that most creative directors don't assess you simply by how creative you are. We also consider how deep, how fast, and how willing to return you are. And how much of a pain in the ass you aren't.

A freelancer and early mentor of mine, Ernie Schenck, was telling me about someone he'd worked with who wasn't able to rebound: *"This went on for a few years, so nobody was surprised when he turned into a pathetic, defeated little puddle of awesome talent that never amounted to jack."* Sad.

Fallon account manager Rob Buchner says, *"Stamina is a constant virtue I see in the best creative people; emotional and intellectual stamina. Without perseverance, their talent surrenders to the uglier dynamics of the business."*

Fourth, while still developing their talent, some people decide to follow the scent of money instead of continuing to follow the trail of great work. One of my partners at Fallon, Mark Goldstein, says truly great creative people are able to recognize "quicksand" agencies. These are places where no matter how good you are, the internal processes and culture conspire to make you horrible. The lure is the short-term financial gain. Goldstein says, *"That's because bad agencies are happy to overpay for badness; they don't know the difference."* But you'll know the difference.

Fifth, some people become intoxicated with the idea of titles, puff pieces in the trades, and becoming "a manager." Fallon legend, Bob Barrie, warns, *"The first time you do a decent campaign, you'll get calls from bad agencies. You'll decide to 'move up' and join one of them and then you'll disappear. Never make a decision based on a coin. Do brilliant work and you'll be rewarded more in the end anyway."*

199

As far as managing goes, Bob says, *"You can't manage till you've done tons of great work yourself. How can you be a credible judge of other people's stuff when you're still figuring out how to do it yourself?"*

This segues nicely into my **sixth** point. Some people appear to be unconcerned with building a body of brilliant work over time. A question: who's had a richer career, Neil Young or Donovan? Young has been making brilliant records for 35 years. Donovan had some hits in the '60s. Who's Donovan? Exactly. The point is, you can't put together a few good campaigns and hope to live off the fumes forever. You're only as good as the last thing you did, and you should've done that today. Current greats like Lee Clow and Phil Dusenberry are Neil Youngs.

Seventh, some people seem closed to new ways of doing things. Another Fallon partner, Rich Stoddart, says, *"The successful creative is totally objective about his or her own work. If it's not working, if it isn't right, they just move on. Bad creatives think 'protect, protect, protect.'"*

Eighth, some people don't exercise their brains enough. Our planning director, Anne Bologna, observes, *"The awesome ones are extraordinarily curious and ask 'why?' all the time. They're part planners in that they're empathetic to the human condition. They don't see the world through their own eyes only."*

Stoddart adds, *"They're sponges. They read everything they can get their hands on. Two or three newspapers, novels, business magazines – everything. When they sit with clients, they're better able to understand the context of people and business."*

Ninth, some people actually believe their initial good press and listen when industry sycophants whisper in their ears.

Here's the thing, though. The guy who cured polio was important. Even though you created a great campaign, you're not all that important in the grand scheme of things.

Yes, you're in a nice industry that can reward well. Yes, you're creative and people admire that. Yes, you may attain some level of status. But, I mean, come on.

Here's what is important: humility. It's great to be around people like Pat Fallon, Laurel Cutler, and Maurice Levy, who demonstrate every day that the greater the success, the greater the opportunity to remain humble.

And if just being classy isn't reason enough to be humble, then consider the practical side. The guy who gave me my start, Jon Goward, says, *"Once you start thinking too highly of yourself, your ears fall off. You stop listening to anyone who criticizes anything you do because you think you know better. And that feeds itself. Success tends to attract people who tell you how great you are. The tricky part is maintaining a strong sense of yourself — being sensitive enough to hear what clients and other people who disagree with you say."*

If you're really great, let other people talk about you. Your job is fairly simple: be quiet, sit down, and create some more work. (In fact, why are you reading this when you could be working on you craft right now? Put this down. You'll learn more by doing than reading about doing.)

I heard a guy say something a few years ago that sums up the whole thing for me. He said, *"My best people come to work every day worrying that they're about to be fired, while the mediocre people are always shocked when they actually are fired."*

How do you feel when you come to work?

David Lubars has won every major creative award in the world, several times over, including Gold Cannes, Grand Clio, Grand Andy, Gold One Show, Gold Effie, D&AD and Communications Arts. His work has been written about in the New York Times, *the* Wall Street Journal, USA Today *and* Time. *He has appeared on the cover of Archive magazine. Twice.*

He began his career at Leonard Monahan Saaybe in 1982. He was recruited by Chiat/Day LA in 1985, where he did highly visible work for Apple, Nissan, and Pizza Hut. He then returned in 1988 as a partner to the renamed Leonard Monahan Lubars.

He then moved to BBDO/LA as CEO and Chief Creative Officer of BBDO West, where he created lauded work for Apple Computer. In 1998 he was named chief creative at Fallon Minneapolis. Since joining Fallon in June 1998, he has launched acclaimed and internationally award-winning campaigns for clients ranging from Nordstrom, EDS, United Airlines, Nuveen, Lee, and Holiday Inn, to Sports Illustrated, BMW, Timex, PBS, and Archipelago.

This article originally appeared in Communication Arts.

CATS, DOGS, CONSUMER, DIRECT

by Lee Margolis
Senior Art Director
J. Walter Thompson Direct, New York

I'd been a dog guy for years. Golden Retrievers. Labradors. Boxers. Never a cat guy. That was until recently. I adopted a cat.

Now I guess I'm a cat guy. No fetching the stick. No barking at the mailman. No major drooling to speak of.
Why am I telling you this?

Well, much like I was a dog guy, I guess you could say I was also an ad-man in consumer for a brief time. Image. Concept. The big idea. Beer to the masses. Candy to everyone. Clothing to all.
That all changed for me, too. But why am I telling you this?

Well, from what I've been told, with the advent of remote controls, VCRs, and cable television (just to name a few), belts tightened, egos shrunk (ever so slightly), and budgets decreased.
Gone were the days of three Orwellian networks. Gone were the days of a captured audience. Gone were the days of a multitude of creative jobs. And besides, by this point, clients were looking for more than just proof that their advertising worked. They wanted numbers.

At about this time, I graduated college. Lofty thoughts embedded my head. Big, beautiful, conceptual work. Television, radio, print, and outdoor. But the '80s were just a memory in the rearview mirror.

Ladies and germs, friends and relatives... say hello to "the proof is in the puddin'." Answers at last. Our hero and yours – Direct Marketing (start theme to *2001*).

Remember now, I was a dog guy in general; now I'm a cat guy in direct. After a few years in general, direct is where I landed. Like Dorothy in Oz, I thought. Like Alice in Wonderland. Like Bill in the White House. Me, a dog guy, in direct. MEOW.

Direct Marketing. Speak to the individual. Get a response.
Listen to who's listening.

Sure I was worried the fun was gone. Sure I was worried there was less "Hollywood" in direct. But get over yourself, you're not making movies, you're making advertising.

If you want to make movies, go to film school, write a screenplay, send it to Spielberg (not Spievogel), but for God sakes, don't get an ego and confuse advertising with Hollywood. And for those who do, I bid my warmest, "Get a grip."

What I found was direct marketing and general advertising are different animals. Like cats and dogs. Just remember: A good idea is a good idea whether you're mailing it or broadcasting it. Whether it barks or purrs. But why am I telling you this?

Well, in theory, all agencies should be armed with concrete, salesmanlike, cutting-edge (can't forget cutting edge) concepts in one hand and an understanding of television, print, radio, outdoor, point of purchase, direct mail, interactive, virtual, and any other vehicle we can think of, in the other.

All working the same strategy to the right people in the right manner. Resulting in the right goal: SALES.

Which brings me back to the analogy I've chosen. I was a dog guy, but now I'm a cat guy. Someday, I'd like to be bi-petual.

Why am I telling you this?

I've gotta get home and feed my cat.

Mr. Margolis, a graduate of Syracuse University, is a Senior Art Director in Direct at J. Walter Thompson in New York.

He says the survival of agencies will be more and more dependent on the integration of direct and consumer in the future, and his position proves that he believes what he says.

I'M NOT CREATIVE ENOUGH

by Tom Monahan
Creative thinking expert, Author, Creative Director

As I sit down to write this article, a cold shiver goes down the center of my back.

"What do I write about?"

"*CA* readers are a pretty savvy audience."

"Will they like it?"

"Will it be meaningful?"

"Will it be valuable?"

"Will it be useful?"

"Will the column be good enough?"

"Am I creative enough?"

These are just a few of the frightful thoughts that flash through my mind, with a few side trips to my sweat glands.

The blank sheet of paper has been haunting writers and artists for centuries. Or the blank canvas, or the solid slab of marble, or the empty stage... All creative people have their boogey men.

In fact, today, as I sit down at my PowerBook – screen glowing, machinery humming – with this subject on my mind, I feel the intimidation is even more present.

When I turn on this device I'm even told how many megabytes are available, in effect reminded just how huge, in technological terms, this blank sheet of paper really is.

As an advertising writer for 20 years I've faced the blank sheet of paper on thousands of occasions. And each time I've asked myself the same question, "Am I creative enough?"

Yes, I've pulled through many, many times before.

But each time it's a new challenge.

And each time I have to ask myself all over again, "Am I creative enough? Can I do it this time? Am I good enough?"

That's the question, psychologists tell us, that plagues most people with "problems."

"Am I good enough?"

Well, I'm not a psychologist. Will never pretend to be. And I don't intend to make light of such a deep, potentially damaging notion as a human being asking for such an all-telling judgment.

But I will tell you that I believe the insecurity articulated in the expression "Am I creative enough?" can actually be one of the more powerful motivators in any creative pursuit.

I've always felt that the best creative people are an odd combination of security and insecurity. Secure in knowing what they want to do, insecure as to whether they've nailed it "this time."

Always knowing that real creativity is the goal. Yet forever asking, "Am I creative enough?"

Over the years as I've interviewed creative people for jobs I always looked for a degree of self-confidence. Because advertising is such a brutal business when it comes to ego assault that I feel people need a certain amount of emotional armor. But if that cocky side isn't balanced by a shadow of doubt, I'm quite leery as to how creative the individual truly is.

You see, I believe to be creative is to be insecure.

Whether it's worn on the outside or not, whether it's recognized by others or not.

To be creative means you are forever stepping into the dark, uncharted unknown. That place I affectionately call "The Void." (Welcoming concept, isn't it?)

Few of us operate in "The Great Void," where Einstein, da Vinci, Picasso and other masters played. But when we aim to do something truly creative, something the likes of which has never been done before, that means we are approaching The Void, or at least putting one foot into it.

The deep, dark Void. The territory where no one else has been before. It's a bit scary. And that's understandable.

Now the reason it's so scary being in or near The Void is because there are no signposts telling us where we are. And, if we are truly in The Void, there are also no indicators telling us that we're doing something well or not. Good or bad... Right or wrong...

Have you ever come up with a concept and asked yourself "Is this any good?" If you had to ask, you were probably in or near The Void.

When you're in or near The Void you're where no one's ever been, so you simply have little or no known criteria to evaluate how good it is. And that's a good sign.

It's a good sign that you really are doing something creative. Not necessarily a sign that it's right or wrong.

When you come up with a concept and you don't have to ask "Is this any good?"because it's pretty easy to tell, then I'm sorry to say you're probably not being particularly creative.

Again, that doesn't mean it's right or wrong. It just means that if it's easy to qualify, then it's probably been done before, or at least it's in a category of things that have been done before, so it's really not very creative.

A conclusion? If you're scared, that's usually a good sign. If you're not scared, then it's usually a bad sign. When it comes to pure creativity, that is.

This is often a new concept to many people.

But it's a welcomed one for most.

I'm doing more and more creative training these days.

Companies or trade organizations bring me in to light a creative spark under their people.

I conduct creativity workshops. I don't teach creativity. I don't believe that can be done. I believe creativity is in everyone, to varying degrees. I feel my job as a creative trainer is simply to help people access more of what they already have. In most cases it's creativity that they had unlimited access to as children, but has since been locked away in the dark, damp corners created by years of judgment as adults. Years of training in insecurity.

One of the most valuable purposes my creative trainings serve is to help people break through the blocks that inhibit their creativity. Some people might help others achieve this by having them "conquer" their fears. I do it by helping people "see the value" of these gremlins.

When fear wells up in us (and it does for any mortal creative person), if we recognize that as a good sign, a sign that we might be approaching that deep, dark, mysterious unknown, The Void, the only place where true creativity ever happens, then perhaps we can see the usefulness of all this insecurity, make friends with it, and use it to our advantage. (Hey, maybe I am a psychologist?)

In my workshops we spend a lot of effort performing exercises that illustrate the value of fear in the creative process. When you see it as a constructive element and not a destructive one, it makes a world of difference.

So in this *CA Annual*, our perennial tribute to outstanding creativity in advertising, I'd be willing to bet that most of the great pieces of communications we see reproduced in these pages didn't come into being without just a little doubt, or fear, or insecurity chilling the spines of the people who conceived them.

I'd like to acknowledge all of you for your wonderful bravery. Or wonderful lunacy, for that matter. Because you faced the blank page. You brushed aside the fear. And you succeeded.

And to those wet-behind-the-ears newcomers – don't think for a minute those seasoned veterans don't experience these subtle horrors most every time they confront a new creative challenge.

And to those seasoned veterans – don't think for a minute that those wet-behind-the-ears newcomers don't confront their new creative challenges any more fearlessly than you might.

I'll contend that fear is a necessary component of this crazy process we call creativity. And I'll further contend that when its role is understood, it's one of the more constructive aspects as well.

Now, as I finish writing this article, I take a deep breath and ponder the results of my creative efforts here. I reread it one last time. A cool haze of fear engulfs me. And I smile to myself and say, "Maybe that's a sign that I am creative enough."

And then another even deeper feeling chills my bones…
"Or, maybe I'm not?"

One of the top authorities on creative thinking as it applies to advertising and other areas of business, Tom Monahan has helped more than one hundred thousand people on three continents master creative thinking in his popular creative workshops. Through his consulting company, Before & After, he has worked with clients such as Capitol One, Frito-lay, AT&T, Viacom and Virgin Atlantic Airways. He is also author of one of the top business-oriented books on creative thinking, The Do-It-Yourself Lobotomy: Open your mind to greater Creative Thinking. *This article originally appeared in* Communication Arts.
Tom can be reached at tom@before-after.com

MONROE'S DOCTRINE

by Evelyn Monroe Neill
Sr. VP/Group CD, Deutsch New York

Rachel just came into the office. She's an art director stuck on a project. She said it could be worse. "I could be a pregnant slave with festering wounds all over my body."

It's not easy to live with high standards. Are you really sure you want to work at a creative shop? Sometimes I think people try to get into a great agency with the ambition of a fish jumping out of the bowl. What is it going to do when it gets there? Gasp?

I was hired by Wieden + Kennedy as a part of a team with my buddy Charlotte. Evelyn Monroe, the copywriter and Charlotte Moore, the art director. You hadn't heard of us. At that time, we were young and awardless.

Although we had worked together for a short time at another agency, we got this job on an entirely speculative photo-comp book. (Our produced work wasn't good enough and we knew it. You'll probably do some God-awful work at some point in your youth. Don't let anyone tell you that it should be put in your book just because it's been produced.) So, I'd say this one ad got us the job. It was actually a single in a three-ad campaign for Jagermeister. The strange thing about this campaign is that some people absolutely hated it. It became *a barometer of people we like,* as Charlotte says. Do you like our ad? We like you too.

I've asked myself: What I can say that would be insightful for someone trying to get a book together? I don't know. I think it's a matter of talent, taste, and learning. If you have talent, but don't know what's in good taste, you'll have to learn. If you learn and you're lucky, you'll move to great shops. If you don't learn, you can still make great money doing tasteless ads. It's a forgiving business. You'll probably end up where you're supposed to be.

"Don't you hate giving advice?" Charlotte says. Charlotte's advice as she stares at a hideous sculpture I just completed for my office: "Cultivate other talents in case you fail in advertising." Well, there it is then.

Ms. Monroe says she's done lots of work for Nike in Europe that you'll probably never see! She has, however, won awards at the Cannes Film Festival and is now Sr. VP/Group CD at Deutsch.

208

WITH KNOWLEDGE, MAN MAY JUDGE HIMSELF

by Charlotte Moore
Creative Person of Note

In a vast world of opinions, some prevail for a period of time.
Some are compelling, but short-lived.
Some are insignificant and malformed.
Some are sheer genius.
But all of them swim in the same pool and affect the environment, which gives rise to the others. We are creatures (with few exceptions) who care what others think, and the creative industry is based on this human characteristic.

Some opinions are strong enough to swing advertising trends into orbit. Others kill agencies and products. Some are thinly disguised, egoistic, self-rationalizations, and others seem to have the allure of a much more slippery force: truth.

It would be restful for a person marching courageously through a career in advertising to lean briefly against something as solid as fact, or as close to certainty as the numerical value of pi.

For better or worse, however, it's a job choice that weds you to uncertainty and interpretation and, therefore, to faith and conviction. You won't escape opinion, and you shouldn't. That's what the business is about. But it's best to be armed.

In more concrete terms, your book will be judged. Your best thinking and greatest efforts will be assessed. Something very close to your heart will be held up to scrutiny. Your instincts will be questioned. Your professional career will be sifted through a mesh of the opinions of associate creative directors, creative directors, executive creative directors, account managers, clients, headhunters, and peers all merely doing their jobs by offering a critique and you doing yours by listening.

Prepare yourself for the onslaught of opinion and have something to hold onto if it all ceases to make sense: your own opinion.

If you haven't been in the business very long, you may suspect your opinion is of the insignificant, malformed variety I mentioned earlier. Maybe it is. But it's valuable to you nonetheless.

Your opinion keeps you focused. Like faith, which ultimately can't be explained, your opinion gives you sustenance. Without it, you couldn't move forward. Or even backward.

Your opinion is the direct result of your world view – or the cause of it. (It's a chicken and egg thing.) It's intrinsically linked to your life experience: the place of your birth, your marriage or break-up, your education, what you ate for breakfast.

Your opinion is both your security blanket and your worst enemy. It lets you know where you stand relative to the rest of the world. It helps you define your location. But it also reflects the shortcomings of your knowledge and whether your mind is open or closed.

Your opinion is an editing tool that lets you make hard and easy decisions: where to go next, with whom to align yourself, which photographer to hire.

At my first large-scale photo shoot in New York, I was listening and cautiously inserting my opinions in a whisper among a voluble crowd of European and Manhattanite stylists, models, and makeup artists. The Italian hair stylist caught bits and pieces of my barely uttered opinions and said forcefully, "I agree!" or "No, I do not think so!"

I don't remember what prompted these bursts of opinion, but I remember they continued in the same vein: "Nice! Very nice! Very beautiful!" "I would not do that! It is not good."

All this, coming from the sidelines, was received eagerly by the photographer, who eventually commented: "It is so great to deal with firm opinions. Europeans are full of them, but Americans just aren't. It's 'What do you think?' 'I don't know, what do you think?' Why don't people know what they think?"

This changed me. I realized four things:

1. If you are going to express an opinion, believe in it. Do not espouse a point of view because you think it might look cool on you like a particular pair of pants. You may be called upon to defend it, and "because it's cool" will be regarded as an unimpressive response. Why is it cool?

2. It is OK not to be right. But it is not OK to always value openness and receptivity above and beyond the ability to identify, articulate, and assert your own point of view.

3. There's nothing like a strong opinion – lobbed gleefully into an otherwise laconic group – for sending people scuttling to their own suddenly clear opinions or even for evoking total polarity. When the hair stylist said, "That is not good!" I suddenly knew with clarity whether I agreed with him.

4. The free exchange of opinion is a wellspring of learning and liberated thinking. Particularly when you start probing into why an opinion is held. This is when the opinions of lots of other people will be very important to you – and ultimately, yours to them. It's a tricky business, I suppose: determing what you will accept and possibly incorporate into your own body of opinion and what you will reject. But the process is illuminating.

As you move forward in this field, it will take strength to adhere to your own opinions. Adhere to them. Develop them.

Identify your own likes and dislikes. Your own principles, ethics, and beliefs. Listen to others but with an understanding that truth, as it falls from their lips, is not absolute. It is their truth, and only true for you if you feel it is the direction you must take.

Pursue this career the best way you can. Give your best self to it. Listen to people, but don't believe everyone.

Your career's work should be the development of sound, exciting opinions. Some day you'll be paid for them.

Or you'll be happy, like me, to hand them out for free.

Sometimes.

Charlotte Moore, formerly of Wieden + Kennedy, helped develop campaigns for Coca-Cola, Microsoft, and Nike. She received the MPA Kelly Award in 1991 and 1992, and today is a freelancer. Her thoughts here are from an article she wrote for the "Enough Said" column in CMYK magazine.

THE HIDDEN AGENDA PHENOMENON
(It's All About the Work, Sort Of)

by Professor Deborah Morrison, University of Texas

One of the best campaigns I ever saw grow from a student's brain, spill onto paper, then finally move into production was a gorgeous little poster set for Martinelli Apple Juice by art director Rossana Bardales.

Each of the pieces played the perfect balance of knowing exactly who to talk to and how to reward that reader.

The design was simple and easily read, the colors beautifully selected to pop and zing across the layout. The illustrations were original and full of attitude, the design a bit quirky yet elegant. In all, that was a perfect campaign.

It's been six years since that campaign was created, but I still like to haul it out as a perfect example of what to do in a junior book. And though the strategy and execution were spot on, what I really want creative students here at UT to understand is this: Rossana showed who she was, how her brain makes ideas, and her take on how the world works. It showed beautifully what I call "The Hidden Agenda Phenomenon" in building a junior portfolio.

As an aspiring writer or art director – that is, someone trying to break into the industry for the first time – you show the best speculative work you can muster.

Read the book you have in your hands for countless tips and inspiration. Create insightful strategy.

Communicate honestly and originally. Know Quark and Photoshop and use them as tools, not as concept-makers.

Surprise your audience. Be relevant. Become your own good planner. Let your education and experience carry you to some personal place in the creative process. Do all this, and you'll make good advertising. That's the agenda for a good spec book.

But there's more to selling your work than simply creating effective ads at this stage of your career.

That's where The Hidden Agenda comes in.

Consider the hiring process from the point-of-view of a busy creative director or creative manager. There's a stack of 25, 30 books on their desk.

These portfolios – from the outside – all look pretty much alike.

The creative director with five quick minutes to look through a dozen, opens and pages through (ouch! she's going fast) to see what she can find. What she sees are the interesting ads, the almost right strategies. But they're almost (almost) secondary to the real reason she's looking. She wants to see potential.

Actually, what she's looking for is the right person. She wants to see a brain at work, someone with quick wit, deeper intelligence than the guy who uses one more stock photo with a clever line.

She wants someone she can trust to have more depth and passion about this job than others right out of a program, someone she can push along to get stronger at the ad stuff in a hurry. She wants to know when she sees those ads in that junior spec portfolio that this person will be someone who works and plays well.

That hiring moment is all about the work. Except for the part that is all about the person who created that work.

That agency is buying a brain; and that, my friends, is the hidden agenda in portfolio building.

Throughout these 15 to 20 pieces of carefully crafted, beautifully executed advertising concepts you've created, there has to be a strong sense of who you are. Yes, you're selling Martinelli Apple Juice and Smith & Hawken and Pepperidge Farm Soups and Orbitz.com. But in bottom-line terms, at this point in your career you're selling yourself more than you will ever have to.

You're explaining – without the cheat sheet of work produced for stellar clients or a too-long résumé – that you love to laugh. That the summer you spent in Venice changed your life. That this weird thing with clowns is something you've thought about for a while and you realize others feel the same. That the way you think and feel and process is an essential part of who you are and the package an agency will buy.

In Rossana's work for Martinelli, she showed she possesses cool elegance with an unbelievable charm. You could feel that in her work from that smart campaign.

You could almost hear her contagious laugh as you looked at it.

How does it happen?

It's certainly the sense of originality we talk about when looking at any great creative work. It's not derivative, it's not a stolen idea or an also-ran in the category.

To show who you are, there should be elements you love about what you've done. Sure you're proud of the strategy and the concept, but more… Does the honesty of the work tell something about how you approach a problem? About where you land with a solution? Are there clues as to who you are and what you do?

Does it show that you love a product – a particular racquet or a camera, for instance – and know all there is to know, even if there's only an image and headline in the ad?

Does your book show a strong sense of humor (it's good to be funny) without being wacky on every page? Do you show how you've traveled (family vacations count) or a quirky love of science (you're a nut for Einstein)? The essential parts of you are fair game for weaving a picture of who you are via your work.

And that may be the hardest part of putting together this magical junior book that you hope will land a Go-to-Goodby-and-Live-Happily-Ever-After fantasy job.

Your book has to front a person who is the definition of the creative life. That person does not simply study advertising and awards books. That person studies life, lives fully, and becomes a better conduit of the human condition because of it.

So it's easy. You make stellar advertising with strong strategy. You craft language with joy and you make visual concepts that make us take note. Then you show that it's you and you alone who could deliver all this. And your book says it all.

Dr. Morrison presides over one of the very best advertising creative sequences for the Department of Advertising at the University of Texas. Their agenda is not hidden – they want to do a better job teaching advertising and help everyone do better work. Seeing what they're doing and visiting one of the very best advertising sites is as easy as going to www.utexas.edu/world

STOP ADVERTISING

by Jim Patterson
Author and former World Wide Creative Director
J. Walter Thompson Company, North America

How exactly do we make advertising that talks to people – to the way people really are, the way they really feel?

A strong case can be made for us to begin by *stopping* all advertising.

That is, advertising that looks and sounds like advertising.

That is, advertising that *imitates* the advertising of the past.

Let's begin with print. How do we make print advertising that doesn't look and sound like advertising?

I once had a very smart client who told me his idea of a powerful newspaper headline. The man was absolutely, positively brilliant in his perception about print.

The headline he chose – "Roosevelt Dies"

He offered another powerful headline – "Man Lands On Moon!"

Those sorts of headline are the competition our print advertising has in magazines and newspapers. The competition is news itself.

But headlines such as those also give us a feeling for the true power that is achievable on the printed page.

About TV.

I am personally uninterested in television commercials; I am especially uninterested in their subject matter.

I can't begin to describe my lack of interest in those primitive white-prints for TV commercials; those "storyboards" with nothing even faintly resembling a story, with neither beginning nor end, without plot; with the feeblest, stereotype characterizations – which keep appearing, day after day.

I tell the creators, and this is the absolute, honest-to-God truth, that I have no interest in iced tea made from a canned mix, in cameras that operate with discs instead of film (who cares?), in cars or any of their accoutrements, in removing plaque, in fast food burgers, in anything they have come to my door to sell.

In short, *I am the average consumer*.

I look at commercials out of the corner of my eye only.

Commercials have to come to me, not vice versa.

I try my damnedest to avoid, then to forget, every single TV commercial I see.

Nevertheless, I have found over the years, that certain tricks – certain "secrets" – employed by these creatives seem to work.

Here are some of those "secrets."

One. Be slaves to stimulus-response.

Make stimulus-response an automatic in the evaluation process. Evaluate everything in terms of these questions: What is the response we want? Is this the best way to get that response?

Two. Demand a cream pie in the face in every TV commercial.

I used to lie to the trainees every year.

I used to tell them I knew the secret of how to make $500,000 a year in advertising before they were 30 years old.

I told them – hit the consumer in the face with a cream pie – then, while you've got their attention – say something very intelligent.

If there is no cream pie in the ad, there is no ad. That's the truth... only it won't make you $500,000 a year. (The secret to making $500,000 a year before you're 30 is write trashy novels on the side.)

Three. All TV must be a poster – a sight poster; a sound poster.

The TV spot can have a hundred cuts, but the viewer must be able to take a single mind-poster away from it.

Four. Ask two questions over and over.

In the creating/evaluating process, you must constantly ask...
Who are you talking to – literally who?
What, exactly, is the response you want from them?

Five. Then, try to be intense about it.

Make them laugh, make them cry, make them sad, cute them to death, even insult them if nothing else works. Do something to them!
Because. . .
They don't want to hear your message.
They don't want to remember your message.
Once they turn on the TV, *they are zombies!*

Six. Design, craft, calculate.

Do it so that every frame, every word, every note works to elicit the response we want.

Seven. If even then, you're still not excited about shooting a spot, if you're not moved viscerally, kill it without mercy.

Finally, all writers of Irish descent must end each and every diatribe with… an Epiphany.

I guess it's about doing this thing, advertising, as well as it can possibly be done.

It's about having an honest work ethic, which demands that we make advertising that's better than any advertising before us.

It's about a way of life, a choice we make or don't make.

When I was a boy, in the summers I used to spend every Tuesday riding with my grandfather on his delivery route.

My grandfather had a deep, truly awful voice, and he used to *sing, every morning, at 5:30 A.M.* as he drove over the Storm King Mountains in Upstate New York.

He told me he really didn't care what I became when I grew up – the President, a ditch-digger – the only important thing was that I sang a happy song as I went over the mountain to work every morning.

And I do.

In addition to his major responsibilities with JWT, Mr. Patterson was a leader in the search for new creative talent. He made his mark at the agency with award-winning campaigns for Kodak, Burger King, Torys R Us, Bell Atlantic, and more.

But that's not all. He is one of the top-selling novelists in the world today. His debut novel, The Thomas Berryman Number *was published when he was 27 – after having been turned down by more than two dozen other publishers. He has since written a string of major national bestsellers, including* Along Came a Spider, Kiss the Girls, Jack & Jill, Cat & Mouse, Pop Goes the Weasel *and more – with three or more new novels coming out every year – always at the top ten of the* New York Times *Bestseller List!*

HOW TO BECOME GOOD AT ADVERTISING: ONE PERSON'S POINT OF VIEW

by Robin Raj
Collaborate, San Francisco

So how exactly does one become "creative?"

What makes one ad brilliant and another seem like a walking strategy statement?

The answer to these Zen-like questions could fill a book.

Apparently, they have. The only advice I might give anyone starting in this business is this. Don't just develop your portfolio. Start developing your point of view. A way of seeing things and expressing things that has a piece of you in it. It's never too early.

In the end, it's all any creative person in this business gets paid to do – offer a fresh perspective. At a moment's notice, you may be called to draw upon the dramatic, the fantastic, the useful, the sarcastic, the absurd.

So it follows that the broader your sensibilities, the better you'll be. It's been my experience that some of the best people in this business never consciously set out to be in it. Instead, they brought with them a wide range of not-necessarily related experiences. And were better for it.

Every good ad person needs to be a student of the culture – past, present, and future. And the more you feed your consciousness, the more your subconscious will feed you.

Here are some obvious places to begin.

1. Get out your scissors. Clip out the ads you admire. Ask yourself, "Why?" Then start a file. Not to emulate others, but to appreciate the thinking that was put in. See? You do have a point of view.

2. Read. Of the three R's, the first two are inseparable if you're to make a career of communication. Devour as much as you can – newspapers, magazines, whatever. (Try this: for every article you're interested in, read one you're not.)

3. If you get the chance to travel, travel. If you get the chance to go bowling, go bowling. Put down the books. Nothing beats personal experience. It may be the grandest rationale of all for goofing off.

4. Art directors, force yourself to think verbally. Writers, force yourself to look at the world visually. Become conversant with both languages, and you'll become more than twice as valuable.

5. Become a student of advertising history. See what others have done before you. Learn to appreciate it, and then learn to defy it. Just because it's in an award annual doesn't mean it's enshrined. Or that you can't do better.

6. Contributing to the mass media is a humbling prospect. Your innocent and well-intentioned ad will be seen by millions. Think about it. And develop a point of view about what you think is ethical and responsible.

7. Know your audience. Not just in some generalized "demographic" sense, but as people with flesh and bones. Talk to them. Ask them questions. And then, as you write, speak with them one-on-one across the table.

8. Be selective about where you want to work. (Easy for me to say, right?) Ironically, this may be the best time of all for you to guide your career – before you're conforming to someone else's expectations. Make a short list of agencies you respect. And pursue them with a passion.

9. Perhaps the hardest lesson of all – learn to be patient. Great ideas sometimes happen on the first try, but not often enough. Develop the resilience to go beyond your last idea until you have something both your heart and head can't ignore. Who knows? You might have solved the problem.

10. Remember, no one in advertising ever stops learning. Unless, of course, they retire. If you enjoy the process, you probably chose well. Advertising sure could use you.

Mr. Raj is best known as the writer of the NYNEX Yellow Pages campaign, which The One Show voted "one of the ten best campaigns of the decade."

NO, REALLY, I LOVE IT. I'VE ALWAYS WANTED A JUMBO PENCIL WITH A TROLL ON THE END

by Amy Krouse Rosenthal

"Nothing compares with the paperweight as a bad gift. To me, there is no better way than a paperweight to express to someone, 'I refuse to put any thought into this at all.'"
– Jerry Seinfeld

There's so much dreck out there. I'm not just talking about "bad" advertising. But stupid movies; lobotomy-compatible TV; honking taxis; mean, icky people. There's no escape. It's like the game dodgeball you played in the 5th grade. You'd run. You'd duck. But somehow you always ended up getting smacked across the face.

Now think about how refreshing it is when you see a movie you can't stop playing over in your mind. Or read a cartoon that makes you rip it out and tape it to your wall. Or you're 3 cents short and a stranger in line just hands it to you.

Or see a commercial that assumes you have a brain.

The respected designer Rick Valicenti once said to me, *"We're in the business of giving gifts."* That is exactly what these rare moments are: Gifts. A little gem in the middle of an otherwise blah-filled day. It feels great. You appreciate it. You *remember* it.

Instead of asking ourselves the same, unanswerable questions – "Is this ad good?" "Will it break through?" "Will the client like it?" – maybe we should be asking, "Is this ad a *gift?*" "Will it change someone's life for the better?" "Is it something I would want to receive myself?" Or is it a case of "I sure as hell don't want this, but I think I'll wrap it up again real nice and unload it on someone else."

As we all know, making a big production out of the wrapping paper doesn't make a dumb gift any more desirable.

Creating this kind of meaningful advertising takes a fair amount of generosity and honesty. Take a step back from it. Have you created something the other person (the consumer) truly wants? Or just something you want? Or the client wants?

It's like dreams.

I believe dreams are phenomenally intriguing, but only to the person who had them. Other people's dreams are boring. With a capital Zzzzzz. "It was so weird. We were in this field, there was this guy and all these little cucumbers, and then..." Likewise, the story of the specially formulated thingamajig is truly interesting to the advertiser, but the consumer couldn't care less.

I'm looking at a package of Pepperidge Farm cookies. On the side is an illustration showing how a man looks in a well-tailored suit versus a poorly tailored one. The caption says, "This has absolutely nothing to do with Pepperidge Farm cookies." I *love* that. Instead of boring me with how scrumptiously scrumptious their cookies are, they charmed me with their silliness. I'm left thinking, "What a cookie company. You made me smile. Here, take my money."

And here's a standard fax cover sheet. What could be interesting about that? I quote, from the bottom of a Mad Dogs and Englishmen fax, "If you experience trouble with this transmission, it's probably not our machine...we got the deluxe model." I bet their clients smile and think, "That's *exactly* why we hired them!"

If the smallest, most mundane pieces of communication can be turned into gifts, what's our excuse with 30 seconds or a two-page spread?

The Aztecs would have been great at advertising.

When the sun set each night, they were terrified it wouldn't rise again in the morning; they were extraordinarily grateful for every dawn. So I bet the Aztec Ad Chief would have approached each assignment thinking, "We'd better do something special here; this may be our last chance."

We're really lucky – as the creators and purveyors of advertising, we have countless opportunities to really do something special. We're given all these blank spaces, and what we fill them with affects a ton of people. It would be so much nicer – and much more – to tap the consumer on the shoulder and say, "Here, this is for you, I want you to have this gift."

Amy Krouse Rosenthal, a self-styled "ad-junkie," started her career at Goodby, then moved on to what she calls,"a very happy 10-year career in advertising." She now writes books and hosts the radio show Writers' Block Party. *www.mommymommy.com is where she resides cyberly. This article originally appeared in* AdWeek.

THE KEYS TO THE KINGDOM

by Ernie Schenck
Creative Director, Co-Founder Pagano, Schenck & Kay

I'm going to make this simple, okay?

You want a job in advertising. I, or others like me, have the power to give you one. Or not give you one.

Really, it's just like good ads and bad ads. Get my attention, and you'll score big. Don't and you won't. And at the risk of depressing many of you clear down to your bone marrow, I have to be honest. Most of you won't.

Hey, but that's good! All the more opportunity to stand out, right?

In some ways, it's not unlike those video games where you've got to work your way through level after level looking for the magic keys that'll open the gate to the kingdom.

Well, I don't know about the magic part. But there are definitely keys that, for me, can get you inside the great walled city we call advertising.

One is The Work. The other is The Attitude.

Let's start with The Work. I look for stuff that reeks of intelligence. That's insightful. Perceptive. That reflects an understanding of human nature. That shows you know how to come up with compelling ideas. That you can build a case. That you realize a piece of communication should reflect the voice of the brand – not you.

Irreverent and smart-ass is fine if we're talking, say, skateboards and tattoo parlors. But business jets? Please. I know it's easy to fall into the MTV thing, but work hard to develop a wide range of thinking. It pays off.

A couple of small points regarding the craft.

If you're an art director, resist the temptation to think on a computer. I'd suggest following the lead of John Doyle, in my opinion one of the truly great print ADs in the world, and one who still conceptualizes on paper.

Computers are great. But only after you've nailed the idea.

222

Another thing to resist, and this goes for copywriters, too. Get your head out of the awards books once in a while. Read novels. Newspapers. Go to museums. Lots of movies. Be aware of what's going on in the world. That's where the original ideas come from.

If you're a copywriter, I'm not just asking you – I'm begging you. No "intrigue-y" headlines, okay? You know, the kind that are supposed to make sense once I read the copy.

One problem, though. What happens if I don't? I can tell you right now, most consumers absolutely do not.

Lesson for the day. Fail to communicate in the headline and you fail to communicate. Period.

After the work, The Attitude is the big deal. Monstrous deal. More than you know. Here's the thing. I've been doing this stuff for over two decades now and guess what? I still don't think I've learned all there is to learn. And yet, year after year, I see kids fresh out of ad school who think they're Bill Bernbach incarnate.

Well, they're not.

So do yourself a favor. Be open. Be flexible. Be receptive to constructive criticism. And definitely be willing to take on anything that's thrown at you.

Yeah, I know you think you should be hanging out in London with guys like Tarsem or Tony Kaye, but do us both a favor. When you're trying to get your first job, come on like you think even a matchbook can be a winner. Because I'll tell you something. It can. And it does. I know. I've seen it happen.

Advertising is a tough fortress to penetrate.

But with The Work and The Attitude both going for you, you'll be inside in no time.

Ernie Schenck is a freelance writer and creative director, a co-founder of Pagano Schenck & Kay, and the winner of many awards for his outstanding work.

THE BEST OF TIMES, THE WORST OF TIMES

by Ron Seichrist
Founder, Miami Ad School

I'm not young anymore. I was young in the '50s. Back when layouts were done with pastels and paints by people who could indicate 10 point type with a camel's-hair brush.

I remember the magic marker revolution that put the pastel wrists to pasture with layouts that always looked better than the printed ads. And I remember the Letraset/Xerox revolution.

I was also around for the computer revolution a few years ago. And what a marvelous revolution it was.

These days if you have bus fare to any Office Depot, you have access to the same technology as the largest mega-agency.

Students have professional-level computer skills. And no one school has the edge on another school.

Why, a student can rip out a fantastic photograph from a stock photo book, scan it, type in a clever headline from any of five million fonts, print this masterpiece in 64-bit color and 20 trillion pixels, make a dozen copies, laminate the whole shebang, slip one copy into a black portfolio case, ship the others to both coasts, and wait for the phone to ring from Wieden & Kennedy or Mad Dogs.

Or they can simply take stock photos off CDs and e-mail everything to the entire ad agency universe, from San Francisco to Sao Paulo or Sri Lanka. What a brave new world!

But I'm from the old world. And I don't like what's happening.

Oh, don't get me wrong; I think today's students are talented, intelligent young men and women who can do extraordinary work. (For example, the student illustration work in the last *CMYK* magazine I read was absolutely fantastic.)

What I don't like is how easy it has become to produce mediocre work and how easy it is to plagiarize.

It really isn't a mark of someone's creativity to simply thumb through stock photos and write a clever headline.

At the last One Club exhibit of student work, I saw a few examples where students had used photographs from current campaigns straight out of awards annuals! Oh, my.

That's not a nice thing to do. What happens when one of those students graduates and inadvertently shows his or her portfolio to the art director who was really responsible for the photo so easily lifted from the *CA Annual*?

The policy at our school requires students to take or at least art direct photos themselves. They're permitted to use stock only in special circumstances – like if they need a photo of a penguin, a bird hard to find in Miami.

But they must have had the idea before finding the photo, and they can't use great stock photos.

Speaking of ideas, let me share with you what we're hearing as we visit ad agencies across the United States.

Creative directors say most student books from most schools show extraordinary computer skills but a lack of concept skills.

These creative directors are not impressed by slick portfolios full of stock photos and one-copy-line ads. They don't give a flying "S" about your wrist; it's your brain they're interested in.

Perhaps another revolution is fermenting. Or maybe this is really what creative directors have been telling schools all along.

While you're tossing your stock photo catalogs out the window, consider locking up your awards annuals too – at least while developing your portfolio.

There's really nothing useful to you in last year's D&AD or One Club annual. By the time an ad appears in the awards book, it's already at least a year old, an eternity in advertising.

Collect old books instead. Read taxidermy manuals. Study semaphore flags. Spend a day in an art museum, for Christ's sake. Try copying a Winslow Homer seascape. Or take your tape recorder into a high school locker room.

Meditate in a Mexican chapel. Rub the letters from old gravestones. If you must browse through awards annuals, look only at those published before you were born.

Have you ever seen the early work of Herb Lubalin, George Lois, Gene Frederico, Helmut Krone, Bob Gage, Hal Riney, and Howard Gossage?

Wait. Forget what I just said.

I remember saying the same thing years ago when I first started teaching in Minneapolis, and in the first group I bored with this diatribe were such young people as Nancy Rice, Pat Burnham, Mark Johnson and Dean Hanson.

I also remember spouting this BS years later when I started Portfolio Center – to people like Charlotte Moore and Michael Wilde. Fortunately, all these guys ignored this stuffy advice and did their own thing.

Maybe, after all, that's what this business is all about; do what's in you. The next superstar creative directors you sit in front of shouldn't turn your knees to water.

Instead, put them in awe of you by doing what they can't. You sure as hell can't beat them at their game.

But all those cool things in your head – from your own personal experience, in your words, through your eyes – are what they don't have and what they want from you.

Simply be yourself. It's called rawness. You've got what it takes to make people say, *"Hey, kid. I wish I'd done that ad."*

The last thing you need to do is copy ideas from old farts.

Ron Seichrist is the founder of the Miami Ad School. In 1979, Seichrist founded the Portfolio Center, the first portfolio school in the United States.

Seichrist was chosen by AdWeek *as one of the ten people who shaped advertising in the last decade.*

HOW TO LOVE PACKAGED GOODS ADVERTISING

by Susan Spiegel
Sr. VP, Group Creative Director
Grey Advertising, New York

I don't know about you, but I can easily spend the afternoon in a drugstore, buying a shampoo. Probably because I get lost in the siren song of the hand lotion aisle first, certain that "Now, with Aloe" spells the miraculous end to my dry hands.

Then I might spend a quick half hour choosing, say, a dental floss flavor and width. I steal a moment for lip gloss to make my lips look wet and talc to make my toes feel dry.

It's exhilarating! I leave the store with armfuls of promise. And some of these products really do make me feel terrific. And the others? Well, I've wasted $2.50 on the thrill, but it's cheaper than Atlantic City, with slightly better odds.

Maybe this is why I've always found it easy to work on packaged goods assignments. I understand that brands "talk" to you from their perch on the shelf.

They promise to make you feel just a little better with them than you did without.

And the brand's impression is built from all the words and images you've stored up about the product. The name, the package, the TV commercials, the images of the people in the ads, maybe a jingle, maybe a set of words; it's all so quick, I doubt many people are aware of it.

As an artist and writer, what a delicious job it is to help form that impression!

What's more, it's not as hard as some people would have you think. *You just have to love your product.* Then it's awfully simple to get other people to love it too.

That's why, when you're starting a portfolio, take Maxine's advice. Start from what you know and love. If you find it hard to get enthused, start considering another line of work.

Because once you've got a job, you don't get to choose your product assignments from your own bathroom or kitchen cabinets.

That's when you learn to be unashamed about learning why other people use the products they use.

There is always a reason. That's one of the beauties of advertising. People don't part with their money without a reason. You can't make people buy things they don't feel they need.

Hold on, you say. (I know your next question. I've been teaching advertising classes for six years.) Aren't there a lot of useless products out there? What do you do when you have to work on something you think is boring?

Well, in the grand scheme of things, some products really do seem useless. I mean, did the world really need 2,000 flushes? Or a new scent of carpet freshener?

The answer is: *You* may not need it, but someone else does.

Otherwise the company that made it would not have bothered. In the best of all worlds, manufacturers look for unmet consumer needs before inventing products to fit those needs.

And the second answer is: You work on it just like anything else you do. You learn to love it. Become the person who needs it.

Wear their shoes for a while. And then turn your insights into the brightest, most impactful communication you can.

So you can stop people, and reach them with your wonderful promise. Whatever it may be.

As long as there's someone who needs to know that Crest fights cavities better, or that Clorox smells lemony now, or that Sure keeps you drier, and Pond's keeps you moister – as long as there's a product with a promise, there're going to be people like me filling pages up with ideas of how to tell the world about it.

And I'm going to be having a lot of fun doing it.

Ms. Spiegel has made a career of winning awards on packaged goods assignments that most people would run from. She co-created well-known campaigns like "The Best Part of Waking Up is Folger's in Your Cup" and "Sure/Unsure."

She has been instrumental in updating the images of age-old brands like Jif Peanut Butter, and Downy Fabric Softener.

She and her husband write theme songs and lyrics for movies and television, and more importantly, silly songs to roast friends on their birthdays.

ADVERTISING ISN'T EVERYTHING

by Helayne Spivak
Legendary Creative Talent, NY

A friend of mine was a paramedic. She rode around in ambulances all over Manhattan for a few years.

Another friend assembled flags in a factory in Queens. And then went on to work in the Post Office for a while.

Someone else I know particularly well worked in the garment center as a pattern cutter.

The ex-postal worker, Tom Messner, heads an advertising agency with his name (and a few others) on the door.

The ex-paramedic, Jamie Seltzer, became one of the few female creative directors in New York.

The ex-pattern cutter is me.

The point of these mini-résumés is this: Some of the most successful advertising writers and art directors have everything but advertising in their backgrounds.

Exciting ads come from excited people with incredibly diverse backgrounds and interests. And while most creative advertising people have a healthy interest in their field, they have an even healthier interest in the world around them.

In other words, the single-minded study of advertising and advertising alone will not make you a better writer or art director.

In fact, the best advice I've ever heard for aspiring young creatives is something my mother said to me years ago: *"Turn off the damned television and go outside and play."*

Ms. Spivak has taken every major award the advertising industry offers, and refuses to return any of them. Her storied career includes Ally & Gargano, Ammirati & Puris, Y&R, and JWT. Perhaps she will tell you the stories sometime.
She taught copywriting at the School of Visual Arts, the Miami Ad School (as featured in Fast Company), *and is a member of the board of directors of The One Club for Art & Copy.*

THE GOSPEL ACCORDING TO LUKE
by Luke Sullivan
Senior Vice President & Chief Creative Officer,
Westwayne, Inc., Atlanta

Get to know your client's business as well as you can.

Bill Bernbach said, "The magic is in the product. You've got to live with your product. You've got to get steeped in it. You've got to get saturated with it."

Your clients are going to trust you more if you can talk to them about their industry in *their* terms. They'll quickly find you boring or irrelevant if all you can speak about with authority is Century Italic. Your grasp of the client's marketing situation has to be as well-versed as any account executive's. There are no shortcuts. Know the client. Know their product. Know their market. It will pay off.

Insist on a tight strategy.

Creative director Norman Berry wrote: *"English strategies are very tight, very precise. Satisfy the strategy and the idea cannot be faulted even though it may appear outrageous. Many strategies are often too vague, too open to interpretation. 'The strategy for this product is taste,' they'll say. But that is not a strategy. Vague strategies inhibit. Precise strategies <u>liberate</u>."*

You need a tight strategy.

On the other hand, a strategy can become too tight. When there's no play in the wheel, an overly specific strategy demands a very narrow range of executions and becomes, by proxy, an execution itself. Good AEs and account planners can fine tune a strategy by moving it up and down a continuum between broad, meaningless statements and little pursed-lipped creative dictums masquerading as strategies.

Make sure what you have to say matters.

It must be relevant. It must matter to somebody, somewhere. It has to offer something customers want or solve a problem they have, whether it's a car that won't start or a drip that won't stop.

If you don't have something relevant to say, tell your client to put their wallets away.

Because no matter how well you execute it, an unimportant message has no receiver. The tree falls in the forest.

Find the central truth about your product.

Find the central truth about your whole product category. The central *human* truth. Hair coloring isn't about looking younger. It's about self-esteem. Cameras aren't about pictures. They're about stopping time and holding life as the sands run out.

There are ads to be written all around the edges of any product. But get to the ones written right from the *essence* of the thing.

Let your subconscious mind do it.

Where do ideas come from? I have no earthly idea. Around 1900, a writer named Charles Haanel said true creativity comes from "a benevolent stranger, working on our behalf." Novelist Isaac Bashevia Singer said, "There are powers who take care of you, who send you patience and stories." And film director Joe Pytka said, "Good ideas come from God." I think they're probably all correct. It's not so much *our* coming up with great ideas as it is creating a canvas where a painting can appear.

Stop the chatter in your head. Go into what author Joseph Heller called a "controlled daydream." Breathe from your stomach. If you're lucky, sometimes the ideas just begin to appear. What does the *ad* want to say? Not you, the ad. Shut up. Listen.

Try writing down words from the product's category.

You're selling outboard engines. Start a list on the side of the page: Fish. Water. Pelicans. Flotsam. Jetsam. Atlantic. Titanic. Ishmael.

What do these words make you think of? Pick up two of them and put them together like Tinker Toys. You have to start somewhere. Sure, it sounds stupid. The whole creative *process* is stupid.

It's like washing a pig. It's messy, it has no rules, no clear beginning, middle, or end; it's kind of a pain in the ass, and when you're done, you're not sure if the pig is clean or even why you were washing a pig in the first place.

Welcome to the creative department.

Be visual and go short on the copy.

The screensaver on the computers at London's Bartle Bogle Hegarty reads: *"Words are a barrier to communication."* Creative Director John Hegarty says, *"I just don't think people read ads."*

I don't think most people read ads, either, at least not the body copy. There's a reason they say a picture is worth a thousand words.

231

Granted, if you interest a reader with a good visual or headline, yes, they may go on to read your copy. But the point is, you should try to solve the problem visually if you can.

Relying on one simple visual means it assumes added responsibilities and a bigger job description. You can't bury your main selling idea down in the copy. If the reader doesn't get what you're trying to say from the visual, he won't get it. The page is turned.

Don't take my word for it. Watch someone in the airport read a magazine. They whip through (usually backwards) at about two seconds per page. They glance at the clock on the wall. They turn a page. They think about the desperate, pimpled loneliness of their high school years. They look at a page. They see your ad.

If you can get them to take in your visual (or read your headline), your ad is a *resounding* success. Break out the Champale. Call your parents. You are a genius.

Get the visual clichés out of your system right away.

Certain visuals are just old. Somewhere out there is a Home for Tired Old Visuals. Sitting there in rocking chairs on the porch are visuals like Uncle Sam, a devil with a pitchfork, and a proud lion just rocking back and forth waiting for someone to use them in an ad once again. And grousing. "When we were young, we were in all kinds of ads. People used to *love* us."

It's good to pay a short visit to the icons at the Home for Tired Old Visuals. Tell them you really liked their stuff when you first saw them in '84. And when you saw them in 1985. Loved you in '86. You still had it in '87, baby. They will nod off after a while. This is when you sneak away, never to return.

Move back and forth between wide-open, blue-sky thinking and critical analysis.

It's like this: Up there in my brain, there's this poet guy. Smokes a lot. Wears black. He's *so* creative. And "chicks dig 'im." He's got a million ideas. But 999,000 of them suck. He knows this because there's also a certified public accountant up there who tells him so.

"That won't work. You *suck*."

The CPA is a no-nonsense guy who clips coupons and knows how to fix the car when the poet runs it into the ditch on his way to "Beret World."

Between the two of them, though, I manage to come up with a few ideas that actually work.

The trick is to give each one his say. Let the poet go first. Be loose. Be wild. Then let the CPA come in, take measurements, and just bow out here by saying go back and forth between wild dorm-room creativity and Dad's basement analysis, always keeping your strategy statement in mind.

Make the claim in your ad something that is uncontestable. When you have a fact at your command, use it. When you can say, "This product lasts 20 years," what's to argue with? State fact, not manufactured nonsense about, oh say, how "We Put the 'Qua' in Quality."

Come up with a lot of ideas. Cover the wall.

It's tempting to think that the best advertsing people just peel off great campaigns 10 minutes before they're due. But that is perception, not reality.

In fact, "Perception/Reality" (the famous *Rolling Stone* campaign from Fallon McElligott) is a perfect case in point. Those great ads that you may have seen in all the awards annuals are only the tip of the iceberg.

The rest of it, a four-foot-high pile of other layouts, sat in the writer, Bill Miller's, office for years. So massive was the pile of ideas, what he didn't use as ads actually served as a small table.

As a creative person, you will discover your brain has a built-in tendency to want to reach closure, even rush to it.

Evolution has left us with circuitry that doesn't like ambiguity or unsolved problems. Its pattern-recognition wiring evolved to keep us out of the jaws of lions, tigers, and bears – not for making lateral jumps to discover unexpected solutions.

But in order to get to a great idea, which is usually the 500th one to come along, you'll need to resist the temptation to give into the anxiety and sign off on the first passable idea that shows up.

Write hot. Edit cold.

Get it on paper, fast furious. Be hot. Let it pour out.

Don't edit anything when you're coming up with the ads.

Then later, be *ruthless*. Cut everything that is not A+ work. Put all the A- and B+ stuff off in another pile you'll revisit later. Everything that's B- or below, put on the shelf for emergencies.

"The wastepaper basket is the writer's best friend." – Isaac Bashevis Singer

233

Eschew obfuscation.

Get puns out of your system right away.

Puns, in addition to being the lowest thing on the joke food-chain, have no persuasive value. It's okay to think them. It's okay to write them down. Just make sure you toss them.

Certain headlines are currently checked out. You may use them when they are returned.

Lines like "Contrary to popular belief..." or "Something is wrong when..." These are dead. Elvis is dead. Deal with it.

Remember, anything that you even think you've seen, forget about. The stuff you've never seen? You'll know that when you see it, too. It raises the hair on the back of your neck.

Sweat the details.

Don't let even the smallest thing slide.

If it bothers you, work on it until it doesn't.

"A poem is never finished, only abandoned." – Paul Valery

Kill off the weak sister.

If your campaign has even one sort-of-okay ad in it, replace it with one as great as the others. Good is the enemy of great.

Remember that you aren't saving lives.

When you get stressed and the walls are closing in and you're going nuts trying to crack a problem and you find yourself getting depressed, try to remember that you're just doing an ad. That is all. It's just an *ad*. Bertrand Russell said, *"One of the symptoms of an approaching nervous breakdown is the belief that one's work is terribly important."*

Don't drink or do drugs.

You may think that drinking, smoking pot, or doing coke makes you more creative. I used to think so, too. In a business where we all purport to avoid clichés, a lot of people buy into this cliché-as-lifestyle. I can assure you it is illusion.

Keep your eye on the ball, not on the players.

Don't get into office politics. Not all offices have them. If yours does, remember your priority – doing ads. Keep your eye on the ad on your desk.

You are a member of a team.

Never get into the "I did the visual" or "I did the headline" thing. You work as a team, you lose as a team, you win as a team.

You are not genetically superior to account executives.

During my first years in the business I was trained to look down on AEs. At the time it seemed kind of cool to have a bad guy to make fun of. (*"Oh, he couldn't sell a joint at Woodstock." "She couldn't sell a compass to Amelia Earhart."*) But I was an idiot. It's wrong to think that way. They are on my side. Make sure they are on yours.

Don't let advertising mess up your life.

I must warn you against working to the exclusion of all else. We all seem to take this silly advertising stuff so seriously.

Some of us end up working way too hard and ignoring our spouses, our partners, our friends, and our lives. Remember, ultimately, it's just advertising. Compared to the important things in life, even a commercial that runs on the Super Bowl is still just an overblown coupon ad for Jell-O. Love, happiness, stability, sanity – *those* are the important things. Don't forget it.

Don't underestimate yourself.

Don't think, "I shouldn't bother sending my book to that agency. They're too good."

All people are subject to low self-esteem, and I think creative people are particularly prone to it. I can think of several people in our creative department who didn't think they were "good enough," but sent their book on a lark and we took them up on it.

Don't overestimate yourself.

For some reason, a lot of people in this business develop huge egos. Yet none of us is saving lives. We are glorified sign painters and nothing more.

Stay humble.

Mr. Sullivan has been in the business some 18 years, with stints at Bozell & Jacobs, Della Femina, The Martin Agency, and at Fallon in his hometown of Minneapolis.

He is now Chief Creative Officer at WestWayne in Atlanta.

This essay is an excerpt from his wonderful book, Hey Whipple, Squeeze This: A Guide to Creating Great Ads, *available from AdWeek Books Division of John Wiley & Sons, New York.*

BAD ADVERTISING CAN RUN, BUT IT CAN'T HIDE

by Ross Sutherland
Ogilvy & Mather

How many times have you heard this: "Any fool can write an advertisement?"

It's annoying, but I can appreciate why these words drip like honey from the mouths of the uninitiated.

The question on the table today is the same question that has plagued advertising since the early days: How can so many immaculately educated people in advertising agencies and in client companies conspire to produce so much drivel?

Only three things are needed to create great advertising:
1. Management that wants it
2. Clients that will buy it
3. People who can create it

This is the holy trinity that prevents work from becoming ordinary – even, dare I say it, bad.

Advertising is as easy, and as difficult, as that.

You have ambitions to become one of those people.

Good luck.

Consumers are very put-upon souls.

They don't buy magazines to read advertisments. They don't watch television to see commercials.

They resent advertising and will go to extraordinary lengths to ignore it.

Your new job will be to make it impossible for them to ignore it. And there can be no better time than now to announce precisely how you plan to go about that.

You and everybody else.

When I look through a spec book, I like to pretend I am thumbing through a magazine.

When I look at a reel, I act like I would rather be somewhere else.

Occasionally, one or two ads indelibly stamp themselves on my memory. When that's the case, it's only because of the following:

The ad is built on an idea. It credits me with a brain.

And it promises me something I want more than my own money.

Of the three things needed to create great advertising, you are the part that creates.

Have an idea.

Credit me with a brain.

And promise me something I'll be happy to pay for.

Good luck.

Ross Sutherland is a New Zealander whose first job in advertising followed his discovery that the future held little promise for a "triumphantly average landscape artist."

What followed were stints as creative director in Thailand, Singapore, Kenya, and Hong Kong, as well as San Francisco and New York. In 1994, Ross left Ogilvy New York for a two-year period to see "if the grass was greener." It wasn't.

Ross currently serves as Senior Partner Creative Director at Ogilvy & Mather, New York.

THEY LAUGHED
WHEN I SAT DOWN TO WRITE

by Phil Theibert
Senior Communications Specialist

Want to write compelling letters and memos? Want to write persuasive copy? Study your direct mail.

"You cannot bore people into buying." The years I spent writing direct mail copy drilled that classic David Ogilvy line into my head. That's why I love junk mail! It provides the best writing course in the world. Every word is designed to produce results. The pros have five seconds to hook you. If you don't call that 800 number, they're fired.

They know how to use word and phrase cues like no one else in the business: "Cent" is masculine; "penny" is feminine. "Take the quiz inside" beats "Take the Test Inside" (people love quizzes, hate tests). "Postage-free" beats "Postage paid." With upscale customers use "complimentary" rather than "free." "Do you make these mistakes in English?" beats "Are you afraid of making mistakes in English?" And always include a "P.S." Around 80% of all direct mail recipients read them.

You can use the same kind of psychology to make sure your own memos get read. Here are some corporate writing tips that can be found in your direct mail.

Emphasize control.

"The Optima Card puts the right person in charge of your interest rate. You." People want to be in control of their lives. For a memo: "This seminar puts the right person in charge. You."

Tap into fear.

A great headline: "I'll never lose my job. I'll never lose my job..." It tapped right into my sense of security (and my sense of insecurity). In a memo, you could ask: "What is the one mistake that could ruin us?" Or simply begin by saying, "Protect yourself."

Promise to unlock a puzzle.

"The Deaf Hear Whispers" compels you to read on. For a letter to your sales force: "How I doubled my client list in one evening."

Promise exclusivity.

"Quite frankly, our credit card is not for everyone. And everyone who applies for membership is not approved." If it works for them, it can work for you. "I'm sending this to only a select few."

Tantalize.

"Think how wonderful it would feel to walk without pain." This can be applied to most company problems. For a memo: "Think how wonderful it would be reduce our inventory costs."

Show what's in it for me.

"Save up to 60% on the books you order." For a letter: "Save up to 60% on our long-distance calls."

Use headline grabbers.

"Golf pros banned from using new 'hot ball' – flies too far." To announce a training program: "Learn to use a computer in less than an hour."

Paint a picture.

"Listen to 500 dolphins shrieking in panic as they gasp for air." For a memo: "Listen to 500 angry customers screaming for refunds unless you..."

Stress convenience.

"Never waste another evening returning videos. We pick them up." Tell your employees how you can make their lives easier. To promote your travel desk, write: "Never stand in line for another ticket."

Emphasize the negative.

"Are you making these seven common mistakes in your golf game?" In your office, ask: "Are you making these seven common mistakes in your entries?"

Play on underdog appeal.

Remember the brilliant ad, "They laughed when I sat down at the piano"? People love underdogs who succeed. Use, "They laughed when I ordered 100 new..." or "They thought I was nuts when I..."

Ask provocative questions.

"When an employee gets sick, how long does it take your company to recover?" For a memo: "Are our pumps costing more to operate than they should?"

Use the "barker" technique.

"Call your friends... check your fuse box... and get ready to rock... because we're bringing the world's loudest, most awesome..."

Those people are excited! Show passion and excitement in your letters. "This company is about to take off like never before!"

Appeal to curiosity/greed.

"If you think you could never get a boat, a car, and a trip for $22.50, think again." For a memo: "If you think we can't earn $100,000 with this new product, think again."

Elicit guilt. Stress urgency.

"In the 10 seconds it took you to open and begin to read this letter, four children died from the effects of malnutrition or disease." Ow! Right to the heart. Perhaps you could use: "In one week our company will waste $10,000 unless you..."

Use bullets.

People skip-read. Pro's bullet important points. For example, when selling driving glasses they write:
- Beat headlight glare.
- Drive through blinding rain.
- Increase vision and safety.

P.S. Don't throw away that direct mail! It'll beat any writing course you can ever take.

Mr. Theibert, author of five books on the art of communication, lives in Jackson, Mississippi, and is Senior Communications Specialist for Entergy, a large regional utility.

LOGIC TO MAGIC

by Eric Weber
One of our favorite creative people

The creative process is hard. It's *hard* to think up great work... and once thought up, it's hard to sell to clients.

A question I am constantly being asked is, "How does a creative person think up great work? How does it actually happen in a creative person's head?"

In my mind, the Creative Process is the leaping from the Logic of a sound strategy to the Magic of an extraordinary execution that makes one internalize and believe the strategic proposition. The strategy is crucial; I believe in primitive, fundamental, non-esoteric strategies because I am certain that advertising *has* to be very fundamental.

I remember a speculative ad for Tonka toys done by a young man named Harold Kaplan.

I first saw this ad in Harold's original portfolio, and kept a Xerox of it over the years because I think it's a superb example of the leap from Logic to Magic.

Harold had been given the assignment of proving that Tonka toys last. That, in fact, is the theme line in the ad – "Tonka Toys Last." If, Tonka, however, had run an ad that showed a picture of a Tonka truck with the headline "Tonka Toys Last," parents might think, *Maybe, possibly,* or *Yeah, I kind of know that.*

Harold started with Logic and created Magic. The picture, which is very crudely drawn, is of a little boy dropping a truck. The headline says, "Tonka Toys Can't Fly, But They Sure Can Land." Same idea, same strategy, but delivered in a truly magical way. I suspect that if parents saw *that* ad in a magazine they would believe the idea and internalize it vastly more than if the ad simply said, "Tonka Toys Last."

That, to me, in a nutshell, is what advertising is all about; that's the mystery and the magic of it. It's what creative people have to try to do every moment of their working and perhaps waking lives. The goal is simple; the accomplishing of it hard.

One might legitimately ask, "Well, is it worth it? Why not just run solid advertising that's clear and on strategy and get on with it?" I'll tell you why.

Let's draw from the annals of advertising and look at a couple of examples where the leap from Logic to Magic has yielded the most extraordinary business success, generating billions upon billions of dollars for clients. First, I will relate a little anecdote that has really crystallized some of my strongest feelings about advertising.

A number of years ago, I created a new campaign for Molson beer. It said, "In Canada, winter comes a little earlier, the snows mount a little higher, the rivers run a little swifter. Some people say you can taste it in the beer." Perhaps you remember it.

I was very proud of that campaign, and so every couple of weeks I would go down to the candy/magazine/beer store in town and I'd ask the owner, Ed Lazzara, who was a bit of a marketing genius in his own right, how Molson was selling. "Well, Eric, for an import beer it sells pretty well, but you know what really sells in my store? Three products. In fact, if I had to do it all over again, I'd open little kiosks all over the Northeast and sell only three products."

According to Edward Lazzara, those three products are Coca-Cola Classic at lunch, Budweiser beer Friday evening and for the weekend, and Marlboro cigarettes right here in the shirt pocket. Every construction crew, every college kid with a summer job, every middle-aged insurance salesmen – Bud, Coke, and Marlboro.

I found this really fascinating because over the last three decades or so these three products have had extraordinary advertising.

Think about it: "Coke is it," Mean Joe Green. "The Real Thing," Max Headroom. "I'd like to buy the world a Coke." For Budweiser, the two farmers cheering the Olympic torchbearer. "For all you do this Bud's for you." Spuds. "Give me a light." The immigrant carpenter being initiated into Americanhood with a Bud – extraordinary, uplifting, advertising.

And of course Marlboro Country, which took what was considered a girls' cigarette in the '50s and turned it into a boys' cigarette in a few short years. That one campaign, which has run for close to three decades now, has generated so much money that Phillip Morris, which was a small U.S. tobacco company, has been able to buy Miller beer, General Foods, and Kraft Foods, making it a true global marketing giant.

And what has funded it? Marlboro Country. It's worked brilliantly in every single country it's run in.

What interests me in particular about the advertising of these three great brands is the extraordinary added value it has brought to what are in reality some pretty mundane products. Think about it. Cola. A sugary, sweet liquid with bubbles in it. Beer. Mead, man's oldest, and next to water, most common drink. And tobacco... which, with all due respect to our client Phillip Morris, doesn't exactly improve one's time in the 100-yard dash.

And yet America, and the world, views these three products with the most powerful and positive feelings. Why? I submit, primarily, because of the superior advertising they've had year in and year out.

Patriotism, masculinity, friendliness, popularity, attractiveness, wholesomeness – all these positive traits are associated with these great brands because of what has been projected in their advertising.

What consistency! What brilliance!

Whose inspiration was it to link a cola to youthful, active, tribal America? To link beer with working men's camaraderie? To link a filtered cigarette with the independence and ruggedness of the cowboy?

We've come to accept these connections as perfectly natural. But somewhere, a creative person made the leap from the Logic of a dry strategic document to magical, inspirational, motivating feelings and thoughts... and then, even more significantly, a client bought it, approved it, went with it.

Now think about other businesses. Maybe there is a way to make a connection between any product and the way people want to see themselves, the way they want to feel. I liked the Apple line, "The power to be your best." It's just a computer, and somehow they've got me excited about my whole life, because I have the power to be my best. (And today, I like to "Think Different." It's still magic.)

I want to relate one case in which I went from Logic to Magic, to give you a little clearer picture of how it actually happens in a creative person's head. A couple of years ago Frank DeVito, President/Creative Director of Lintas, asked me to help on one of his accounts. *"Eric, I need your help. I have a crisis on Dr. Pepper."*

We were both associate creative directors at Y&R, handling a lot of business. Dr. Pepper was one of Frank's accounts, and I agreed to help him out.

We didn't have any time during the day, so we met for dinner every night for a week straight, 3 or 4 hours each night, and we made Dr. Pepper commercials. Dr. Pepper was the most glamorous account at Y&R at the time, and it still arguably is, so we felt we had to do some really terrific stuff.

This was the strategy: *You will enjoy the deliciously unique, increasingly popular taste of Dr. Pepper.* Frank and I came up with a lot of good stuff, but none of it felt MAGICAL. About the fifth or sixth night of working – we'd had a bottle of wine and were getting a little crazy – Frank said, "How about a couple of tough teenage girls walking along, wearing jackets that say *Peppers* on the back – like it's a gang?" Then he quickly said, "No, that's stupid."

I said, "I don't think it's stupid – what if everybody who drinks Dr. Pepper *IS a* Pepper? You know, like, *Be a Pepper.* Peppers are lively, peppery, spicy individualistic people."

"Be a Pepper." What an idea! We knew, after nearly a week of working, that we had pulled the Magic out of the Logic. . . that we had struck gold.

I hope I have given you some idea of how creative people actually get from Logic to Magic. Of course, after we *got* that far, we still had the great challenge of selling the campaign, which we obviously also lived to tell about.

I'd like to shift gears now and tell you about a lesson I recently learned when I let someone else take the leap from Logic to Magic.

A couple of years ago, my wife and I had our fourth kid, and the house suddenly began to feel small. My daughters both came down to the kitchen one morning sobbing, "We hate each other, and we can't stand being in the same room." So we decided we would end the sibling wars by adding on a bedroom.

Now, I'm a practical Head of Household, and I didn't want to spend a lot of money. I also know how architects can lose control, especially in collusion with wives who have *Architectural Digest*-scale dreams.

So I said, "Roland" – I knew the architect – " I want it over here; I want it to be a box. I want it to be very basic. I don't want any fancy roofs, gargoyles, anything. A box."

Fortunately, I got extremely busy at work and the architect and my wife forged ahead with their own plans. I was horrified when I saw them. I thought their ideas were impractical and totally excessive.

I didn't know why I needed some stupid connection between the box and the house... and I knew it would cost me more.

Fortunately, I was very busy at work. In a moment of total distraction, I said, "All right, go ahead and do it."

Am I happy I did! I know now that if I'd gotten what I'd asked for, I'd have gotten something that I didn't particularly want. I got something I didn't ask for, which made me a little uncomfortable at first, but I have really come to love it – it's added an enormous amount of aesthetic and, I suspect, financial value to my house.

I didn't control the Magic. I let it happen.

Mr. Weber is a bit of a writer – 30 books, two movies (including the entirely too popular How To Pick Up Girls), *several hundred commercials, and lots of direct mail pieces. He has held top creative jobs at Young & Rubicam and FCB.*

[Editor's Note: Though the author of How To Pick Up Girls, *Mr. Weber was and is quite happily married, which just goes to show that you don't have to live like your target audience to communicate with them.]*

He wrote and directed the ad agency comedy Suits, *which is on cable fairly regularly. Check it out. (If you'd like your own copy, e-mail* thecopyworkshop@aol.com *and we'll get you one for a very special price – we know the director.)*

AFTERWORD:
Keynote address to the Miami Ad School graduating class.

by Maxine Paetro

First, I want to congratulate you for working so hard and for graduating tonight. As I look out at all of you, I know you're wondering, maybe worrying, about your future.

I've interviewed many thousands of graduates as they've stood on the brink of who-knows-what. And I want to be among the first to tell you that things are going to be very different when you leave school and get your first job in advertising.

Things won't necessarily be better or worse, but life will be more real, because your school experience is quite different from what life will be like when you have a job.

Right now, what's going on for you in school is about you; it's about your ads, your book, and your job potential. When you step outside these doors and join an advertising agency, it is not going to be about you any more. There will be many more people involved in "your" ad, a cast of dozens, because the end result will be analyzed, judged, and paid for by the client, who may be spending many millions for advertising that must pay off in sales of product or services.

I want to tell you about a time in the early '80s when I was working as a recruiter at Saatchi & Saatchi – a very large agency that almost no one wanted to work for. And the reason that no one wanted to work at Saatchi & Saatchi and agencies like Saatchi & Saatchi – that is to say big agencies with *big account clients* – was because they thought they weren't going to get to do very good work at those places.

They thought they'd be doing cereal ads and detergent commercials and that they couldn't win awards with those kinds of ads. And if they were unable to do award-winning advertising, their careers would go down the drain.

And because of this kind of thinking, under most circumstances, an agency like ours probably couldn't have attracted as many good people as it did. But we had a secret weapon.

246

Within Saatchi & Saatchi was a small division, a group of very talented people who were winning awards for a hamburger chain and a long-life light bulb.

The agency was called Cliff Freeman & Partners.

In fact *all* the people who worked at Saatchi & Saatchi had talent, but Cliff's group had the kind of talent that was rewarded with statues, and that was the kind of talent that attracted kids from schools like this one, and we wanted you guys.

So we set up a recruitment and training program and it was my mission at the time to bring as many good young people as we possibly could and expose them to advertising and pick their brains and have them infuse the agency with their vision of what they thought the world was going to be like and how they saw products and how they connected with people their own age.

Our ultimate goal, of course, was to hold on to some number of these kids, who would become true assets to the agency and a real part of the company going into the future.

I'm going to use the word "kids" a lot. I can't help it; it's how we think of you guys. I hope you understand that it is a term that we use with a great deal of affection.

Anyway, I was in charge of creative operations at this large packaged goods agency with a small frisky boutique, and over the course of five years – 1982 to 1987 – we hired fifty kids.

That was a while ago, about fifteen years, and I still remember those kids, every single one of them. And this will interest you because it goes to the heart of what you're all wondering now. What will happen to me? What will happen if I take the wrong job? Where will I be two or ten or fifteen years from now?

Here's what happened to those fifty kids who were very much like you are today.

First, it's interesting but not surprising that the largest number of the kids that came out of that program have been very successful by any standards, that is to say many are secure, doing work that is often satisfying, and they're making over $250,000 a year.

It's not surprising because these were talented kids, and it would almost have been harder for them to fail than succeed. And succeed they did.

Ten to fifteen years after graduating from our training program, it turns out that five of those former kids are still having their careers at Saatchi & Saatchi, and that means mutual satisfaction between themselves and the agency over the long haul.

One of these former trainees, a particularly shy young man, is now an Executive Vice President, heading a division that has to do with advertising to children, and this is a special interest of his.

Another one of those kids is a brain when it comes to new technology. He's been heading a division that has to do with the Web and interactive TV.

The other three are also respected ad people with solid careers.

Four of the kids from the first group were scooped up immediately by Cliff Freeman & Partners, and they stayed for a number of years and almost immediately started getting awards, the good kind; lions that come in a box lined with velvet.

It was pretty damned thrilling, let me tell you, to go to the Cannes Film Festival in NY and see young people that I had interviewed when they were sitting in groups like this, going up to collect their awards.

One of our kids wanted to go back to Hungary, where he was born and Saatchi sent him. He lived his dream to be a creative director of an entire office, and then he came back to the United States, and he is doing well.

While some of our kids stayed at Saatchi for their entire careers, others found similar large agency homes and have not moved from them. One team has been at Y&R for twelve years, another has spent thirteen years at DMB&B, another is a lifer at Leo Burnett.

One of those original kids became a creative director of a soft drink account at another gigantic agency, and he quit because he thought the management of the agency was racist.

He went off to California and started a business of his own, then came back to New York to work for Spike Lee. He's made a film I've seen on the Sundance channel, and he's still in advertising.

Several of the others got jobs in smaller agencies throughout the country, and others, notably a writer/writer team who got married a few years back, make their living as professional freelancers.

Three – count 'em, three – of our kids became hugely successful commercial TV directors on a short list of best directors in New York. Two of them were from our first group of ten.

The third came to the agency a year later. I remember him well because he was so talented it was scary and he was also very attractive. But he refused to date – he stayed home to work on his ads and didn't want to be distracted by relationships.

He left Cliff Freeman after a few years, went to work at a big agency, won some awards, became a little disillusioned with the reality of advertising, and then he got over it. As I said, he became a director and he is doing very, very well.

Over the past fifteen years nearly every one of the trainees who stayed in advertising has distinguished him or herself with statues, titles, and those big pay checks I've told you about.

But some of them took time off, stepped out, gathered their thoughts and figured out what they where going to do next.

Some resurfaced a year or two later and went back into advertising. Some opted out for good because they knew it wasn't for them.

One very precocious young woman dropped out in the middle of the training program. I was trying to expand our program to our offices overseas, and this young woman got to our London offices and decided she wanted to see France! So she quit.

I didn't forgive her easily for doing this, because that was a pilot international program and I wanted all my kids to get circulated through European offices.

Anyway, she quit, and then maybe a year later, she was rehired by the agency at three times her former salary and moved up the ladder as well. Years later, she quit again, went to a few other agencies, and now is selling real estate in East Hampton. She got a call just last week; an agency wanting to hire her for a lucrative freelance assignment. She said, "No, thanks, I'm not interested."

One of our kids co-wrote a screenplay two years after graduating from our training program. He and his teammate sold it for $400,000, and as far as I know he is still out in Hollywood and he is still writing screenplays. One of our kids just got his own syndicated cartoon column. Another has a big career as a fine artist.

Another of our former trainees wrote to me recently to tell me that after fifteen years as a Creative Director, he ditched it all and bought himself a tiny house on a tiny island in the South Pacific.

He's eating fruit that tastes like candy, sleeping in a hammock, and thinking things over.

Not all of the kid stories have happy endings.

A couple of our wunderkind got busted out of our business because they were arrogant and had bad business manners, and actually, I kind of knew they had bad business manners and that they where arrogant when I participated in the decision to hire them.

But I didn't really care because I didn't think it was going to be a problem. I thought that I could keep my hand on the reins and help them and teach them. In a way I guess that was my arrogance that I thought I could do that.

I remember one of them in particular. He was a rule breaker, and we kind of liked rule breakers in this business then, and maybe now, too. Back then, in order to get in the training program he had to submit a test as well as his portfolio.

There was a deadline, and this kid decided that the date of the deadline was midnight, not the end of business day.

He convinced the security guard to let him into my office at midnight, not a good thing. The security guard involved got in trouble, and even my secretary asked me not to consider this kid whatsoever, he was such a bad kid.

I took a chance and guess what: He was in trouble every single day. He was contentious, difficult, and told everybody else that his work was brilliant and that theirs was crap. But he was great in his way. It's funny because there was an endearing side to him, and he was one of those who quit and came back to the agency more than once. He'd had a terrible childhood, and some of us wanted to take care of him. Too late to make a long story short, but to tell you the ending, this kid married an exceptional art director, a better art director than he is, and the world that doesn't care about his early childhood is turning its back. Actually, at this writing, his wife is working and he's unemployed.

The other youngster who led with his arrogance was also endearing, a little broken and demonstrably talented.

Two years after hiring him, he told me he was a convicted felon. That was after he convinced some account guy to let him go and shoot a television commercial when he actually had no idea what he was doing.

Luckily it was a commercial for a local retail account, but still $30, $40, $50, thousand later, we had film that was unusable, and the agency had to eat the cost.

The kid got pulled down from his high horse, and he truly never recovered his reputation at our agency. He dropped out of sight and last I heard, he was sleeping under the Santa Monica Pier. I guess you could say he pretty much washed out of the business.

Another of our kids died of AIDS. That was a big tragedy.

He was a talented young man, and I'm sorry he didn't live to realize his dream.

I feel the same way about one of our kids who became a heroin addict. She was the last person in the world that I thought would have a drug problem. She was a darling little girl from South Florida, an illustrator/art director and I remember her riding through Greenwich Village on her bicycle just enjoying life.

She was kind of very innocent and for her own reasons, she decided not to be in the business any more, dropped out and became an artists' model, and then I saw her on a television commercial. You may have seen it, too. An attractive blonde woman takes off her wig, takes off her make-up, takes out her teeth – to show the cadaverous results of heroin addiction. A true story.

Some of our kids who dropped out of advertising went off our radar screen. They got married, moved away, became tennis pros or I just don't know what happened to them, but chances are, they are having very good lives.

In sum, all fifty of those kids were very bright and very talented.

Every one of those kids started their advertising career with a great book and a squeaking clean endorsement and went to work in an agency most didn't want to admit to their friends.

Why some didn't work out and why some did leads me to conclude something.

The first job you get is not as important as you think it is.

I know from meeting some 30,000 beginners, talking to them as I look at their books, that this is what you're thinking: "If I don't get hired by Fallon (or whatever the agency of your dreams is), life is over." It's not true.

Fifty kids like you. Half of them have done extraordinary well in advertising, another 25% have been successful in a related field. The other 25% have left advertising forever, where they either crashed or found happiness in some other kind of work.

So, what I think is more important than your first job is this: it's who you are as a person.

You've heard the expression, "It's only advertising" and it's not an expression you really want to hear when you are working a hundred hours a week on your portfolio and projecting fantasies of what your life is going to be.

But advertising is a business, and your life is your life.

Your real job from this moment on is to make your life as long and as rich as you can make it.

So this is my advice: When you get that first job, whatever it is, work hard at it. Respect the agency that hires you and the people who give you your first chance. There are talented people everywhere, so take the time to learn from them and to give them more than they hoped or expected from you.

Do things for others, and I don't really mean in the agency itself. Do something that has to do with giving, because there are going to be times when you're sitting at your desk trying to define yourself by doing an ad for a product that seems to have a negative value in the world, or you'll be working with someone you dislike, and it would really be a good idea if you had something in your mind that reminded you that you are not only a copywriter, art director, designer.

That you are also a person who took a kid to the park or delivered meals on wheels or made sure to call home every Sunday.

It's also a good idea to develop other interests, feed your mind, and be a good friend.

And lastly, most of you *will* get that job in advertising that fueled your dreams and brought you to this school – or you will find a path that suits you even better.

Keep the faith. Henry David Thoreau said it best: "*If one advances confidently in the direction of his dreams, and endeavors to live the life which he has imagined, he will meet with a success unexpected in common hours.*"

Thank you for listening.

I wish you all the best of everything.

READING & RESOURCES:

Magazines:
Most of these magazines are available at larger newstands.

Advertising Age
1-800-678-9595
www.adage.com
Crain Communications, Chicago
Student subscription rates available.

AdWeek
1-800-722-6658
www.adweek.com
Regional editions available.
Student subscription rates available.

Archive
1-800-989-9494
Published quarterly.
Excellent collection of
cutting-edge work.

CMYK
www.cmykmag.com
Get this! A magazine dedicated to
student advertising work!!

Communication Arts
650-326-6040
www.commarts.com/CA
Published 8 times a year.
(Advertising Annual is a favorite.)

Creativity
Published 10 times a year by
Advertising Age
1-800-678-9595

WIRED
1-800-SOWIRED
Published Monthly
Important writing on the future
of advertising and technology.

Award Books:
Check a good art supply store.
Many award annuals are available.

ADDY Award Books
Most ad clubs publish books that salute
the winners of their local and regional
ADDY Award. Check with your local
ad club to track one down. (Hint: the
Minneapolis book is particularly good.)

Communication Arts
Advertising Annual
Copies from previous years are also
available through their Web site.

The One Show
Published by The One Club
212-979-1900

Print Casebooks
The Best in Advertising
Published annually
RC Publications, Bethesda, MD

Basic Bookshelf:
These books are generally regarded
as useful and are generally available
– though you may have to look on a
used book site. There are new books
coming out all the time – go to a
superstore or check the Web stores.

Aitchison, Jim
**Cutting Edge Advertising: How to
Create the World's Best Print for
Brands in the 21st Century.**
Prentice-Hall

Antin, Tony
Great Print Advertising
John Wiley & Sons

Applegate, Edd
The Ad Men and Women
Greenwood Press

Bendinger, Bruce
The Copy Workshop Workbook
The Copy Workshop

Chiat/Day: The First 20 Years
Rizzoli
(A great look at a great agency.)

Designers and Art Directors of the UK
The Copy Book: How 32 of the World's Best Advertising Writers Write Their Advertising

Dru, Jean-Marie
Disruption: Overturning Conventions and Shaking Up the Marketplace
AdWeek Books – John Wiley & Sons

Fox, Stephen
The Mirror Makers
University of Illinois Press
(Great book on the early days of
advertising – just reprinted!)

Goldberg, Natalie
Writing Down the Bones
Random House (Great book on writing)

Gossage, Howard (and others)
The Book of Gossage
The Copy Workshop
(Unique insights from one of
advertising's true originals.)

Higgins, Denis (Editor)
The Art of Writing Advertising
NTC Books (Now McGraw-Hill)

Kirshenbaum, Richard & Bond, Jonathon
Under the Radar:
Talking to Today's Cynical Consumer
AdWeek Books – John Wiley & Sons

Levenson, Bob
Bill Bernbach's Book
Random House, New York

Marra, James
Advertising Creativity:
Techniques for Generating Ideas
Prentice-Hall (currently out-of-print)

Martin, David
Romancing the Brand:
**The Power of Advertising and
How to Use It.**
AMACOM

Mayer, Martin
**Whatever Happened
to Madison Avenue?**
Little Brown

Minsky, Laurence
**How to Succed in Advertising When
All You Have Is Talent.**
(Ad greats show and talk about the
work that first got them work)
The Copy Workshop (Coming Soon)

Pricken, Mario
Creative Advertising:
**Ideas and Techniques from the
World's Best Campaigns.**
Three Rivers Press

Roman, Kenneth & Maas, Jane
The New How to Advertise
St. Martins Press

Rothenberg, Randall
Where the Suckers Moon:
An Advertising Story
Alfred A. Knopf (The story of the
Subaru pitch and Wieden + Kennedy.)

Stabiner, Karen
Inventing Desire
Simon & Schuster
(A year spent inside Chiat/Day.)

Steel, Jon
Truth, Lies and Advertising:
The Art of Account Planning
AdWeek Books – John Wiley & Sons

Strunk & White
The Elements of Style
Macmillan Publishing
(If you think you're a writer, you should
have this. If you don't have it, get it.)

Sullivan, Luke
Hey Whipple, Squeeze This!
AdWeek Books – John Wiley & Sons
(A new book by one of the best of the
new generation.)

Twitchell, James
20 Ads That Shook the World
Three Rivers Press

Golden Oldies:

Good books, but they usually give you a look at how the business used to be. You may have to search for some of them.

Bedell, Clyde
How to Write Advertising That Sells
©1940 (An old-time classic.)

Buxton, Edward
Advertising Freelancers
Executive Communications, New York

Buxton, Edward
Creative People at Work
Executive Communications, New York

Caples, John
**How to Make Your
Advertising Make Money**
Prentice-Hall (May still be in print.)

Caples, John
Tested Advertising Methods
Prentice-Hall (Ditto.)

Cummings, Bart
The Benevolent Dictators
NTC Business Books, Chicago
(Interviews with ad greats.)

Della Femina, Jerry
From Those Wonderful Folks Who Brought You Pearl Harbor
Simon & Schuster, New York
(A lot of fun!)

Dobrow, Larry
**When Advertising Tried Harder.
The Sixties: The Golden Age of American Advertising.**
Friendly Press

Hopkins, Claude
**My Life in Advertising/
Scientific Advertising**
NTC Business Books, Chicago

Ogilvy, David
Ogilvy on Advertising
Crown Books

Reeves, Rosser
Reality in Advertising
Alfred A. Knopf

Seiden, Hank
Advertising Pure & Simple
AMACOM

Watkins, Julius
100 Greatest Advertisements.
Dover Publications
(Great ads from the early days.)

Young, James Webb
A Technique for Producing Ideas
NTC Business Books

Business Books:

Here are some good books to read about the business of marketing and advertising. Be sure to read at least one Trout & Ries book. Remember, advertising is a *business*.

Beckwith, Harry
Selling the Invisible: A Field Guide to Modern Marketing
Time-Warner Books
(Readable marketing wisdom.)

Drucker, Peter
Managing for the Future
(Read something, anything, by Dr. Peter Drucker – one of the greatest business writers of all time.)

Levitt, Theodore
The Marketing Imagination
Macmillan

Ohmae, Kenichi
The Mind of the Strategist
McGraw-Hill

Ries, Al & Trout, Jack
Bottom-Up Marketing
McGraw Hill

Ries, Al & Trout, Jack
Marketing Warfare
McGraw Hill

Ries, Al & Trout, Jack
**Positioning:
The Battle For Your Mind.**
McGraw Hill
(A classic – must reading.)

Books on Portfolios:

Mine may have been the first, but it's no longer the only one. Some of these emphasize portfolios for art directors or designers,

Berryman, Gregg
Designing Creative Portfolios
Crisp Publications

Linton, Harold
Portfolio Design
W.W. Norton & Company

McKenna, Anne T.
Digital Portfolio:
26 Design Portfolios Unzipped
Rockport Publications

ABOUT THE AUTHOR AND HER BOOK.

Maxine Paetro is one of advertising's leading creative executives.

As creative department manager for some of New York's top agencies – including FCB, Ogilvy & Mather, Dancer Fitzgerald Sample, Saatchi & Saatchi, JWT, and Y&R – she brought a new level of professionalism and insight to this critical job.

When *How to Put Your Book Together* was first published by Ed Buxton, it became an instant classic – helping to make the tough process of job-hunting just a little easier on everyone.

How to... was Max's first book and the beginning of her own career as a writer. She has three published novels, a celebrity biography, and has collaborated with other writers of fiction and non-fiction.

She lives in New York City and also has a garden with a cottage attached in Upstate New York.

THE ILLUSTRATOR AND HIS WORK.

Giff Crosby is Sr. VP Co-Creative Director at Wolf Group in New York.

He is a copywriter, but has been known to draw the odd cartoon.

Sometimes, a very odd cartoon.

He has worked at DDB, Ogilvy & Mather, and the Acme Rivet and Machine Company of Bloomfied, New Jersey.

His many awards include a Gold Lion from the Cannes Film Festival.

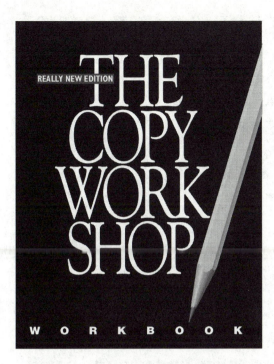

If you don't have your own copy yet, please accept our apologies ...and 20% off.

It's *The Copy Workshop Workbook* – pretty much the #1 book on how to write this stuff.

You'll want a copy even if you're an art director. Maybe specially if.

So… if you don't have yours yet, get 20% off at www.adbuzz.com

Or call us at 773-871-1179.

WHAT'S THE BUZZ?

Visit www.adbuzz.com and find out. Save 20% on advertising books. Let the Ad Museum link you to cool historical sites.

Catch a spot or two in the AdBuzz theater.

And see what else you can find.

SUBSCRIBE TO THE FUTURE OF CREATIVE.

CMYK publishes up to 100 selections from students of advertising, design, illustration and photography. It's the absolutely freshest form of inspiration you'll find on the newstands today.

C M Y K magazine

THE FUTURE OF CREATIVE

Subscribe:
Go to the CMYK Web site –
www.cmykmag.com
Take a look at some of their features.
Subscribe – 4 issues for only $20.
This will be an important resource for you. This is *your* magazine.
It deserves your support. Subscribe online or download a pdf
subscription form and mail to: *CMYK* • 5B Isadora Duncan Lane
San Francisco, CA 94102 • Or call 1-800-574-CMYK

SUBSCRIBE TO "CA."

Or at least get a few Advertising Annuals.
CA (Communication Arts) is the best magazine for staying on
top of the best in our profession. It's as simple as that.

Communication Arts

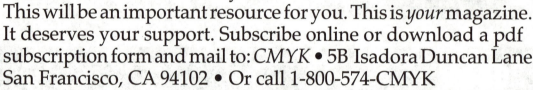

How to Subscribe:
Go to the CA Web site –
www.commarts.com/CA
Subscribe – 8 issues for $53 – includes
Advertising, Design, Illustration, and
InterActive Design Annuals. You can also
get back copies of CA Advertising Annuals.
Subscribing online saves 56% off cover price.
Communication Arts • 110 Constitution Drive • Menlo Park, CA
94025 • (650) 326-6040 FX: (650) 326-1648